MAKING MEN, MAKING CLASS

"new" model of manhood —
p. 27

o reliance on corporate
$
42-43

o p. 51 "manhood
as mediating
agent."

p. 51 bringing the
domestic into labor
relations

p. 72 YMCAs would
actually ~~teach~~ convince
workingmen of injustice

MAKING MEN, MAKING CLASS

〰

The YMCA and Workingmen, 1877–1920

Thomas Winter

The University of Chicago Press
Chicago and London

THOMAS WINTER is assistant professor of American culture and literature at Bilkent University, Turkey.

The University of Chicago Press, Chicago 60637
The University of Chicago Press, Ltd., London
© 2002 by The University of Chicago
All rights reserved. Published 2002
Printed in the United States of America

11 10 09 08 07 06 05 04 03 02   1 2 3 4 5

ISBN: 0-226-90230-7 (cloth)
ISBN: 0-226-90231-5 (paper)

Library of Congress Cataloging-in-Publication Data

Winter, Thomas, 1961–
    Making men, making class : the YMCA and workingmen, 1877–1920 / Thomas Winter.
        p.   cm.
    Includes bibliographical references and index.
    ISBN 0-226-90230-7 (cloth : alk. paper) — ISBN 0-226-90231-5 (paper : alk. paper)
    1. YMCA of the USA. Railroad Dept.—History.   2. Middle class men—United States—History—20th century.   3. Bluecollar workers—United States—History—19th century.   4. Masculinity—Religious aspects—Christianity—History of doctrines—19th century.   5. Middle class men—United States—History—20th century.   6. Bluecollar workers—United States—History—20th century.   7. Masculinity—Religious aspects—Christianity—History of doctrines—20th century.   I. YMCA of the USA. Industrial Dept. History.   II. Title.

BV1040 .W56 2002
267'.3973'0904—dc21   2001052273

For Venitra

CONTENTS

▼

As for every author, the personal and intellectual debts I have incurred in the writing of this book are numerous, and I wish to take the opportunity to acknowledge them. The usual disclaimer applies: all errors are mine.

I want to begin by thanking the universities where I received my undergraduate and graduate training and the scholars who introduced me to the work of a historian. At the University of Hamburg, I would like to thank Reinhard Dörries, now at the University of Nürnberg-Erlangen, who encouraged my interest in American history and supported my plans to study in the United States. I also wish to thank the late Günther Moltmann, who made it possible. On the other side of the Atlantic, I wish to thank the University of Cincinnati and its Department of History, which generously supported me throughout my M.A. and Ph.D. work through teaching assistantships, fellowships, and research and travel grants, and the scholars who were my teachers. In particular, I want to thank Bruce C. Levine, John K. Alexander, and Thomas Sakmyster.

Most of all, I want to thank Joanne Meyerowitz, who supervised my dissertation work. Initially, I had conceived my dissertation on the YMCA's Railroad and Industrial Departments as a case study on philanthropy and labor relations. During an early conversation, she suggested that I should "somewhere in the dissertation" look into "what they say about being men," as I still recall her words. Heeding that advice opened new perspectives on the source material I was just beginning to gather. In the end, it made for a very different and, more importantly, a much more exciting dissertation than the one I had originally intended to write. I want to thank her for directing me on that path and for her confidence that I had something important to say about gender.

I also wish to take this opportunity to thank the members of my dissertation committee: Roger Daniels, Wayne Durrill, and Mary Frederickson. Roger Daniels gave the dissertation a thorough reading, improving my prose and argumentation. Wayne Durrill urged me to look more carefully into the ways the YMCA transformed its language of manhood over time, a suggestion I attempted to follow as I revised the dissertation into a book manuscript. Mary Frederickson saved me and my sanity by generously agreeing to take over as my outside reader at the last minute. She advised me to stay calm and took the dissertation along on her vacation. I am not sure whether it was a scintillating read, but maybe this book is closer to fitting the bill.

I do not want to fail to thank two close friends. Nina Mjagkij took me in when I first arrived in Cincinnati in 1988. Initially, she brought the YMCA's work with industrial and railroad workers to my attention. I do cherish her friendship and her support. I am grateful for her consistent prodding to "get the book out," as I am for her faith in my ability to do so. This book may never have come into being without the assistance of Eric Jackson. When my manuscript floppy disks did not survive the move from Cincinnati to Ankara, Turkey, I was confronted with the daunting task of possibly having to retype it from hard copy. Eric made new copies of the files from my old computer, mailed them to me, and saved me several months of work.

Additional funding for the research that went into the dissertation and the monograph has been provided through research grants from the Rockefeller Archive Center, the Newberry Library, and the Lilly Foundation and the Indiana University Center on Philanthropy, Indianapolis. As I moved beyond the dissertation and into revisions for the book manuscript, an Albert J. Beveridge Grant from the American Historical Association enabled me to go back to the YMCA Archives for further research.

No historical monograph comes into being without assistance from archivists. I want to take this opportunity to thank Andrea Hinding, David Carmichael, and Dagmar Getz at the Kautz Family YMCA Archives at the University of Minnesota, Twin Cities. In particular, I wish to thank David Carmichael, whose detailed knowledge of North American YMCA collections on a number of occasions enabled me to uncover evidence in locations and boxes I thought I had thoroughly explored. In Minneapolis, I also want to thank Jerimiah Moerke, who painstakingly transcribed for me the personal entries for several hundred YMCA railroad secretaries and provided other research assistance.

Two of the chapters in this book have been published before. Chapter 5 appeared as "Contested Spaces: The YMCA and Workingmen on the Railroad, 1877–1917," in *Men and Women Adrift: The YMCA and the YWCA in the City*, edited by Nina Mjagkij and Margaret Spratt (New York: New York University Press, 1997). Chapter 7 appeared as "Personality, Character, and Self-Expression" in *Men and Masculinities* (January 2000): 272–85, copyright © 2000 by Sage Publications and is reprinted by permission of Sage Publications, Inc. I thank these publishers for their permission to reprint this material. Archival material in this book appears courtesy of the Chicago Historical Society; the YMCA of Metropolitan Chicago; the Kautz Family YMCA Archives and YMCA of the USA; the Western Reserve Historical Society, Cleveland, Ohio; the Newberry Library, Chicago; and the Rockefeller Archive Center.

At the University of Chicago Press, I would like to thank Douglas Mitchell and Robert Devens for seeing this manuscript through the publishing process and offering support, good cheer, and patient answers to frantic questions along the way. I also wish to thank Christine Schwab and Clair James for their splendid copyediting, which improved the book in many ways. Last, but not least, I want to thank the readers of my manuscript, Nancy Bristow and a second reader who chose to remain anonymous. Both offered enthusiastic comments and perceptive suggestions for revisions, compelling me to rethink parts of my argument and the way I originally presented it.

I would like to take this opportunity to thank my mother, Ina Winter, and my sister, Sabine Winter, for offering good cheer and support along the way. To my mother, I owe much of my interest in history, and I am grateful for this contribution she has made in my life. Both have remained interested in what I am doing and have been a patient audience over the years.

This acknowledgment would be incomplete without an expression of deep gratitude to my wife, Venitra DeGraffenreid. We met as I was just beginning to work on my dissertation, and she lived with me through the project—chapter by chapter, offering good cheer and good ideas—and still agreed to marry me. I am also deeply indebted to our sons, Rutger and Torbjörn, who provide many delightful distractions. All three of them, in their own ways, continue to remind me that there are more important things than academia. To my wife, who, besides myself, has lived longest with this book, I wish to dedicate it.

The YMCA, Gender, Class, and Social Change, 1877–1920: An Introduction

❖

Historians have shown that ideals of manhood fundamentally changed during the Gilded Age and the Progressive Era. That half-century witnessed the transformation of U.S. society from a predominantly rural society of small towns to a rapidly expanding urban society, the transition from proprietorial to corporate capitalism, the concomitant emergence of a working class and the formation of a new middle class, the rise of a modern women's rights movement, and the birth of a mass consumer society. While it would be going too far to speak of a "crisis of masculinity,"[1] all of these developments amounted to a social transformation that affected the ways in which men understood themselves as gendered beings. While the so-called men's history has produced new and exciting insights into a wide range of men's lives, the ways in which cultural constructions of manhood relied on articulations of class have received only marginal attention.[2]

Using the Young Men's Christian Association's (YMCA's) programs for railroad and industrial workers from the 1870s to the end of World War I as a case study, I argue that definitions of class difference were an integral part of newly emerging articulations of manhood among middle-class men. As YMCA officials set out to make men, they ended up making class as well.

In the second half of the nineteenth century, the YMCA joined a growing matrix of reform-oriented urban institutions that targeted conflicts incited by rapid social change. Urbanization led to the creation of a range of new public spaces in the United States, such as libraries, parks, playgrounds, settlement houses, and YMCAs. Such spaces played important roles in the attempts of urban, entrepreneurial elites and an emerging new, professional, managerial middle class to define themselves and their social purpose and to give shape and direction to social change. These spaces reflected the sense of mission of self-conscious urban elites, who assisted in their creation in a time of increasing social and industrial unrest. With the aid of such public spaces, urban elites hoped to regulate the attitudes and behavior of the cities' masses and to imprint their cultural mark on the nation's rapidly sprawling cities. In turn, at a time when the composition of the middle class and the meaning of the term itself were in a state of transformation, Americans from a disparate set of occupations coalesced around such spaces into a more unified middle class of professionals and experts. Such professionals sought to offer their knowledge and leadership in finding solutions for a range of social issues. In the late nineteenth century, the Young Men's Christian Association became host to a certain subset of middle-class professionals. In a society which yet lacked a defined national administrative core, groups such as the YMCA sought to intervene and to steer social change.[3]

Part of a tradition of voluntarist activism in American society, the YMCA offered an institutional home to a growing segment of middle-class men who sought for ways and means to apply Christian solutions to problems associated with urbanization and industrialization. Founded in England in 1844 by George Williams, a sales clerk who was inspired by revivalistic meetings held by Charles Grandison Finney, the YMCA began to expand onto the North American continent as visitors from New York, Philadelphia, Boston, Washington, D.C., and Montreal took notice of the first association at London's Gresham Street. Initially, only the efforts in Boston and Montreal led to the founding of associations in late 1851. While numerous American cities had young men's societies in the 1840s, it was the arrival of the YMCA in North America that gave such efforts organizational focus and institutional cohesion. After gaining a foothold in American society in the antebellum era, the YMCA reconstituted itself as a nationwide movement in the years after the Civil War. Central to this development was the YMCA's deliberate pursuit of financial benefactors, the holding of funding drives to raise the money necessary for new buildings, and the creation of a paid, professional cadre, called secretaries, to staff them.

As the YMCA moved from rented rooms, storefronts, and shared quarters into buildings of its own by the late 1860s, the association could no longer rely on volunteers for its work. The need for professional staff became evident, and in 1871 the association created out of a diverse range of job descriptions used by YMCAs the position of "General Secretary." A professional organization, the Association of General Secretaries, was created in 1873. Whereas YMCA officials initially had to carry out the tasks of janitor, librarian, and minister, the secretary assumed a wider range of tasks, increasingly resembling those of a business manager, such as handling all applicable accounts, fund raising, and directing staff at larger associations. The so-called traveling secretaries of the YMCA International Committee also had to maintain lines of communication with state and local associations and cultivate relations with the YMCA's benefactors. While the position of a YMCA secretary retained many of its earlier functions, it took on more and more managerial characteristics. This growth and expansion of the YMCA was intricately connected to a shift in the association's purpose toward a more active engagement of the social problems and conflicts created by urbanization, industrialization, and the emergence of a working class in the United States.[4]

The YMCA, which had initially targeted a middle-class, white-collar male audience, began to experiment with ways to carry the association's message to the working classes in the 1870s. Traditionally allied with families that represented the nation's urban, industrial elites, such as the Vanderbilts, Rockefellers, Dodges, and McCormicks, who provided funding and often held positions in association governance as well, the YMCA combined concerns for the physical and moral well-being of workers with grave apprehensions about the potential political radicalism of workingmen. In an era of heightened industrial unrest, YMCA officials regarded an emerging urban, and frequently boisterous, working-class culture as a threat to the fabric of American society. In 1877 the YMCA turned its attention toward the nation's working people and created a Railroad Department, followed by an Industrial Department in 1902.[5]

Directing its attention to workingmen and industrial conflict, the YMCA attempted to intervene in labor relations at a critical stage of the development of industrial capitalism. New technologies of mass production and distribution contributed to a deflationary crisis and falling profit rates in the Gilded Age. Entrepreneurs sought to compensate by extending their control over labor processes. This strategy conflicted with the managerial prerogatives of skilled craftworkers in particular, resulting in heightened labor unrest during the final three decades of the nineteenth century. In response, employers, as they became more aware of the human factor in production, tried to find ways to expand their control over labor and production processes to their workers as well.[6]

In launching programs aimed at workingmen, then, the YMCA bene-fited from employers' concern with labor strife and interest in new ways of handling their workers and shaping their behavior on and off the job. The YMCA conducted such programs, often in connection with newly emerg-ing company welfare policies (usually referred to as welfare capitalism) to subject work, the workers, and their communities to more rational plan-ning and to ensure their employees' allegiance to the corporation.[7]

YMCA officials believed that building workingmen's allegiance to the company, and thus resolving labor conflict, lay not with wages, hours, or work conditions but with developing proper standards of manhood among workingmen. From the YMCA's viewpoint, proper manliness was simply irreconcilable with political radicalism, class conflict, and labor unrest. Re-lying on the premise that proper leisure activities in an appropriate environ-ment would foster moral conduct, the YMCA aimed to raise workingmen's standards of manliness. Building the right standards of manhood would subdue the destructive impulses of a potentially restive working class. The YMCA hoped to overcome social tensions and to direct workers toward desirable standards of manhood by involving them in a wide range of activ-ities, such as shop Bible classes, English and citizenship classes for immi-grants, thrift classes, or interfactory athletic leagues.[8]

While the YMCA set out to reform and uplift workingmen, the asso-ciation also served as an outlet for middle-class men to unite on the basis of a shared manhood and to restore their sense of manliness and cultural authority. Such voluntary associations and professional groups had emerged in the early nineteenth century as a main channel through which the mid-dle class defined itself and its interests, reconciled differences, and forged alliances. By the late nineteenth century the YMCA had emerged as a ma-jor institutional outlet through which middle-class men articulated new definitions of manliness, adding their own distinct set of ideas to a rapidly swelling chorus of voices exhorting middle-class men on ways to restore self-confidence in their own manliness.[9]

Exploring changing ideals of middle-class manhood in turn-of-the-century American society, historians have pointed to the emergence of a "cult of masculinity." Rapid urbanization and the rise of bureaucratic struc-tures, new forms of work and altering career paths for middle-class men, historians have argued, no longer provided men with a sense of economic independence and manly achievement and heightened their anxieties about their manhood. Historians such as Elliot Gorn, Anthony Rotundo, Mi-chael Anton Budd, Gail Bederman, and Michael Kimmel have described how these conditions gave rise to a hedonistic cult of masculinity, which sanctioned a more aggressive, physical type of manhood that encouraged middle-class men to seek self-realization through strenuous, abundant experience as a therapeutic release from the pressures of modernity. Bederman, in particular, has identified a cultural shift from "manhood," defined by moral character and self-restraint, to a more aggressive ideal of "masculinity," distinguished by individual self-assertion and physical and sexual prowess. According to this interpretation, middle-class men embraced a cult of masculinity that encouraged toughness and physical strength outside of the workplace to compensate for a perceived loss of authority. Through living the "strenuous life," in Theodore Roosevelt's memorable phrase, middle-class men hoped to counter any perceived threats of effeminization and cultural emasculation and to recapture a purer form of manliness. In short, middle-class men endeavored to regain abundant, authentic experience as a way to recapture an idealized, fading past.[10] My research suggests differently.

In a period distinguished by rapid social change and mounting class conflict, some middle-class men eschewed the more hedonistic notions of masculinity and instead sought to reconcile the quest for new definitions of manliness with a sense of mission and a social purpose. Middle-class men, concerned about signs of social disintegration, I suggest, may have found a single-minded pursuit of individual development an unsatisfactory response to the predicaments of the time. While this segment among American middle-class men sought to revitalize middle-class manhood, they also set out to restore a sense of community and unity under their leadership, with the goal of gaining a renewed sense of social purpose. I further suggest that the YMCA attracted this segment of middle-class men and offered it an institutional home and an outlet for its social activism. Certainly, there can be no doubt that the YMCA was in the forefront of promoting physical exercise and a "muscular Christianity" among its clientele. However, YMCA programs with railroad and industrial workers also provided an opportunity for middle-class men to articulate ideals of manhood that restored their sense of manly authority, while eschewing hedonistic forms of masculinity and attaining a sense of social mission.[11]

Such men, however, had to confront a notable challenge. In the early nineteenth century, a functional separation of middle-class society and culture into private and public realms had emerged. This division of social life into private and public spheres, structurally differentiating home from work, consumption and reproduction from production, female from male activity, had identified female sentiment as a source of regeneration from the marketplace and assigned it to the domestic sphere of the home. By the

1830s, women reformers had begun to redefine notions of female domesticity and sentiment into foundations of reform politics. As a result, this separation of private and public spheres limited men's activism to (albeit profitable) acquisitive individualism in the marketplace and to politics. In turn, the gendered distinction of social life into private and public realms left little room for socially permissible forms of male homosocial expressiveness or for the articulation of reform ideas outside the cultural context and private vocabulary of female domestic sentiment. While these men may have longed for a place of emotional expressiveness and male camaraderie, they also looked for cultural sites through which they could define their moral mission along with a manly purpose. Institutions such as the YMCA offered these men a space and an institutional platform.[12]

I suggest that this segment of middle-class men used YMCA programs for railroad workers and, later, workers in urban industries as a means to institutionally mediate a language of manhood—a language that articulated their concerns, identified problems, and proposed solutions—to construct a new ideal of a middle-class manhood that would enable them to come to terms with the pressures of social change. YMCA secretaries relied on this language of manhood to construct social relations and to represent themselves and their relations with the association's benefactors in industry and the workers the YMCA hoped to serve and uplift morally. In that sense, then, the YMCA's language of manhood facilitated a common set of social relations among association officials from a wide range of social and occupational backgrounds, generating a shared set of concepts and practices around which to organize. This language of manhood performed cultural work by constructing meaning, organizing cultural practices, conceiving social relations, and establishing collective identity.[13]

As YMCA secretaries articulated an ideal of manhood for workingmen, they also rethought their own. Subduing the danger posed by working-class men, increasingly of immigrant background, to the fabric of American society was crucial on two levels. First, taming workingmen offered to middle-class men in the YMCA an opportunity for a renewed sense of social purpose. Second, subduing workingmen played a critical role in how YMCA officials redefined their own understanding of what it meant to be a man. Defining an ideal of manhood for workingmen and creating programs aimed at taming their behavior enabled YMCA officials to articulate a suitable ideal of manhood for themselves. The YMCA's programs for workingmen, framed by a language of manhood, enabled YMCA secretaries to validate their own manliness as they also sought to shape their workers' behavior on and off the job.

Bringing an ideal of Christian manhood to the workers, the YMCA presumed, could engender a workforce that would set examples of sacrifice and service and exude goodwill and selflessness. Once the workers adopted a higher ideal of manhood, rooted in values of Christian brotherhood and service, YMCA officials were convinced that workingmen would abstain from political radicalism and labor unrest. Engulfed by Christian piety and enmeshed in a web of edifying and uplifting activities, workers would abandon disruptive and destructive impulses and turn their energies upon becoming better men, which meant, most of all, becoming more faithful and diligent workers. Thus, by subsuming relations between management and workers under a shared ideal of manliness, YMCA officials believed they could dispel class conflict. Ironically, emerging definitions of middle-class manliness within the YMCA's language of manhood came to rely on maintaining and managing class difference.[14]

This book pursues, then, what I consider to be the central ambiguity, and possibly irony, of the YMCA's project: in the context of a social setting plagued by class strife, the association's attempt to transcend class lines and unite men on the basis of manhood ultimately led them to articulate new definitions of manhood structured by class difference.[15] Hoping to restore unity and community among men, YMCA officials cast themselves and the association they represented as mediators across boundaries of class. United on a higher plane of Christian manhood, YMCA officials and workers would serve a greater good. But, whereas YMCA secretaries would demonstrate an assertive manliness, lost in the white-collar world, through their "strenuous" efforts to tame the workers, workingmen were to accept their subordination. Reaching out across class lines and attempting to lead workingmen on the path to a higher ideal of manhood enabled YMCA officials to reconcile traditional ideals of service with new ideals of manly self-assertion, as they took charge of other, physically more powerful men. As YMCA officials redefined ideas of manhood and class, they not only took part in the remaking of middle-class men's notions of the meaning of manhood, but also constructed and affirmed class differences through their cultural practices.[16] Class-based challenges and social differences, then, played a key role in the ways in which some middle-class men rearticulated ideals of manhood around the turn of the century. I argue that middle-class manhood, as YMCA secretaries came to define it, became contingent upon managing cross-class interaction while maintaining class difference.

My emphasis on middle-class men's desire for a renewed sense of mission as they articulated a new ideal of manhood, grounded in an articulation of class difference, offers a corrective to current scholarship on changing definitions of manhood among middle-class men in Gilded Age and Progressive Era U.S. culture. In their studies of turn-of-the-century middle-class ideals of manhood, scholars such as Mary Ann Clawson and Nancy Bristow have emphasized how middle-class definitions of manhood relied on eschewing social class as a focus of identity.[17] While it is understood that concepts of gender differ across lines of class, how manhood and class became articulated in connection with one another in the Gilded Age and the Progressive Era has not been sufficiently investigated. Instead, scholarly investigations into late nineteenth- and early twentieth-century middle-class redefinitions of manhood have been preoccupied with representational strategies of exclusion along lines of race or gender. These studies represent valuable contributions to an expanding literature on the history of men and manhood. However, historians have largely neglected to explore the ways in which emerging constructions of middle-class manhood were contingent upon defining class difference.

In her groundbreaking study of race and manhood within a larger discourse on civilization, Gail Bederman asserts that definitions of middle-class manhood relied on exclusion along lines of race. Early on in the book, she concedes that "class issues underlay" changes in manhood. Further, Bederman points out that "challenges by working-class and immigrant men, reinforced [middle-class men's] focus on manhood" and that "class, too, provided materials to remake manhood." However, "class-based challenges to the power of middle-class manhood," Bederman claims, "seemed to disappear behind civilization's promise that the hard-working, meritorious, virile Anglo-Saxon man was inexorably moving towards racial dominance and the highest evolutionary advancement."[18] In brief, Bederman argues that white, middle-class men were more concerned about issues of race than class. While there can be no doubt that race functioned as a critical cultural domain against which manhood was defined, and white males were rather confident of their racial superiority, I suggest that class issues were far more troubling to middle-class men than Bederman suggests.

Angus McLaren has explored how constructions of class are bound up with constructions of gender. McLaren, too, argues that middle-class men relied on exclusion as a representational strategy for affirming their manliness. According to McLaren, turn-of-the-century legal and medical middle-class discourses of manhood invested working-class men with feminine qualities, representing them as an "other" that required control and guidance.[19] Like race, femininity or womanhood served as a critical cultural domain against which manhood was defined. As Barbara Melosh has reminded us, "the discourses of gender . . . become ways . . . of maintaining hierarchies of all kinds" and, as such, "describe a fundamental relationship of difference that organizes and produces other relationships of difference—and of power and inequality."[20] Social class is one such relation of difference, power, and inequality. I suggest that the relationship between manhood and class was more complex than either Bederman or McLaren pursue.

We need to look, then, at the connections between class and gender in U.S. middle-class culture. Over the course of the nineteenth century, class difference and concepts of gender had become contingent on the notion of separate spheres in American Victorian culture.[21] Based on a separation of work and home, of production and reproduction, this concept of public and private cultural domains had become increasingly pronounced in the antebellum era and had formed not only the foundation for middle-class concepts of gender, but for the cultural reproduction of the middle class as well. By the late nineteenth century, previously clear-cut public-private distinctions became increasingly porous. The social and economic transformation that reordered the cultural matrix of American society also challenged middle-class definitions of public and private. This shift in boundaries between public and private domains undermined middle-class concepts of gender and prompted middle-class men to redefine their concept of manhood. Because the ideal of separate spheres sustained concepts not only of gender difference but also of class difference, however, this shift forced middle-class men to rethink their identity not only as men, but as middle class as well. Realizing their precarious position in the marketplace, middle-class men sought to generate new definitions of manhood that would enable them to restore a sense of cultural authority.[22]

The YMCA's language of manhood, then, was embroiled in a larger shift between private and public realms in U.S. culture in the Gilded Age and the Progressive Era: Victorian Americans had developed an extensive vocabulary to deal with private strife out of the initial differentiation of private from public realms in the antebellum era. Into the Gilded Age and the Progressive Era, men and women who sought to deny the existence or significance of class and class differences in public life relied on this private vocabulary to frame the debates of public issues. Over three decades ago, Robert Wiebe pointed to "an earnest desire to remake the world upon their *private* models" as key to what he called a "revolution in identity"— the emergence of a new professional, managerial middle class that embraced corporate, bureaucratic solutions to social problems.[23] As members of an emerging middle class, YMCA secretaries sought to come to terms with their gender and class identities and they, too, relied on a vocabulary grounded in the cultural division between public and private realms. Reaching into the treasure trove of Victorian middle-class culture, profoundly shaped by the distinction of social life into private and public spheres, they found conceptual tools that matched their cultural perceptions and predispositions in terms of character and personality.

Both *character* and *personality* have a fairly long history in the English language, according to the *Oxford English Dictionary*.[24] While both terms represent concepts of individual identity, they have carried very different connotations since their initial appearance in the English language.

Upon its first appearance in 1315, *character* referred to a "significant," or "distinctive mark impressed [or] engraved." By the seventeenth century, the word came into more regular use with a slightly different meaning. *Character* now also referred to a person's individual style of writing, in itself a way of marking. Character, then, emerges as an expression of individuality. The word *character* begins to denote "the sum of the moral and mental qualities which distinguish an individual," "moral qualities strongly developed or strikingly displayed," and one's reputation as an employee. By the late eighteenth century, the word also emerges as a quality sanctioning an individual's ability to carry out economic transactions. In the nineteenth century, character was seen as a set of qualities subject to shaping. *Character* became more often used in conjunction with *forming, molding,* or *building,* for example. As character becomes more and more understood to be a malleable quality, it also opened up to forms of surveillance and discipline, such as the "science of character-reading" (1892) or "character-training" (1898).

Whereas *character* initially carried connotations of marking or engraving, *personality* carried spiritual and sacred connotations of the self being a part of the divine. Beginning in the fifteenth century, we can find references to the holy trinity as consisting of different personalities. Carrying inflections of the divine in human beings, *personality* also comes into use as a term referring to an individual's possessions and belongings. By the late eighteenth century, according to the *Oxford English Dictionary*, *personality* came to refer to "that quality or assemblage of qualities which makes a person what he is, as distinct from other persons." It appears, then, that a shift in the meaning of *personality* was set in motion around the period of bourgeois revolutions.[25] In the nineteenth century, the use of *personality* develops further in the direction of denoting a distinct, elevated form of individuality: a person who stands out due to unusually strong character. In addition, *personality* picks up rather material and even embodied meanings, such as a "physiological unity of organic functions, which is something deep consciousness and constitutes our fundamental personality" (1879).

Certainly, it is difficult to make a generalization about the changes that occurred in the usage and meaning of these two words from the fourteenth to the late nineteenth centuries. Both denote types of individuality; both carry meanings of belongings and possessions and stand for outward reflections of the self. However, it seems that character, while denoting a distinct set of qualities making an individual, was also very much understood as a rather material quality to be created, shaped, or acted upon, whereas personality was associated with the sacred as well as the body—a higher state of individuality and self-possession.

Concepts of character and personality played a central role in the ways in which YMCA officials mutually constructed manhood and class in their quest for a renewed sense of community in industrial relations. My interpretation of these two concepts and their relations to articulations of gender and class differs from that of previous scholars.

Historians such as Warren Susman, Jackson Lears, Richard Wightman Fox, or Joan Shelley Rubin have seen character and personality in juxtaposition, linking them to a shift in U.S. culture from a producer society to a consumer society. These scholars have suggested that in an increasingly interdependent economic sphere, and with the emergence of a burgeoning consumer culture, the ideal of an independent self, defined through its character, gave way to the idea of an interdependent self. This new idea of the self found expression through personality, directed at winning and influencing others—the ideal quality of a successful salesman. This interpretation associates character with the values of a nineteenth-century producer culture, offering a self-sustained notion of the self, grounded in ideals of independence, sobriety, self-control, and civilized morality, whereas personality, as a new notion of the self, came into being alongside an emerging consumer culture, requiring the ability to play act, to win friends, and to influence and convince others. Although some scholars have noted the close association between character and manhood, they have not fully explored the gender- and class-specific dimensions of these concepts.[26] Critical concepts in nineteenth-century U.S. middle-class culture, personality and character were closely intertwined with the public/private distinction that emerged in antebellum America.

Victorian middle-class men and women saw close ties between personality, character, and the private sphere of the home. Karen Lystra has argued that while Victorian public life was dominated by a notion of character, "in the protected realm of private reality, a culture of personality was also taking form." This private culture of personality centered on "expression of one's true self," or "self-expression," revealing the "essence of an individual."[27] Whereas Victorians preferred self-restraint in public, in the privacy of their homes they emphasized emotional self-expression between spouses and family members.

This private culture of personality and self-expression fostered and affirmed individuality—the formation of public character—through practices of reciprocal self-disclosure. As Lystra puts it, "these introspective practices strengthened, shaped and gave further definition to an individual's identity." Practices of private self-disclosure had implications for public life, because, as Lystra points out, "in a social order that increasingly emphasized individual motivation and achievement, the fostering of self-esteem and nurturing individual ego strength served an important purpose." In that sense, self-expression was fraught with notions of self-disclosure and of the self coming into being by exchanging true expressions of the self for self-revelations from others.[28] What appears at first glance to be an equal exchange, however, became in the hands of YMCA secretaries a means to inscribe class difference into their language of manhood.

Building on this historiography, I suggest that character and personality figured prominently in the ways in which YMCA secretaries articulated a new ideal of middle-class manhood contingent upon class difference. Initially meant to sanction acquisitive individualism, within the YMCA's language of manhood, character became a quality required of workmen to fulfill their role as effective and efficient producers of commodities and services while deferring to their social betters. Though such deference to one's alleged social betters was always a part of the character ideal, it also used to carry the promise of opening, if not guaranteeing, opportunities for social mobility. By 1920 deference and self-sacrificing labor had superseded the promise of social advancement. Instead, character found its affirmation through selfless service to the company. The YMCA believed that such selfless service would build manly character, which was to be its own reward. Proffering the workers an ideal of manhood that was contingent upon self-sacrificing service to their employer aimed at enmeshing them in a web of social relations of production, which I have chosen to call here workplace domesticity.[29] In turn, personality encapsulated all the qualities required of a YMCA secretary, qualifying him to guide workingmen on the path toward character through example, advice, and counsel. A YMCA secretary was to gain validation of his manliness by facilitating workingmen's

self-expression into desirable channels, guiding them on the pa.
character.[30]

In the YMCA's language of manhood, association secretaries' pers.
ality facilitated the cultural reproduction of labor by abetting workingmen's character formation. In admonishing workers to strive to be faithful,
diligent laborers, this language validated and culturally reproduced the
social relations of production between employers and workers. More than
simply validating an existing set of class relations, however, YMCA secretaries relied on this language of manhood to situate themselves as interme-
diaries and managers of social relations of production through personality.
By means of concepts of character and personality, the YMCA's language
of manhood metonymically extended a given set of capitalist relations of
production into the cultural make-up of the selves of working-class and
middle-class men. Binding concepts of character and personality into patterns of cultural exchange, this language of manhood invested YMCA secretaries with the charismatic power to shape and regulate this set of relations
and validated their superior manliness.[31] This language of manhood gave
the YMCA secretary the means to demarcate and delineate boundaries of
class, affirming his manhood by exercising power over workingmen.

The YMCA's language of manhood, then, did not simply attempt to
represent workingmen as an excluded "other,"[32] but instead affirmed
middle-class manliness through a more complex representational tactic that
inscribed class relations into the YMCA's language of manhood through
concepts of character and personality. By assigning YMCA secretaries and
the workingmen they purported to serve different positions in the social
processes of the production and reproduction of labor, this language enabled YMCA secretaries to construct manhood around class relations and
class difference. Capitalism as a "process of deterritorialization," Klaus
Theweleit has suggested, constantly replaces cultural codes and boundaries, generating new cultural resources for stabilizing markets, in a concomitant process of "reterritorialization," generating new boundaries and
codes of class and gender.[33]

The chapters that follow develop my argument along both topical and
chronological lines. Chapter 2 outlines the social and cultural background
of the YMCA secretaries involved in the railroad and industrial departments. Based on the sources available for a select group of major YMCA activists and policymakers in the railroad and industrial departments, I sketch
out their family and class background, their upbringing and education, their

motivations for joining the YMCA, and the cultural forces that contributed to shaping them. It also provides a brief introduction of the YMCA at the point of the founding of the YMCA Railroad Department in 1877.

Chapters 3 through 6 introduce different topics pertaining to the main argument. Chapter 3 supplies a narrative of the institutional expansion of the YMCA, its connections to employers' attempts to find new ways to shape and control their workers behavior in the face of surging labor unrest, and the political constraints this relationship created for the association. Chapter 4 supplements chapter 3 by looking at employers' underlying motivations for funding the YMCA. It shows how the associations benefactors and YMCA secretaries articulated a language of manhood to express their vision of labor relations and their ideal of workers' behavior. After all, theirs was a language of social anxiety. YMCA officials believed they could harness the forces of industrialization to their own project, creating a society in which Christian manhood would serve as a matrix for social order—a society in which moral, pious men, regardless of social standing, would self-sacrificingly cooperate in the production of industrial wealth, while bringing about the Kingdom of God on earth. While the workingmen the YMCA purported to serve shared some of the association's assumptions concerning manhood, their response to the ideas and programs offered varied. Chapter 5 documents the ways in which workingmen responded to the YMCA through forms of resisting and appropriating the spaces the association provided. Initially, YMCA secretaries, employers, union leaders, and workingmen appeared to share a language of manhood that invoked images of independence, self-control, responsibility, and sobriety and the notion that hard work should guarantee social advancement. Around the turn of the century, however, a language of manhood that purported to transcend class lines began to reflect a widening gap between classes. Together, chapters 4 and 5 explore the ways in which the YMCA, company officials and proprietors, and workingmen understood and defined manhood and how these relations placed certain restraints on the association's work but also made for at times creative fields of tension. Between employers' demands for worker compliance, workers' resistance to attempts at moral uplift, and the concerns of YMCA officials with fulfilling their obligations to benefactors and patrons alike, these men had to find a way to define their own role as professionals with a concomitant understanding of manhood. This was not an uncomplicated undertaking. As I will demonstrate, while many YMCA secretaries embraced their benefactors' position and interests as their own, on a number of occasions YMCA secretaries at least tacitly sided with the workers. Accordingly, chapter 6 follows the emergence of YMCA secretaries as a cadre of professionals. How their concerns with the validity of the YMCA as an institution and as a provider of company-sponsored industrial betterment programs and with their own status as professionals shaped their understanding of themselves as men is key to this chapter. By the 1890s, as YMCA officials elaborated further their language of manhood, a more distinct middle-class position became visible, manifesting itself in an ideal of manhood grounded in the demarcation of class difference and in the management of cross-class interaction.

Chapter 7 concludes the book's argument. It addresses a crucial turn of events within YMCA institutional expansion and its impact on the ways in which association officials understood the meanings of manhood. This final chapter documents the impact of the institutional expansion from railroad workers to urban, industrial workers. The ways in which the YMCA's response to these workers differed from its response to railroad workers had significant repercussions for YMCA secretaries' perceptions of their relations to their working-class clientele. YMCA secretaries reconfigured their ideal of manhood to regain a sense of male selfhood and cultural authority. Crucial to this reconfiguration was the articulation of an ideal of manhood segmented along lines of class. As YMCA secretaries articulated new definitions of manhood for themselves and for workingmen along the railroads and in urban industrial centers, they also played a significant role in reproducing a capitalist set of social relations of production on the cultural level.

It is all too easy to dismiss YMCA secretaries as the rear guard of the open shop and to see the association's programs and the support it received from industrialists as a hand-in-glove attempt to culturally mollify employers' union-breaking efforts. While there is some truth to such an understanding of the YMCA's railroad and industrial departments and the YMCA secretaries who ran these programs, it is also important to look at these YMCA officials as men with concerns of their own—men who made considerable sacrifices for their calling, who often worked under stressful conditions and took poor pay. Looking at these men, their problems, and the solutions they devised will help us to better understand how middle-class men articulated new definitions of manhood in conjunction with class difference.

"A Zeal for Religious Work and an Open Door of Opportunity": YMCA Secretaries and Nineteenth-Century Ideals of Manhood

▼

As YMCA secretaries rearticulated white, middle-class manhood in the Gilded Age and the Progressive Era, they had to reconcile their past with a rapidly changing present. Industrialization, urbanization, and the formation of a national core of institutional and administrative capacities in post–Civil War U.S. society altered the life course and career patterns of middle-class men, confronting them with changing expectations of manhood. The Gilded Age brought new constraints and expectations but also new means and opportunities for middle-class men to reinvent themselves as gendered beings and to culturally authorize manhood. Faced with the need to confront change in their daily lives, middle-class men had to reconcile conflicting traditions, expectations and realities, and paths of how one could attain a secure sense of male selfhood. Grounded by their social background in antebellum ideals of manhood, YMCA secretaries had abundant cultural resources from which to draw as they set out to rearticulate white, middle-class manhood: Second Great Awakening ideals of evangelical piety, the ideal of the self-made man, and the notion of work as a contribution to both personal fulfillment and the well-being of the community. The past, then, served as a viable source out of which YMCA secretaries hoped to reconstruct a stable present and a promising, fulfilling future. In that sense, the rearticulation of white, middle-class manhood in the Gilded Age and the Progressive Era was part of a transition that began earlier in the nineteenth century.

The first half of the nineteenth century witnessed a transition in cultural constructions of manliness as a weakening of institutional and communal restraints offered men new opportunities for experimentation and self-invention. In the colonial era, a concept of communal manhood had prevailed. Originating in the tightly knit communities of colonial New England, this ideal identified a man's identity with the fulfillment of his duties to family and community. This communal concept of manhood, portraying men as duty-bound providers, family patriarchs, and republican citizens, slowly lost validity by the early nineteenth century. An emerging market economy, Western expansion, improved transportation, and population growth freed men from many traditional communal restraints and the social discipline imposed by small neighborhoods, replacing it with a society of strangers. In this changing social context of increasing spatial and social mobility, the earlier, communal concept of manhood began to receive competition from a newly emerging ideal of the self-made man. With manhood often no longer tied to land ownership or an artisan shop, this new ideal fit well with a high degree of social and geographical mobility and the opportunities offered by an expanding national market. According to this new concept of self-made manhood, free competition would reward the best man. Market values, emphasizing the autonomous individual, slowly eclipsed the older emphasis on community restraints on individual conduct, both public and private. The self-made man was quintessentially a "marketplace man."[1]

This new ideal of middle-class manhood entreated men to savor their possibilities and opportunities and enabled economically acquisitive conduct in the marketplace. While society continued to expect that men would engage in purposeful behavior, constrained by civilized conduct, social norms suggested that men's accomplishments were limited only by their talents. Independence and autonomy substituted for duty as the primary virtues of a true man. This self-made man, as Karen Halttunen phrased it, through "exercising self-possession, self-government, and above all, self-reliance, . . . placed himself beyond evil influences and became a law unto himself."[2] Individual traits that earlier generations had regarded as selfish and dangerous passions were now free to express themselves in the marketplace. Men's self-worth came to depend more and more on their economic achievements, and those hinged on an increasingly volatile market economy that witnessed major swings from its inception. The ideal of the self-made man was satisfying to many men drawn into an emerging market economy, while its new demands were discomfiting at the same time: self-made manhood, although sanctioning new opportunities, was subject to material challenge on a daily basis and required constant affirmation through continued success. Middle-class ideas of manliness, then, had reached a juncture, torn between ebullient individualism and powerlessness, between assertive self-reliance and a longing for communal bonds and affirmation.[3] Men sought to balance the new opportunities available and the requirements placed on them by an emerging capitalist marketplace with ideals rooted in their communal past.

Victorian men found this balance in a concept of character that propelled a man to diligent, industrious behavior, while simultaneously demanding self-restraint. Most of all understood as the moral and rational capacity for control over one's emotions, character encompassed a range of qualities—all of which emphasized self-sacrifice and self-control—associated with a nineteenth-century producer ethic and identified its bearer with republican civic virtue. Often used interchangeably with *manhood*, the term *character* was applied to the man who had successfully synthesized communal moral standards with productive, acquisitive habits into a unified whole. As the cornerstone of self-made manhood, character comprised a collection of qualities best summarized as acquisitive individualism. It proved especially advantageous to the members of an emerging middle class, offering them a prescription for how to represent an integrated self.[4]

Mediating between past and present, character played a central role in American Victorian culture. In limbo between a social structure based on small communities and a new society based on market exchanges, Antebellum Victorians insisted on mutual self-disclosure, or sincerity, to protect market relations against the corruption by the so-called confidence man.[5] This ideal of sentimental sincerity conformed to the logic of capitalist exchange by representing a quality to be exchanged or reciprocated by trust. With regard to men, Victorian culture invested that quality in an ideal of character that signified that sincere trustworthiness that middle-class Americans expected in all walks of life from one another. While guaranteeing the much longed-for trustworthiness, character also encompassed and allowed for an individual drive toward productivity and acquisitiveness, though urging self-restraint. Enabling men's performance in the marketplace, character reflected an internalization of communal norms; a "civilizing process," to use Norbert Elias's phrase, concomitant with the emergence of a capitalist marketplace.[6] In the nation's burgeoning urban marketplaces, composed of strangers, character both sanctioned the pursuit of economic gain and offered a new way of knowing, recognizing, and evaluating those in one's surroundings.

This balanced ideal of manhood, grounded in character, received reinforcement in the Second Great Awakening. The match between the acquisitive self-made man and evangelical theology reflects the transitional quality of the character ideal itself. In Karen Halttunen's words, "The concept of character represented an effort to reconcile two different views of human nature: the premodern concept of soul, which focused on man's inner spiritual being as he confronted God alone, and the modern concept of personality, which turned attention to man's external standing before other men."[7] Character found an outlet for its sacred component in the Second Great Awakening. As a new generation of men no longer saw themselves as fixed parts of organic communities, they welcomed the opportunity to reinvent themselves as free moral agents as the theological prescriptions of the Second Great Awakening demanded. Great Awakening theology, like the character ideal, emphasized the responsibility of the autonomous individual, balanced by "a new level of instinctual repression and disciplined effort."[8] At the same time, the revivalistic experience and the emphasis on same-sex bonds offer a renewed sense of community. One outcome of this evangelical reform spirit was an emphasis on male same-sex emotional intimacy and expressiveness, referred to as "fraternal love" or "brotherly love," which gave men a new firm anchor for a gendered identity in a changing social and economic environment, assuring them of the continuing significance and meaning of communal ideals and values.[9] This ideal of "brotherly love" and the evangelical revivalistic reform spirit that it was part of, satisfied the longings of American middle-class men for both individuality and community. A tradition of voluntarist organizing, evident in organizations such as the YMCA, gave this impulse institutional shape and direction.

The very emergence of the YMCA in Great Britain and the United States was closely tied to evangelical revivals, largely associated with Charles G. Finney. In England, Finney's writings had already exercised "a powerful influence upon [George] Williams," the founder of the British YMCA. Subsequently, in his own attempts at drawing other clerks and salesmen such as himself to Christ, Williams heavily relied on Finney's works. The founding of the YMCA in 1844 in England by George Williams, son of a Somerset farmer and clerk with a London dry goods merchant, was in part the result of Finney's revivals there. This connection was not a mere coincidence, as Finney tirelessly urged his listeners to take on voluntarist activism as their life calling. Thus, the first YMCAs in North America were founded as a direct consequence of Great Awakening theology.

This theology proffered evangelical piety as the basis for a new institutional matrix of reform, substituting personal piety for earlier communal restraints on public and private conduct.[10]

An institutional offspring of the Second Great Awakening, the YMCA played an important role in the cultural transition from a social fabric maintained by communal restraints to new social patterns that emphasized the autonomous individual as self-regulating moral agent. As Daniel Walker Howe has noted, with fewer communal or institutional constraints than preceding generations, antebellum American men not only reinvented themselves, they also set out to remake the social fabric by replacing communal restraints with bonds of voluntary association, like the YMCA. Joining a new ideal of the autonomous male self to bonds of voluntary association, such men hoped, would guarantee that male passions would be reigned in by fraternal discipline.[11] Creating new institutions such as the YMCA enabled Victorian Americans to generate new values and cultural perceptions suitable to their changing surroundings.

In the second half of the nineteenth century, however, the YMCA entered a phase of introspection, searching for new directions and opportunities to apply protestant Christian theology to some of the social problems of the day. When the YMCA reconstituted itself as a national movement in the aftermath of the Civil War, growth and expansion of the association became closely tied to the industrial transformations that changed the country. The YMCA, itself searching for direction in the decades after the Civil War, attracted men looking for a purpose, a mission, and an identity—both as men and as professionals. Growing up in the shadow of the market revolution, these men shared many of the concerns and problems of a generation of men that, in Charles Sellers's words, "had to compete for elusive manhood rather than grow into secure manhood by replicating fathers."[12] The YMCA offered them an institutional platform to find fulfilling careers and the opportunity to articulate an ideal of manhood that promised to bridge past and present.

The biographies of several YMCA officials who took on positions of leadership in the association's railroad and industrial work display close personal and cultural ties to the market revolution and the Second Great Awakening, influences that, in turn, critically shaped their understanding of what it meant to be a man. Their life courses followed often remarkably similar patterns. Place and time of birth, family and class background, evangelical affiliation, career path, and the challenges of social mobility eventually interwove their lives with the YMCA—shaping expectations and exposing them to cultural influences, molding their understanding of themselves as men and their expectations of others as well.[13]

These men formed a fairly homogeneous group. The majority were born during the 1860s: George Warburton was born in 1860, Henry Orison Williams in 1861, George Davis McDill and Clarence J. Hicks in 1862, Charles R. Towson in 1863, Joseph M. Dudley and William H. Day in 1864, Edwin Lorenzo Hamilton in 1866, John Ferguson Moore in 1867, and Frederic Burton Shipp in 1868. Only two of this group were born in the 1870s: Ward W. Adair was born in 1870, and Aaron G. Knebel was born in 1874. Still, the proximity in birth dates places them within the same generation.[14] These men were also united by religious background and geographical affinities.

A look at the birthplaces of railroad secretaries entering association work between the late 1870s and 1900 indicates that these men shared both regional and cultural ties to the Second Great Awakening. Several leading YMCA officials in the railroad and industrial departments were born in upstate New York: John Ferguson Moore in Albany, Ward W. Adair in Pembroke, Genesee County, Henry Orison Williams in Watertown, Jefferson County, and Edwin Lorenzo Hamilton in Auburn, near Rochester. George Warburton was born in Sanford, Somersetshire Hamlet, England, but his family immigrated in 1869, settling in Auburn, New York. While the precise origin of Hicks's family is difficult to trace, his father, too, came from New York state. All these locations had witnessed antebellum revivals— part of or on the fringes of what has been called the "burned-over-district." Finney had held revivals in Auburn and in Jefferson County. In addition, revivals took place in Albany, Watertown, and Auburn. Many more revivals took place in western and northern New York, most importantly at Utica and at Rome, spreading their evangelistic message among the population of the area. Not all members of this group could trace their origins to northern and western New York state. However, Baltimore, Charles Towson's place of birth, also witnessed intense revivals as part of the Second Great Awakening.[15] Their birthplaces connected these men to cultural environments infused with revivalist theology.

This affinity was not limited to leading YMCA officials. Out of 645 railroad secretaries listed in the *Roster of Paid Secretaries*, vol. 1, *1880–1900*, 140 listed cities and towns in New York as birthplace, 50 in New England states, 95 in Pennsylvania, and 152 in states belonging to the Midwest. Certainly, it should be not at all surprising that most secretaries came from the more populated states, like New York. And while it would be a leap of historical faith to assume that every secretary born in an area affected by the Second Great Awakening, such as upstate New York, brought a certain set of cultural assumptions to his work, I would hazard nonetheless that this was not unlikely either, as Finney held revivals all over New York, as well as in Reading, Lancaster, and Philadelphia, Pennsylvania, and even visited Boston.[16] In the life courses of these men and their families, then, geographical ties often received reinforcement from similarities in religious background.

The evidence available supports an argument regarding the connection between the YMCA and evangelical churches, affected by the Second Great Awakening. The YMCA *Roster of Paid Secretaries* lists George Warburton and Clarence Hicks as Methodist, Ward Adair, Joseph M. Dudley, and Edwin Ingersoll as Presbyterian, and Charles Towson as Baptist. Peter Roberts had served as a Congregational minister before coming to the YMCA. In any case, most YMCA officials came from a Presbyterian, Congregationalist, Episcopalian, Baptist, Methodist, or Methodist Episcopal background. As a recent historian pointed out, the vast majority of YMCA recruits came from pious families of an evangelical background.[17] Similarities in religious background and place of origin also extended into social origins.

As far as records are extant, the majority of the group come from middle-class backgrounds, and their fathers' status and achievements probably set examples for their sons. In all likelihood, their fathers were no different from other fathers of the time, who "encouraged aggressive achievement that they associated with masculinity" among their sons.[18] Towson's father, Obadiah, had made it from artisan and shop owner to farmer of modest means. The 1860 Baltimore Census lists Obadiah Towson as a master tobacconist with a shop in the city of Baltimore. Ten years later, the census taker found Obadiah Towson and his family in different surroundings as farmer and resident of Towsontown, Baltimore County. Since the family's move out of the city of Baltimore, Charles (1863) and another son had been born. By the expectations of the midnineteenth century, Obadiah Towson had lived the life of modest success and become a yeoman farmer. However, born third of four children, Charles could hardly expect to inherit the farm and would be on his own, while his father's success in all likelihood set high standards for him. Young Charles Towson attempted to make a living in positions as diverse as director of Baltimore's Sunday Schools, real estate agent, and traveling salesman for a Baltimore paper manufacturer before finding his calling in the YMCA. Clarence Hicks's family situation represented a similar picture. The census lists his father,

Robert J. Hicks, as a carpenter and partner in a wagon shop, but the two-acre farm was both demanding and too small to be divided among several sons. Clarence, too, would have to be on his own. Clarence Hicks worked as a farm hand and as a molder in his brother's foundry. Later he took jobs as a barrel handler, tutor, and, like Towson, a traveling salesman. The fathers set examples their sons possibly hoped to emulate but must have found difficult to accomplish. Towson and Hicks had to realize at a relatively early age that they would have to make it on their own—both had to become self-made men.

The examples that these fathers set for their sons was not always without problems. Edwin Hamilton's father, a lawyer, not only had been convicted of forgery, but he died when Edwin was only eight years old, forcing him to leave school. Thus, Edwin Hamilton was forced to realize at the young age of eight that he would have to make it on his own. Simple self-made manhood would appear to have offered limited rewards to these men who, in their youth and adolescence, experienced its shortcomings.

Whereas their family background exposed them to the limitations of the ideal of the acquisitive self-made man, the Civil War exhibited the problems of the antebellum ideal of a pious manhood that would balance a man's material, acquisitive drives. The war itself held out the promise of real manhood to the pragmatic can-do, go-getter, giving rise to the notion of "the strenuous life." Earlier hopes for an ideal of manliness that subjected social reality to high cultural principles seemed to have outlived their usefulness and practicality, while the war also masculinized ideas about benevolence.[19] In that sense, the war had an ambivalent impact on the generation of men born around the Civil War. Grounded in a set of values and ideals that the war had put in question, this generation had to recreate the social world surrounding them, finding a new balance between the acquisitive energies and the longing for communal and spiritual affirmation.

Confronting this ambiguity, these men faced the challenge of choosing careers that held out the prospect of not only a livelihood but also personal, spiritual fulfillment, maybe more than their fathers' prospects had. Precisely because they sought more than a livelihood, they were also quite sensitive to the pressures of economic transformation that altered career paths and foreclosed many opportunities. In addition to earning a livelihood and finding personal fulfillment, Victorians perceived their work as a contribution to the well-being of the community. Work was to be socially useful. Victorians had high expectations of their work. Settling on a career path often resembled a spiritual quest.[20]

It is probably no coincidence, then, that Charles Towson and Clarence Hicks, both one-time traveling salesmen, would rise to such prominence in the YMCA: as Olivier Zunz has argued, salesmen represented the spearhead of a corporate culture, which began to reshape large aspects of American culture in the late nineteenth century. To succeed, salesmen had to reconcile the communitarian spirit that often still prevailed in many rural communities with an appeal to the individual self-interest of their customers. At the forefront of a corporate culture that emphasized service, carrying connotations of an older communitarian vision, salesmen also had to be confident in themselves and their products and forceful in presenting their wares. A salesman's success depended on his own self-confidence and on his ability to convince customers of his good moral and ethical intentions.[21] In that sense, the career paths of Towson and Hicks, and possibly others like them, had already prepared them to fuse missionary zeal to an emerging corporate capitalist order. For such men, who were ideally prepared to serve as cultural mediators and who themselves sought to join a desire for individual advancement to socially purposeful effort on the quest for a meaningful and fulfilling career, the YMCA must have come as a natural home.

For the men who became YMCA secretaries, their decision to join the work of the YMCA often reflected a mixture of grasping the opportunity of self-made manhood and the desire to help others on their path. Of some help here are replies some of these men gave in a YMCA-conducted questionnaire in the 1930s. In these questionnaires, the YMCA asked retired YMCA secretaries about their family and religious background and their reasons for taking on positions in the YMCA. On the question asking why he joined the YMCA work, Henry Orison Williams replied, "because of a controlling desire to help young men to find themselves, find Christ, and find a field of service." Other shared Williams's feelings. Hamilton entered railroad work "because of an earnest desire to tell others about Jesus . . . the Association seemed to offer the best opportunity." Charles R. Towson made the connection between professional opportunity and religious conviction most clear, inflecting both the ideal of character and a strong evangelical missionary spirit. Towson said he joined because of a "zeal for religious work and an open door of opportunity."[22] While such statements were solicited by their former employer and given years after the men had retired, and as such certainly represented a rationalization of their lives and career paths, they also powerfully ring with nineteenth-century concepts of manhood and the cultural tensions these man had to confront and sought to reconcile. The careers of these men reflected an updated version of the self-made man. But compared to their fathers' generation, they were liminal men—men on the make. Their very identity as men had become malleable, a product of their own efforts.[23] And the YMCA offered them an institutional basis in their endeavor to reinvent themselves as men.

The majority entered YMCA service in the 1880s and 1890s. Moore, Williams, Hamilton, and Towson became active in the YMCA in the 1880s, Dudley, Day, and Knebel in the 1890s. Between 1880 and 1881, Williams was a member of the finance committee of the Watertown YMCA, when George A. Warburton was General Secretary there. It appears that older, already established secretaries often recruited others in the group. Explaining his reasons for joining the YMCA work, Henry Orison Williams stated, "because Warburton [General Secretary of the New York Railroad YMCA], Richard Cary Morse [General Secretary of the YMCA International Committee], and Robert McBurney [General Secretary of the New York YMCA] urged [me]."[24]

In several cases, the career break was far from being as abrupt as it appears at first glance. George McDill, who had begun to work as a clerk with the Chicago Northwestern Railroad in 1884, came in contact with Augustus Nash in 1889. Nash was doing pathbreaking work with the Cleveland YMCA in designing shop Bible classes, which enabled YMCA secretaries to carry the message to workers in the shops. In 1898 McDill, by that time general manager of the vice president's offices, left the employ of the Chicago Northwestern to become traveling railroad secretary with the YMCA. Clarence Hicks first served as college secretary for the Wisconsin YMCA state committee. In November 1889, he was offered the position of Secretary of the YMCA Railroad Department, which he held until 1911. Peter Roberts served as ordained minister of the Congregational church at Scranton, Olyphant, and Mahanoy City, in the anthracite coal region of Pennsylvania between 1886 and 1907, interrupted by a return to Yale University for a Ph.D. in sociology. As a minister in the Pennsylvania anthracite region, Roberts had first-hand exposure to issues of Americanization and had the opportunity to observe the efforts of the Pennsylvania YMCA. In 1907 he followed a call from the YMCA to become special secretary for immigration and Americanization with the YMCA Industrial Department, a position he held until 1921.

Others among this group had a more indirect path to the YMCA. Charles Towson, who would later become a leading figure in the YMCA's industrial work, was down on his luck at least once in his life, and his experience with the YMCA during that time was not particularly positive. He later recalled the event in an article on the "Power of Friendliness." Criticizing many of his colleagues, Towson wrote on the first page of that month's issue of *Association Men* that "most [secretaries] . . . are like the secretaries in a big Young Men's Christian Association where I went once when I was broke and needed something to eat as well as a good bath." He recalled "a big sign made like a hand pointing towards that door, on which it said in big letters 'Welcome Strangers.'" Thus drawn into the YMCA, he walked in, but "was there anybody to welcome me—well, I should say not!" Towson wrote that he "walked out just as dirty and hungry as when . . . [he] went in."[25] That experience apparently did not deter him from making the YMCA his calling later in his life.

Towson began his career with the YMCA when he became the Director of its Baltimore East Branch in 1889. In the fall of 1893 Towson accepted a position as General Secretary of the Roanoke, Virginia, YMCA, from where he moved on to become General Secretary of the Norfolk, Virginia, YMCA in May 1895. Praised for his "energy, natural wit, readiness of speech and personal magnetism," at six feet four inches, he was also known as "the delegate at length" in Virginia YMCA circles.[26] Later in 1895 he answered a call to become the General Secretary of the Pennsylvania Railroad YMCA in Philadelphia, where he remained until 1907. At that time he was called upon to replace Charles C. Michener as Senior Secretary of the YMCA Industrial Department, a position he held until 1922. From 1923 to 1934 he worked as President of the Silver Bay Association of the YMCA, which sponsored Industrial Relations Conferences.

In addition, Hicks and Towson remained with personnel management and industrial relations after leaving the YMCA. In 1911 Hicks followed a call from Cyrus McCormick to become industrial relations counselor at International Harvester. Four years later, in 1915, Hicks took a similar position with John D. Rockefeller, Jr., at Colorado Fuel and Iron. In 1917, he moved on to Standard Oil Company of New Jersey, another Rockefeller interest. Hicks remained with that company until his retirement in 1933. Charles Towson assumed a position as Personnel Director with Deering and Milliken, a textile manufacturer, in 1934.

Around the turn of the century, so go most accounts, white, American middle-class men abandoned the quest for affirmation and fulfillment through work. But the social and economic changes that began to reshape middle-class men's lives in the late nineteenth century revealed the problems inherent in this shift. The anonymity of large and rapidly growing cities and the newly emerging career paths for middle-class men in corporate offices and municipal and government bureaucracies offered financial rewards but lacked a sense of accomplishment and gendered identity. Large numbers of middle-class men searched for a sense of achievement o of work and projected their competitive impulses into their leisure life, em bracing a hedonistic form of physical manliness.[27]

As the following chapters will demonstrate, a significant segment of American middle-class men sought more than a brief moment of manly affirmation in the gymnasium, but rather sought self-affirmation and a sense of social usefulness in their work. These middle-class men sought to infuse their lives with a sense of mission, recreating the balance inherent in the antebellum ideal of character.

Such men, though, had to confront a profound problem. The functional separation of private and public that had emerged in the early nineteenth century had designated female sentiment as a source of regeneration from the marketplace and relegated it to the domestic sphere of the home. Women reformers, in turn, had redefined the private sphere of the home from a place merely disconnected from productive, value-creating labor, into a well-spring of reform sentiment. This separation of private and public spheres relegated men's activism to acquisitive individualism and the marketplace or to politics. It left little room for socially acceptable forms of male homosocial expressiveness or for the articulation of reform ideals outside the context of domestic sentiment, represented by women. But the self-made man longed not only for a place of emotional expressiveness and male camaraderie but also for cultural space in which to define his moral mission and a manly purpose. Institutions such as the YMCA offered some of these men a space and an institutional platform.[28] Those who became YMCA secretaries found themselves trying to reconcile ideals and expectations of the past with new realities. In the process, they created a new ideal of manhood for themselves—an ideal that, though it carried many marks of the old, was also nonetheless strikingly new and different.

"We Have Only to Step in and Occupy the Land": The YMCA, Labor Conflict, and the Rise of Welfare Capitalism

\/

Increasing strike activity along the railroads in the 1880s provided the impetus for a number of railroads to begin exploring possible ways of guaranteeing the cooperation and loyalty of their workforces. From 1881 to 1886 the total number of strikes increased from 474 to 1,432, with 101,000 and 407,000 workers participating, respectively. In 1894 alone, 1,349 strikes took place with about 505,000 workers participating.[1] As labor unrest had reached cataclysmic proportions in the eyes and minds of many contemporaries, entrepreneurs and managers began to look for new ways to control and discipline their workers.

The first to introduce modern corporate finance and managerial structures, railroads also were among the first to experiment with new approaches toward handling personnel and labor relations. In the late 1870s entrepreneurs and managers began to experiment with paternalistic industrial betterment programs, or welfare capitalism, to morally uplift the workers, increase their productivity, and ensure their allegiance to the company on and off the job. Other industries would soon follow suit.[2]

In the 1870s, concerns with improving control over apparently increasingly restive workforces, shared widely among entrepreneurs, coincided with concerns within YMCA circles over the social relevance of the association, its validity as an institution, and how it could better serve the needs of a rapidly industrializing society. Both entrepreneurs and managers and the YMCA identified labor unrest, fueled by class strife, as the critical issue facing late nineteenth-century U.S. society and acted on this perception. Out of these concerns grew a close relationship between the YMCA and a segment of the nations' urban-industrial elite on levels of funding and governance. This close relationship very much contributed to shaping YMCA policies in the field of industrial relations.

As the YMCA reorganized itself after the Civil War, it also attempted to identify issues and problems that could serve as a new programmatic focus. It found this focus in part in the questions raised by the combined forces of urbanization and industrialization. At the first convention of YMCAs held after the war in Albany, New York, in 1866, the association committed itself to "improving the social conditions of young men." When Chicago received the first modern YMCA building—a five-story structure, named Farwell Hall after the millionaire retailer James V. Farwell, who had provided the site for it—the famous evangelist Dwight Moody linked the building to the city's function as a railroad center. By constructing this building, he said, the YMCA was "raising the beacon of light . . . that shall penetrate with its healing beams of Gospel goodwill every hamlet and town that may be reached by the network of railroads radiating from this centre, and forever to be a Christian home for the stranger young men coming to this city."[3] While it would take another decade for the YMCA to make the above implication explicit by turning its a attention toward railroad workers, the YMCA's expansion was linked early on to the issues raised by industrialization.

Although YMCA efforts with workingmen actually slightly preceded companies' interests in industrial betterment work, the association did not enthusiastically embrace such efforts at first. As a result of meetings held by Rev. Dr. W. H. Goodrich of the First Presbyterian Church of Cleveland for railroad workers at the Union Depot, the Cleveland YMCA began to offer its services and facilities to railroad men in April 1872. In the years that followed, YMCA railroad work slowly gained recognition. In 1873, at the International Conference of YMCAs at Poughkeepsie, New York, George Cobb, the Cleveland railroad secretary, received five minutes to talk about YMCA railroad work. In an action that later became part of YMCA lore, Cobb ingeniously extended his allotted time by beginning his talk as he walked up to the podium and continuing to talk on the way back to his seat.[4] Notwithstanding such creative interventions, it would take the YMCA four more years to make railroad work part of its program.

When railroads, prompted by concerns with labor unrest, began more systematically to implement welfare policies to manage labor relations in the late 1870s, the YMCA took notice. In June 1877 the YMCA International Committee and the delegates at the YMCA International Convention at Louisville decided to begin railroad work on a national basis.[5] One delegate told his audience that "some of the managers of our leading railroads are beginning to realize that no part of their general equipment pays better than a Railroad Christian Association." Urging his fellow YMCA delegates not to miss this opportunity, he stated that railroad officials "are ready to seek the best welfare of their employes [sic] but need our cooperation." With a fair amount of self-confidence, the delegate admonished his audience that "we have only to step in and occupy the land."[6]

In October 1877, only a few months after the inception of the new line of association work, railroad YMCA delegates met at Cleveland, the site of the first railroad YMCA. The conference attracted many more delegates than expected, with representatives from Chicago; Boston; Evansville, Indiana; Detroit and East Saginaw, Michigan; Jersey City, New Jersey; Buffalo, West Albany, and New York, New York; Bradford, Cincinnati, Cleveland, and Columbus, Ohio; and Altoona, Erie, East Liberty, Philadelphia, and Pittsburgh, Pennsylvania. In addition, ten places that had not yet established associations sent delegates.[7]

Railroad YMCAs sought to offer an alternative to the saloon. They provided a place for leisure and for time spent between "runs," offering overnight accommodations and meals—all in combination with non-denominational religious work.[8] Eventually, railroad YMCAs became an important part of early experiments with welfare capitalism. For the first decade after its inception, YMCA railroad work remained a fledgling offspring of the YMCA movement.

After 1889 the work expanded with Clarence J. Hicks's succession to the position of Railroad Secretary. Duplicating the strategy used by railroads to promote their own expansion, Hicks introduced "system work": the YMCA Railroad Department now began to directly approach railroad companies to establish YMCA branches at as many divisional points of an entire railroad system as feasible. With this new approach, first adopted along the Chesapeake and Ohio Railroad, railroad officials dealt directly with a representative of the YMCA Railroad Department instead of having to deal with each railroad association individually, which was initially under the supervisory control of its respective city association. Hicks's effort paid off, as the YMCA became a crucial agency of early welfare capitalism along North American railroads.[9]

By the end of the nineteenth century, the YMCA figured prominently in the efforts of several companies to secure the loyalty of their workforces.

By the 1890s the YMCA railroad work expanded and so did the department's staff. Reprinted from *Railroad Men* 12 (October 1898): 17. (Courtesy of Kautz Family YMCA Archives, University Libraries, University of Minnesota, Twin Cities, and the YMCA of the USA.)

To be sure, only a minority of railroads offered reading rooms in the 1890s. According to an 1892 Interstate Commerce Commission report, out of 350 railroads, 78 offered reading rooms and subsidized accommodations to their employees. Out of those 78, 44 channeled their efforts through the YMCA.[10] By the turn of the century, a majority of railroad systems availed themselves of the services the YMCA had to offer. One railroad official wrote: "I know of no railroad appliance which has been so universally adopted as has the Y.M.C.A., with the single exception of a certain make of lubricating oil." This official also had an explanation ready. With an implied trust in the socially lubricating effects the YMCA might provide in industrial relations, he stated that "the reason that this oil is somewhat more generally adopted than the Y.M.C.A. is no doubt due to the fact that . . . the president and energetic hustler at the head of the oil company is also the president of a Young Men's Christian Association."[11] Paralleling the spirited efforts of the YMCA along the railroads, the association considered expanding its outreach to workers in other industries.

Alongside the inauguration and expansion of YMCA railroad work, associations began to reach out to other groups of workers on the state and local level. First discussions of such attempts actually preceded the YMCA's railroad work. In 1867, the New York state convention of the YMCA "discussed how they could 'best reach and benefit the young mechanics and working men of our cities and towns.'"[12] Notwithstanding such early considerations, the association moved slowly on this issue. In 1881 George Warburton of the YMCA Railroad Department promoted an expansion of YMCA programs to mechanics in an article in the national YMCA newsletter, *The Watchman*. Warburton suggested that the YMCA should do "anything . . . to . . . make their surroundings both in the shop and the boarding house more congenial and helpful."[13]

Such encouragement did not fall on deaf ears in the YMCA. In 1882 the Minnesota state YMCA sent a "gospel wagon" across the state to bring the message of Christ to lumbermen. In addition, the YMCA state committees of Alabama, Colorado, Kentucky, Pennsylvania, and Wisconsin attempted work with mine workers in the late nineteenth century.[14]

The Pennsylvania YMCA was the first state association to approach workers in a more systematic fashion. Its outreach to mine workers and timber crews was a direct outgrowth of the YMCA's railroad work. In 1887 an official of the Pennsylvania Railroad approached YMCA railroad secretary Edwin D. Ingersoll about efforts with mine workers in that state. Ingersoll conferred with the YMCA state secretary, and efforts began in Pittston in 1887 and spread throughout the bituminous coal region during the following decade. In 1898, the year of the United Mine Workers' successful strike for union recognition in the bituminous region, the Pennsylvania YMCA inaugurated work with miners in the state's anthracite region. In 1899 the Pennsylvania YMCA followed with programs for lumbermen. Two secretaries, carrying a small organ, hymnbooks, and Bibles, traveled through eleven logging camps. The *Pennsylvania Association News* reported that "the committee has decided to make this a permanent feature of its work." By 1903 the YMCA had six secretaries in the anthracite region and three in the bituminous coal fields.[15]

As early as 1892 YMCA officials believed that it was necessary to systematically extend its efforts of uplift to workingmen beyond the railroads and put such programs on a broader basis than it had done previously. In its 1892 *Handbook*, the national YMCA asked local branches to put mechanic journals in their reading rooms and standard references on the library shelves and to offer evening classes and practical talks to apprentices. The *Handbook* further suggested that local branches obtain permission from employers to distribute YMCA brochures in workers' pay envelopes.[16]

Association officials believed that YMCAs could provide an ideal meeting ground for its middle-class members and the workers the YMCA now hoped to attract, with the goal to overcome class tensions and mitigate industrial conflict. The YMCA expected difficulties, but those would be outweighed by benefits: "There will be prejudice, possibly an inclination to class jealousy, on the part of some of the young men, which can be overcome by frank and kindly intercourse." Class prejudice, the YMCA felt, was a two-way street. Therefore, "care will be necessary on the part of the membership generally, to do or say nothing likely to offend any or to make them ill at ease." YMCA officials felt they had a distinct mission to mend class conflict. As the *Handbook* stated, "the affiliation of these young men with other classes in the Association will not be without its social significance, and may perhaps help in solving some perplexing problems now pending before the country."[17] The authors of the YMCA *Handbook* believed that in the homosocial environment provided by the YMCA, differences could be overcome and solutions found for the pressing problem of industrial unrest. In practice, however, the YMCA remained far more reluctant than the *Handbook* suggests.

When the YMCA International Committee decided to expand association programs to urban, industrial workingmen in 1903, the work had an experimental character at first. Charles C. Michener, the Industrial Department's first General Secretary, even had to split his time among several positions within the YMCA. The YMCA Executive Committee, too, urged Michener to proceed with little publicity and to organize "a few strong industrial associations." Between 1902 and 1906 Michener and the secretaries in the field laid the basis for the program.[18]

The Industrial Department approached factories and company towns about inaugurating industrial work, while Michener and his staff began to draw the existing YMCA state committees and city associations in industrial centers into cooperation with the Industrial Department's work. Industrial YMCAs were soon established at Vermont Marble Company in Proctor, Vermont, Westinghouse Air Brake Company at Wilmerding, Pennsylvania, National Tube Works in Lorain Ohio, Pearl River Lumber Company in Brookhaven, Mississippi, and Monaghan Mills in Greenville, South Carolina. By 1906, the last year that Michener served as secretary, the Industrial Department had established industrial associations in twenty-four locations in eight states: Arizona, Mississippi, New York, Ohio, Pennsylvania, South Carolina, Tennessee, and Vermont. In 1906 these twenty-four industrial Associations represented a total membership of 3,662 men. In addition, an association for African American mine workers had been established in Buxton, Iowa.[19]

At the beginning, though, there was an occasional misunderstanding regarding the purpose and nature of the Young Men's Christian Association and its policies, much to the dismay of YMCA officials. In Douglas,

Alaska, "before the building was opened, one of the saloon men, not under-standing Young Men's Christian Association ethics, made an offer of $500 a month for the 'bar privileges.' Another would give $200 for running a 'Black Jack' table."[20]

In the early years, the YMCA Industrial Department preferred to set up new branches in isolated company towns and mining and lumber camps, rather than to work out of already established city associations in the na-tion's industrial centers. YMCA officials felt that the geographical isolation would make it easier to reach the workers. While the YMCA would even-tually spread to all kinds of industries, both in isolated settings and in the nation's urban industrial hubs, strike-prone industries in a highly paternal-istic setting, such as cotton mills, were among the most willing benefactors of the YMCA. The YMCA's success in such settings paved the way for the YMCA in other manufacturing industries.[21]

By 1907 the YMCA was ready to expand its industrial work. Charles Towson, who came from the YMCA railroad branch at the Pennsylvania Railroad in Philadelphia, replaced Charles Michener in 1907. Towson's succession to the position of General Secretary of the YMCA Industrial Department in 1907 represented a turning point. Under Towson's tute-lage, YMCA industrial work expanded significantly. The YMCA extended its reach far beyond company towns and mining and lumber villages into the nation's industrial centers, drawing urban associations everywhere into the fold. By 1916 the Industrial Department, in cooperation with urban as-sociations, offered tournaments for shop men, factory athletic and baseball leagues, lectures on workplace safety, educational classes, talks on personal hygiene, neighborhood socials, and Americanization classes.[22]

Classes in English and civics, intended to Americanize immigrants, represented an important departure after 1907. In May 1907 the YMCA Industrial Department hired Dr. Peter Roberts to coordinate that aspect of YMCA industrial work. Setting up offices at American and European ports, such as New York, Boston, Philadelphia, and Baltimore, Liverpool, South-ampton, Hamburg, and Bremen, the YMCA helped immigrants at the ports of arrival with handling formalities, finding relatives, and avoiding fraud and provided them with letters of introduction to the local YMCA secre-tary at the immigrants' final destination.[23]

Through its range of efforts and programs for railroad and factory workers, the YMCA began to reach a substantial number of American workingmen along railroads and in urban industries.[24] Membership figures can serve here only as a rough indicator, as company-sponsored YMCAs offered services to nonmembers as well as to members. In November 1889,

Both the Railroad Department and Industrial Department of the YMCA made the improvement of workingmen their aim. Both programs tied a worker's "efficiency" on the job to the way he spent his leisure. Reprinted from *Association Men* 34 (January 1909): 100, 171. (Courtesy of Kautz Family YMCA Archives, University Libraries, University of Minnesota, Twin Cities, and the YMCA of the USA.)

when the YMCA *Yearbook* reported membership statistics of its railroad associations for the first time, 98 railroad associations reported a total membership of 19,277. By 1911 the total number of railroad associations had increased to 235, reporting 86,091 members. Over the following decade, the YMCA both consolidated and expanded its operations along the nation's railroads. By 1920 the number of railroad associations had decreased to 226, but the membership had increased to 110,253. The YMCA industrial work followed this pattern. The YMCA *Yearbook* reported membership among industrial workers for the first time in 1905. In that year the YMCA reported 3,170 members in 24 industrial associations. From 1907 to 1920 the membership among industrial workers grew from 48,000 to 126,235. This expansion critically relied on the funding offered by YMCA benefactors in industry.

Beginning with railroads, the YMCA began to target companies as patrons, and corporate support became decisive on all levels of the creation and expansion of YMCA programs with railroad workers. Railroad support enabled the YMCA to hire a secretary to coordinate the new programs with railroad workers on the national level. In February 1877 William H. Vanderbilt and Cornelius Vanderbilt, Jr., president and vice president of the New York Central and Hudson River Railroad, Thomas A. Scott, president of the Pennsylvania Railroad, John W. Garrett, president of the Baltimore and Ohio Railroad, and Morris K. Jesup, YMCA International Committee member and philanthropist, contributed funds to enable the committee to hire Edwin D. Ingersoll of the Columbus YMCA as General Secretary for railroad work.[25] However, corporate funding did not turn out to be a cornucopia from which the association could expect a steady outpouring of wealth right away. For eleven years Ingersoll worked "with the understanding that his engagement was subject to thirty (30) days' notice to quit at any time salary might not be in sight."[26] Corporate support, then, was crucial to launching the YMCA Railroad Department and to later YMCA industrial work, also.

The founding of the YMCA Industrial Department followed the pattern set by the Railroad Department earlier. In 1902, encouraged by the success of the railroad work and the corporate support it had received, the YMCA International Committee resolved to create an Industrial Department. Richard Cary Morse, Cephas Brainerd's successor as chairman of the YMCA International Committee, explained in a fund-raising letter to John D. Rockefeller, Jr., that the "success in the [YMCA] railroad department opens our way to other industrial classes of working men." Morse's appeal proved successful. A contribution from John D. Rockefeller, Sr., underwrote the salary for the first YMCA secretary responsible for industrial work.[27] The cases of Ingersoll and Michener were no exception to the rule.

Companies routinely paid the local secretaries' salaries, and staff retention depended on such support. YMCA railroad secretary Edwin Ingersoll reported that "sixteen Railroad Secretaries were reported in the last Year Book. Two of those who were not supported by R. R. Companies have been compelled to seek other employment for support and are dropped from the list." But there was good news as well: "fourteen [secretaries] have been added, making the number now twenty-eight [and] liberal appropriations by Railroad Companies have enabled us to secure men of ability and experience."[28] From 1889 to 1912 the secretarial staff of the YMCA Railroad Department increased from two to nine on the national level, and the number of local railroad secretaries and assistant secretaries increased from 113 to 518. The YMCA Industrial Department started out with just one

Edwin Ingersoll, the first International Secretary for Railroad Work of the YMCA International Committee, began his service in 1877. For eleven years Ingersoll worked under an agreement subject to thirty-days notice, in case the YMCA could not raise his salary for the next month. Health problems forced him to resign his position in 1888. Reprinted from *New York Railroad Men* 11 (November 1897): 1. (Courtesy of Kautz Family YMCA Archives, University Libraries, University of Minnesota, Twin Cities, and the YMCA of the USA.)

secretary. In 1907 two secretaries were exclusively engaged in industrial work on the national level. An additional twenty-four secretaries devoted their time to industrial workers and their needs in local YMCAs. By 1919 the International Committee had increased its industrial staff to 16 secretaries, 84 city YMCAs employed 102 industrial secretaries, and 158 industrial YMCAs had a staff of 347 secretaries. By 1921 218 YMCA secretaries served a working-class population in urban industries, and 226 YMCA secretaries served workingmen along railroads.[29]

At first, though, companies' interest in industrial betterment work remained limited, and YMCA facilities all too frequently reflected that fact. Railroad YMCAs at isolated division points or temporary construction sites had to make do with retired passenger coaches or even freight cars. In some cases, a YMCA branch consisted of abandoned passenger cars placed end to end and the vestibules boarded up to allow visitors to pass from one car to the next regardless of snow or rain.[30] The first reading room of the Cleveland YMCA railroad branch was dedicated on 14 April 1872. Designed to offer a pleasant and morally uplifting environment, the room had been fitted out by the Lake Shore and Michigan Railroad, the Cincinnati, Columbus, Cleveland and Indianapolis Railroad, and Pennsylvania Railroad in the Union Passenger Depot, the main railway station. Described by the President of the Cleveland YMCA, H. A. Sherwin, as "a splendid room, elegantly furnished . . . , the walls hung with portraits and elegant engravings," the YMCA reading room was also shared by travelers, who used the same facility as a waiting room.[31] Even the pioneering and pace-setting railroad

The restaurant facility of the New York Central and Hudson River Railroad YMCA branch in New York City—a far cry from the basement room at Grand Central Station that the YMCA had to occupy initially. Railroad YMCAs were the first to feature restaurant and dormitory facilities, nowadays commonly associated with YMCAs in metropolitan areas. (Courtesy of Kautz Family YMCA Archives, University Libraries, University of Minnesota, Twin Cities, and the YMCA of the USA.)

association at Grand Central Station, New York City, connected with the Vanderbilt-owned New York Central and Hudson River Railroad, occupied rather primitive quarters for quite some time. Officially opened on 20 November 1875, the facility was "a poorly-lighted affair, with a series of vaults behind it." In one of the vaults, "a small closet-like apartment was fitted up with a couple of zinc bath tubs, supplied only with cold water which was brought to the requisite temperature by the injection of live steam after the tub had been filled."[32] Possibly because the major strike waves in late nineteenth-century America would not hit the nation until 1877 and later, these early railroad YMCAs often had to make do with rather crude facilities because railroads and their officials lacked interest.

The majority of railroad YMCAs continued to occupy rooms in railway stations until the late 1880s, when companies began to provide funding for larger buildings as railroad managers became increasingly interested in

The building of the New York Central and Hudson River Railroad YMCA in New York City, one of the finest, most sumptuously appointed YMCA buildings anywhere at the time. Even today the so-called Vanderbilt YMCA, on 46th Street, serves as a reminder of the YMCA's connection to the Vanderbilt railroad interests. (Courtesy of Kautz Family YMCA Archives, University Libraries, University of Minnesota, Twin Cities, and the YMCA of the USA.)

industrial welfare work. In 1887 Cornelius Vanderbilt, Jr., provided for a building for the New York Railroad YMCA at Madison Avenue and 45th Street at a price of $150,000. In 1893 Vanderbilt expanded the facility at an additional cost of $225,000. That building, "with its baths, game rooms, lounges, gymnasiums, lunch rooms, infirmaries, libraries, bowling alleys, but still few sleeping rooms set standards for further facilities."[33]

In the late nineteenth century the quality of the railroad YMCAs' quarters improved and the number of railroad association buildings increased. Whereas in 1890 less than twenty railroad YMCAs had buildings of their own, by 1911 188 railroad YMCAs had their own facilities, offering beds and meals at cost as well as leisure time activities and religious work for railroad workers.[34]

By the beginning of the twentieth century, companies often provided or paid for an association building, which in 1905 usually cost from $10,000 to $50,000, and routinely donated a portion of the annual operating costs.

At Westinghouse Airbrake in Wilmerding, Pennsylvania, the company paid for a building that cost $100,000. At Monaghan Mills in Greensboro, North Carolina, the company paid for a building that cost $10,000 and agreed "to be responsible for whatever money is needed in addition to the fees and subscription from the men."[35] Around the turn of the century the Vanderbilt-owned New York Central Lines alone had expended over $700,000 for railroad YMCA buildings and spent about an additional $40,000 per annum for maintenance.[36]

Not always did the YMCA gain the support of a targeted sponsor. In 1877 James Stokes, a member of the Board of Directors of the YMCA of New York City and of the Executive Committee of the YMCA International Committee, brought a Cleveland railroad worker and YMCA member, Henry Stager, to New York to represent and talk about the YMCA railroad work with potential contributors. Stokes asked Stager to talk to his father about "some incidents of the work." Stager, who is alleged to have played a critical role in the founding of YMCA railroad work at Cleveland, apparently either misunderstood Stokes or did not know the difference between the words *incidents* and *accidents*. Stager "shocked the elder Stokes with such a series of head-on collisions as never had been heard before by mortal man" that he refused to contribute "to the detriment of an already depleted treasury."[37] While the outcome of this meeting, apparently orchestrated with great care by the younger Stokes and the YMCA International Committee, must have been disappointing, such mishaps seem to have represented more an exception than the rule, and many companies made "handsome contributions" toward the YMCA's budget.[38]

In particular, an emergency could open an employer's purse wide. After the infamous "Ludlow Massacre" at the Rockefeller-owned Colorado Fuel and Iron (C.F. & I.), John D. Rockefeller, Jr., too, turned to the YMCA.[39] What began on 23 September 1913 as a walkout of Colorado miners for recognition of the union and other demands turned into a protracted battle between striking miners, state militia, and Baldwin-Felts detectives, costing 200 lives. On 20 April 1914 twenty-four men, women, and children died; eleven of them suffocated in a hideout underneath a burning shack near the Ludlow mines of C.F. & I—hence the name "Ludlow Massacre." The strike ended when Secretary of Labor and former UMW official William B. Wilson convinced the President to restore order by sending in federal troops.

After the events at Ludlow, the public associated the name Rockefeller with coercion, violence, and death in the Colorado coal fields. In an attempt to salvage his damaged reputation, Rockefeller attempted to reconfigure the company's approach to industrial relations. In addition to establishing the Rockefeller Employee Representation Plan, which became the model for company unions adopted by companies all over the United States, Rockefeller brought in the YMCA, with which the Rockefellers had a long-established relationship.

In 1915 John D. Rockefeller, Jr., authorized funding for the YMCA to put a secretary on its Colorado staff full time, and none other than former YMCA Railroad Department official Clarence Hicks took charge of employer-employee relations at C.F. &. I. and served as a liaison to the YMCA. At C.F. & I. the YMCA developed one of its largest operations at a single company. The company appropriated $80,000 for buildings and equipment and $20,000 annually for maintenance. Within ninety days YMCA associations were established in nine C.F. & I. camps, with each building costing approximately $15,000.[40] Clearly, the YMCA benefited from managers' concern with labor strife and interest in welfare capitalism as a solution.

While companies contributed generously toward the YMCA railroad and industrial departments, they commonly made their support contingent upon the workers' own commitment before management would donate out of the company's coffers. Standard Steel Works, a branch of the Baldwin Locomotive Works at Burnham, Pennsylvania, appropriated $20,000 for a building on the condition that the men themselves raised an additional $10,000. Companies such as Standard Steel were afraid to invest money in an endeavor that might draw no positive response from the workers themselves. In addition, management customarily expected that the workers contribute to the cost of YMCA branches through their membership fees of $5.00 annually, which did not include meals and overnight accommodations. This was more than workers customarily paid at company-operated clubhouses. According to a 1919 government survey, railroad workers paid between $0.50 and $1.00 per annum for membership privileges in company clubhouses. Notwithstanding the financial burden to workers' budgets, employee membership fees covered 40 percent of the expenses of YMCA railroad work during the early years. In 1919 Richard C. Morse even claimed that membership fees covered 60 percent of the cost.[41] Insisting on contributions from the workers assured not only that they would help to bear the cost, but also that they had an interest in the programs and activities offered. While it is impossible to say whether the money expended on railroad or industrial YMCA branches ever paid off for the companies, the association's sponsors did not lose sight of cost-accounting either.

Company officials not only allocated funds to support the YMCA, but also took on positions of leadership in the newly created YMCA Railroad Department and in local associations. From the beginnings of national railroad work in 1877, railroad officials and businessmen were consistently involved in railroad YMCA affairs. The first chairman of the Railroad Department of the International Committee, Charles Finney Cox, held positions with three Vanderbilt lines and served as the vice president of the Canada Southern Railroad and treasurer of the Big Four and Nickel Plate lines. In 1881 Edwin Ingersoll reported that "at St. Louis a R.R. President, three Vice-Presidents, General Managers, Superintendents and leading citizens compose the R.R. Committee of the Young Men's Christian Association." Ingersoll himself reported on the results and progress of his work directly to Cornelius Vanderbilt, Jr., who became a member of the YMCA International Committee in 1879 and served as chairman of the Committee of Management of the New York railroad branch of the YMCA until his death in 1899. The composition of the Industrial Department's leadership similarly reflected its close relationship with industrial management: virtually all of the national Industrial Department's committee members held executive posts in industry. Certainly, these man took such positions for practical reasons: their involvement in YMCA governance enabled them to supervise the expenditure of funds, which they often provided themselves. In addition, from the perspective of railroad officials, providing stewardship by sponsoring the YMCA seemed not only a means to defuse potential for unrest, but also a way to demonstrate that they utilized their wealth in service for the betterment and uplift of the community and that they took an active interest in their employees as their moral charges.[42]

Paternalistic motives were clearly on the mind of many company officials and managers. In Ottumwa, Iowa, the YMCA's General Secretary, W. F. Hunting, reported that "the superintendent in one of our factories makes it his business as soon as the whistle blows to visit every department of the factory and personally invite the men to gather for the meeting." And in another factory in the same city, "the president of the concern not only gives his money, time, and influence to the association's interests, but he is one of our lay speakers, and addresses his own men in regard to their personal salvation."[43]

Because merchants, manufacturers, and other members of the business community not only made financial contributions but also often sat on the governing boards of associations, their local control represented a major obstacle to the YMCA's ability to promote reforms—if the association ever attempted to do so. In 1912 reporter John A. Fitch, who had been an investigator with the Pittsburgh Survey, reported a conversation in a steel to\..1 in Pennsylvania.[44] The YMCA secretary told Fitch that the association had only 150 members, a tiny fraction of the steel town's male population. Fitch asked him why he did not have a larger membership, since the steel mill alone employed 5,000 men. The secretary responded that the association mostly attracted the company's office clerks rather than steelworkers, because "the working schedule of the mills is such as to make it very hard for the workmen to use the Y.M.C.A. facilities; they would be too tired, you know, to use the baths and the bowling alleys, even if they were members." Fitch inquired whether that was a result of the twelve-hour day and the seven-day week, which the secretary confirmed.[45]

At that point, Fitch suggested that the association should campaign for a shorter work day: since "the working schedule is a barrier between you and your real work; in order to reach the men at all, your first job apparently, will be to break down that barrier." This the secretary vehemently denied, explaining the possible consequences: the companies are "the heaviest contributors, and it would break it up for me to go into anything like that; anyway, I would be sure to lose my job." He also pointed out that the YMCA did not depend only on the company: "we are backed up everywhere by the substantial business men of the various localities; they would not stand for any such movement."

Company control over the community and its institutional infrastructure played a key role. The YMCA secretary explained how tightly the YMCA was tied to the local business community: "the steel company has done more for the schools here than any other agency. They gave the borough its high school building. [The local YMCA's] president is the chairman of the school board." Therefore, he said, "it would hardly do, you know, under the circumstances, for the association of which he is president to oppose the policies of the steel company. At least, he would look at it that way." The secretary related a previous experience. "Last winter," this somewhat embarrassed secretary explained, "we wanted to get Charles Stelzle here to talk to the men." But "Stelzle always talks to workingmen about bettering their conditions and usually mentions unionism." And he added that "this is a non-union mill—the company would not tolerate unionism." He admitted that "no sane men can deny that there is need here of any agency that will better the conditions of the men, but you see how Stelzle's talk would create unrest, and it would not do. We had to decide against it." This secretary considered "it best to keep pretty quiet and be careful."

While the secretary realized the problems within the community, he emphasized the limitations on the YMCA as an agency advocating reform. "Things are rotten here alright," he added, "but the work of the Y.M.C.A. is not one of social reform." He saw the local YMCA's objectives as limited: "we aim to get good, clean young men, and to help them stay clean. That is our work." This secretary expressed his personal belief in reform, but he considered it "outside of our line of activity." This YMCA staff member hardly felt that he could oppose, or even challenge, the association's benefactors.

To be sure, YMCA officials did not always require subtle forms of coercion, feeling victimized by forces beyond their control as the steel town YMCA secretary did. In at least one case, a local YMCA official rather eagerly lent a helping hand in an effort to suppress radical labor organizing. During the Johnstown steelworkers strike in 1919, a Citizen's Committee, under the leadership of W. R. Lunk, secretary of the Pittsburgh YMCA, and H. L. Tredennick, president of the Pittsburgh Chamber of Commerce, forced William Z. Foster, who would later become one of the leading figures in the Communist Party of the United States, and a group of labor organizers out of town. On 7 November 1919 a group of about forty men apprehended Foster, who was supposed to address the Johnstown strikers, in broad daylight and took him to the railroad station at gun point. Several of the group accompanied Foster on the train eastward to Conemaugh to ensure his departure. The following night the Citizen's Committee surrounded several other socialist labor organizers in their hotel and demanded that they leave town within twenty-four hours. Later, Foster claimed that Lunk and Tredennick "freely stated that the strike could never be broken by peaceful means, and that they were prepared to apply the necessary violence."[46] While we have only Foster's reporting of the event, it seems apparent that YMCA secretary Lunk was not coerced into participating in the forceful deportation of the labor organizers.

Despite such apparent partisan interventions, the YMCA claimed that its works served both employers and employees. In 1916 the YMCA addressed the increasing social significance of management-labor differences. At its Thirty-ninth International Conference in Cleveland in 1916, the Association resolved that "with reference to organized industry, the field of the Association lies in the zone of agreement between the employer and employee." The YMCA "does not attempt to adjust issues, but it creates a spirit which enlarges the field of agreement in which issues may be more than readily adjusted." The association emphasized that "it is not partisan.

It is more than neutral; it is mutual." The YMCA declared that the "a\
support" of employers and workers was desired: it portrayed its own "v\
thy service" as uniting "employers and employees in mutual Association
effort."[47] This statement was reiterated in 1919. The YMCA's approach to
issues of labor relations was based on the assumption that capital and labor
had shared interests, while its actions, at least in some instances, clearly
contradicted such proclamations. The YMCA, in any case, was aware of the
situation and admitted that there was not only "a sense of class distinction"
between the YMCA and the workers it purported to serve, but also a widely
shared "impression that the YMCA is under the control of the capitalistic
class."[48] The YMCA, then, had reached a critical juncture in its own development, displaying contradictions between theory and practice.

In addition, not all industrialists shared the excitement over the
YMCA's efforts and achievements that some of their contemporaries displayed in words and deeds. In 1904 a railroad official complained that
"we farm out our restrooms, our temperance encouraging resorts, to the
Railroad Y.M.C.A. Where comes in the company, whose existence makes
occupation possible, whose capital is invested, whose property is involved?"[49] Some railroad officials began to feel that industrial welfare work
was too important to subcontract it to a third party, and criticism of the
YMCA, casting doubt on the association's ability to handle the job, became
prevalent.

Among the YMCA's most severe critics was the National Civic Federation (NCF), founded in 1900 by Chicago reformer Ralph M. Easley with
the purpose to improve worker-employer relations through mediation. In
the NCF, Republicans such as Marcus A. Hanna, AFL leaders such as Samuel Gompers and John Mitchell, and Progressive reformers such as Louis D.
Brandeis joined hands to achieve a reconciliation between conservative
"bread-and-butter" trade unionists and welfare capitalists. The NCF
wished to see company welfare work in the hands of trained professionals,
hired by the company and working as their employees, rather than under
the control of outside agencies such as the YMCA. The NCF raised many
complaints against the YMCA, implying that funds expended on the YMCA
were a waste of a company's resources.[50] In 1904, at a Conference on Welfare Work, held under the auspices of the Welfare Department of the National Civic Federation, several participants also had questions about the relationship between YMCA officials and the companies. Whereas the YMCA
always claimed to be uniquely qualified as a mediating agency between the
company and the workers, industrial welfare professionals present at the

conference challenged the association's claim to independence and impartiality.[51] By the early twentieth century, the organizational matrix of welfare capitalism began to change.

By the second decade of the twentieth century, labor relations began to change and so did welfare capitalism and companies' ways of handling their personnel. In the 1920s employers altered their approach to personnel issues in two ways. First, employers began to rationalize the handling of their workforce through personnel management departments. Second, proponents of welfare work tried to avoid the charge of paternalism. Instead of character-building, Bible classes, reading rooms, and lectures, companies added new tools to their repertoire and increasingly utilized financial incentives, such as stock ownership, group insurance, paid vacations, and savings plans to increase efficiency and loyalty among their workers.[52] As companies adjusted the ways and means by which they handled their workforces to the requirements of corporate management, they relied less and less on groups such as the YMCA.

"To Aid in the Upbuilding of Character": The YMCA,
Welfare Capitalism, and a Language of Manhood

❧

The YMCA and its benefactors in industry sought to cast the relations
between employer and worker within a cultural framework of benevolent,
manly paternalism in which employer-patriarchs not only provided work,
but also looked after the moral well-being of their employees and built the
workers' manhood. Certainly, a culture which celebrated the ennobling
effects of hard work also readily accepted the more coercive aspects of
such ideas, such as the notion that employers would rescue their workers as
moral charges from a potential descent into immorality by bestowing upon
them the benefits of Christian patriarchal discipline. As both the YMCA
and its benefactors in industry liked to perceive it, employer and employee
were engaged not in conflict but in a relationship of mutual service, based
on a shared manhood. YMCA officials and company executives sought to
contest the workers' mutualistic code of manly loyalty toward one's peers
and a "manly bearing" toward the boss. In place of the workers' communal
ethic, which had been the backbone of artisanal craft culture, the officials
and executives sought to instill loyalty and service to the company. By subsuming relations between management and workers under a shared ideal of
manliness, YMCA officials and company managers believed they could dis-
place class conflict and assert their cultural hegemony through paternalistic governance over the workers.[1] Gender as a central category of workplace relations played a critical role in the social thought of employers and
YMCA officials alike.

YMCA and company officials agreed that the type of manhood required could be subsumed under a concept of "character," inherent in antebellum articulations of middle-class manhood. This character ideal balanced notions of hard work and individual acquisitiveness with a sense of duty, service, self-restraint, and civilized morality. Based on this concept of balanced character, YMCA secretaries and company officials articulated a language of manhood that proffered harmony and interdependence between social classes. Both hoped that workers would shed their propensity for political radicalism and industrial unrest once they adopted the ideal of manhood the YMCA and employers promoted.[2]

As YMCA officials and employers urged workers to build character, however, they also altered the meaning of the concept. An ambivalent concept of the male self when it first made its appearance, character reflected the attempt of American Victorians to culturally connect an emerging marketplace to a vision of a socially and economically more stable communal past. While it sanctioned and enabled market performance, the character ideal also sought to tame men's acquisitive impulses by tying them to self-restraint and civilized morality and reigning in such drives and passions by subjecting them to the refining private bonds of female domesticity.[3] Capitalizing on this ambiguity, employers and YMCA officials redefined the meaning of character in terms of what I call here "workplace domesticity." Accordingly, entrepreneurs, managers, and the YMCA believed that workplace relations should be modeled on the social relations of a patriarchal household, where the *pater familias* would guarantee the well-being of those in his care—both relatives and employees—and receive the products of labor, deference, and unflinching loyalty in return. Manhood, and its complement "character," as defined by entrepreneurs and YMCA officials, was to be the foundation stone of labor relations. The ideal of character did not decline in the late nineteenth century, as Karen Halttunen has suggested, but was redefined.[4] YMCA and employers sought to proffer the upbuilding of character and the resulting gain in manhood as its own reward, disconnected from any expectations of economic advance. Equals as men, the worker bartered his service and pledge of loyalty for his employer's promise of moral guidance that would help him to build character and become a better man, though not necessarily a better paid man. On the basis of a shared gender consciousness, employers and employees were supposed to find common ground, with both playing their parts in a harmonious whole.[5]

This chapter builds on a growing historiography on the role of gender in labor relations and managerial discourse.[6] Most recently, Andrea Tone has focused on the ways in which employers attempted to make the factory an instrument of reform and to rework working-class masculinity by the means of industrial betterment programs. Focusing on the Progressive Era, Tone asserts that, wherever the target group consisted primarily of male workers, "welfare work tried to redefine the requirements of a successful breadwinner . . . emphasizing that the kind of work employees performed was less important than the financial benefits they acquired for performing it."[7] Although Tone's formulations are useful, the picture was more complex than she suggests.

The transition from an understanding of work and labor relations that emphasized skill and the control workers exercised on the shopfloor, to a notion of work that reduced the relation between employer and employee to the wage form was more uneven than appears from Tone's study. It is well understood that employers increasingly rationalized the handling of their workforces after 1900. As employers expanded control over all details of their operations, they turned toward mechanization, which resulted in the so-called deskilling of many work processes. Employers turned to the deskilling of work processes not only to lower the cost of production, but also to break workers' control and power on the shopfloor. Whereas especially skilled artisans regarded their managerial powers on the shopfloor as an integral part of their work and their manhood, companies sought to reduce labor relations to the wage form, proffering salaries and eventually benefits packages as a substitute.[8]

As I will demonstrate, however, while entrepreneurs did expect increases in productivity and revenue by encouraging their workers to be more faithful employees, they emphasized the nonpecuniary rewards of service to the company. I suggest that industrial welfare work often actually reflected the ways in which entrepreneurs attempted to rule their factories like family-based manufacturing establishments earlier in the nineteenth century as they also began to redefine their self-perception as corporate employers and as men.

My interpretation supports a recent reassessment of welfare capitalism. Historians have suggested that welfare capitalism failed to wean workers away from unions or to discourage labor activism and did little, if anything, to increase productivity. Howard Gitelman has argued that "welfare work proved more of a comfort to its proponents than an obstacle to opponents."[9] Managers' concerns over manliness—both their workers and their own, and their desire to validate an emerging entrepreneurial paradigm of manliness—shaped entrepreneurial and managerial thought about labor relations and industrial welfare work and represented a motivating force in creating such programs. Industrial conflict provided the stimulus.

In March 1877 the presidents of the Pennsylvania, New York Central and Hudson River, Erie, and Baltimore and Ohio Railroads, financially strained by recession and competitive overexpansion of railroad networks, decided to cut their losses and optimize profit by reducing wages and increasing workloads. When the Baltimore and Ohio Railroad took the lead in implementing a 20 percent wage cut, railroad workers in Martinsburg, West Virginia, went on strike on 16 July 1877. Soon the strike spread to Pittsburgh, Philadelphia, Baltimore, and other cities as railroads elsewhere took similar measures. At several locations, events took a violent turn. On Sunday, 22 July 1877, a battle between 650 Philadelphia militia and Pittsburgh strikers left 25 dead. Railroad officials turned toward the federal government for help, and President Rutherford B. Hayes proclaimed a state of emergency and dispatched troops.[10]

Not everywhere did events turn violent. On Monday, 23 July 1877, the strike reached Cleveland, where railroads, too, had cut wages and increased workloads. The Cleveland railroad strike, however, remained a comparatively subdued affair.

Explanations differ for why the events in Cleveland took a turn different from other locations, such as Pittsburgh or Chicago. Historian Robert Bruce has argued that widespread public hostility and the prudence and forbearance of both city and railroad management accounted for the more peaceful Cleveland developments.[11] Railroad manager James H. Deveraux, president of the Cleveland, Columbus, Cincinnati and Indianapolis (C.C.C. & I.) Railroad and the Lake Shore and Michigan Railroad offered an alternative explanation of the events. On 24 July Deveraux, who had cut wages by 20 percent like other railroads, assembled the workers in the machine shop and promised to restore one-half of the wage cut by 1 August. With the recent strike events in mind, that was certainly a most prudent step to take. And in all likelihood the assembled workers considered Deveraux's announcement at least modestly pleasant news.

In his own account of the events in the machine shop, however, Deveraux sidestepped the wage issue, instead emphasizing their shared bonds of Christian manhood. Deveraux claimed that he had "appealed to them as Christian men, urging the principles of the gospel as his argument against their proceedings." While "the passions of the men were strong," Deveraux remembered, "he had not spoken long before sour faces grew brighter."

In his rendition of the event, Deveraux accounted for the workers' receptiveness to his appeal to their Christian manhood by pointing to the uplifting activities of the Cleveland YMCA railroad branch, which had been active among the city's railroad workers since 1872: "It was through [the YMCA's] influence that this change had been brought about."[12] On the following day, the C.C.C. & I. Railroad employees went back to work and soon thereafter the strikers at other Cleveland railroads followed. On 4 August 1877 the Cleveland strike was over.[13]

Certainly, this account, published by the YMCA as a pamphlet under the title "Christianity versus Communism," is to a good extent apocryphal. Hardly an accurate account of the events, and certainly not a reliable reflection of the workers' thoughts, the document reflects the attitudes and biases that railroad executives brought to Gilded Age labor relations and how they perceived its problems and possible solutions. Men such as Deveraux regarded manhood as critical to resolving industrial conflicts before violence would erupt, and they believed in the power of their own appeal.

Believing in the power of Christian manhood as a mediating agent in industrial relations enabled Deveraux and others like him to disconnect industrial conflict from the underlying economic issues. Appealing to workers as Christian men reflected an attempt to elevate labor relations above the realm of industrial and class conflict and onto a plane of shared manliness, articulated and defined by men such as Deveraux. In fact, this was a private solution for a public problem: appeal to a shared manhood promised to resolve a public issue—industrial strife—in terms of a private vocabulary of manhood and morality. By emphasizing a shared manliness as the plane upon which employer and employee would interact, tensions in industry appeared as a morality issue that could be resolved through an appeal to the workers' manhood, with only marginal adjustments to wages or work conditions. The primary purpose of work was not a wage, but self-culture, and its dividends were payable in manhood. Simply put, this language of manhood, while it effectively bypassed questions of remuneration and power in the workplace, actually served to reinforce the existing social relations of production by substituting manhood as a reward in and of itself for economic advancement. And there was no better place for true men to affirm their manliness than in the employment of a railroad.

As one contemporary observer suggested, a success in railroad employ represented a proof of manliness and very much a reward in and of itself. YMCA supporter and journalist, St. Clair McKelway, speaking at the 1908 anniversary celebrations of the New York Railroad YMCA building, linked employers' ideals of manliness to good discipline and work ethic: "A blunderer, a slouch, slink, an insubordinate, may get along by hook or by crook in other callings, but in the railroad service the duration of his employment is short." Working on the railroad was regarded as a test of a man's manliness. Echoing social Darwinist ideas prevalent in social and business thought at the time, McKelway proclaimed that the "men whom railroads make have good stuff in them. The men whom railroads smash have not good stuff in them. The railroad service is of an exacting character. Success in it illustrates the law of survival of the fittest." [14] With railroad work dividing real man from the refuse, any man in the employ of a railroad would get a chance to prove his manliness through strenuous struggle in the execution of his tasks. A successful career in service to a railroad validated the manliness of the managerial elite and suggested that the managers' entrepreneurial ideal of manhood represented a suitable model and prescription for success for others employed in railroad service to emulate. Far from becoming "sissy men," a man who succeeded in service to a railroad would gain an exuberant manliness. As McKelway explained, working on the railroad "makes you manly and makes you so independent as almost to make you sassy." [15] Although railroad employment was believed to build and affirm the manliness of those performing it, the type of manhood workers exhibited was problematic in the eyes of employers and YMCA officials.

YMCA officials clearly perceived some of its manifestations as troublesome. YMCA officials believed that railroad workers exhibited a peculiar type of manhood that encompassed both desirable and undesirable traits. George Warburton, the influential railroad secretary of the New York City Railroad YMCA and editor of that association's own publication, *Railroad Association Magazine*, wrote that the "characteristics of [railroad workers'] employment account for the existence of a peculiar type of manhood." Railroad work, Warburton believed, "not only creates a type, but inevitably attracts to itself certain kinds of men." [16] While railroad work made men, the nature of the employment also tended to attract precisely the men considered in many ways least desirable for the job.

Looking back, Warburton wrote in 1921 that "the typical railroad men of the early seventies was [sic] picturesque, daring, clannish, and peculiarly susceptible to these influences of moral degeneration which . . . are most potent in the life of men who spend much of their time away from home." He described the workers in terms of noble savages and ranked them morally with other rowdy workers, referring to "the men . . . [as] a rollicking boisterous lot." Commenting on the particular occupational culture of railroad workers, which not only tolerated but often encouraged risk-taking as

Here shown while secretary of the Toronto, Canada, YMCA railroad association, George A. Warburton served for over a decade as secretary of the influential New York YMCA railroad branch. (Courtesy of Kautz Family YMCA Archives, University Libraries, University of Minnesota, Twin Cities, and the YMCA of the USA.)

part of their workplace culture and their manhood, Warburton observed a "disposition to abandon and reckless daring" among them.[17] Contemporary observers, such as Warburton, regarded railroad workers as exceptionally daring, self-conscious, and independent-minded. In a social setting increasingly shaped by bureaucratic rationality, such behavior became unacceptable. As late nineteenth-century American business culture embraced the financial risks of corporate capitalism, risk-taking that was not related to pecuniary gain, like that involved in railroad workers' occupational culture, came to be considered needless and counterproductive and, therefore, wasteful and immoral.[18] While railroad work seems to have attracted a certain type of men, the nature of the employment further compounded the problems.

Warburton blamed the workers' recklessness and lack of morals on irregular shifts and the nature of their work, which required them to spend long hours on the road away from home. Railroad work often seemed to entice the men away from the path to the desired type of manhood. Warburton explained that "the excitement of their calling kept them keyed up during long hours of labor, drained their vitality, and was followed by abnormal lassitude and weariness." *Vitality*, one of the key words of Victorian biological science, referred to contemporary assumptions about the human body's internal energy supply, which especially men were urged to use sparingly. Concerns with vitality mirrored the widely held belief among biologists that living organisms had an inherent life force on which they drew. Just as immoral and licentious behavior diminished the body's energy, so did exhaustion—the depletion of physical energy—encourage what Warburton refers to as "abnormal lassitude," which could mean any form of behavior Victorians regarded as sinful.[19] Warburton added, "it is no wonder that stimulants made a special appeal to such men, or that grosser forms of sin became too often their common habit."[20] The lack of a home and erratic work schedules created irregular habits among railroad men and led them to moral lapses that were believed to endanger their very manhood. Warburton, then, painted an ambiguous picture of railroad workers. On the one hand, the often dangerous railroad work endowed the workers with a certain rugged nobility. On the other hand, railroad workers were considered a potential threat. Albeit railroad workers seemed to represent serviceable raw material, company officials sought to reshape and redirect the more problematic aspects of their workers' manliness in the appropriate direction.

Concerns and assumptions about manhood shaped managerial and entrepreneurial thinking and decision making about industrial betterment programs and the practice of philanthropic giving in the Gilded Age and the Progressive Era. As railroad and industrial magnates, these entrepreneurs had made critical contributions to the joint projects of nation building and industrialization; as "masculine civic stewards" they considered it as their duty to extend their care and guidance over their workers, fulfilling their obligations to the community. Industrial philanthropists, like the entrepreneurs who supported the YMCA, believed that "masculine largesse preserved the republic, the religious establishment, personal character, business integrity, and private investments in a single stroke." These "masculine civic stewards" pursued a two-fold purpose: conditioning workers to be industrious, cheap and available, while uniting men of different class background in a quest for self-culture, rationalizing social behavior according to the dictates of industrial discipline.[21] Reuben Smith, Assistant General Manager of the Cleveland and Pittsburgh Railroad asserted that it was absolutely necessary to have "men of correct habits . . . sober, honest, faithful" in the railroad's employ.[22] These men believed that developing and nurturing a suitable type of manhood among their workers was in the best interest of the company, and they were willing, as we have seen, to commit the necessary funding. Theodore Vorhees, vice-president of the

The YMCA sought to replace resting places and leisure sites such as "The Bucket of Red Blood," a retired boxcar located in Bush, Illinois, "where the railroad men . . . ate their 'Cockroach Pie,' ran the road, quarreled and fought." Reprinted from "The Bucket of Red Blood," Box 1, Promotional Materials, 1911–1913, YMCA Railroad/Transportation Department Records, 1877–1987. (Courtesy of Kautz Family YMCA Archives, University Libraries, University of Minnesota, Twin Cities, and the YMCA of the USA.)

Philadelphia and Reading Railroad, and former superintendent of the New York Central and Hudson River Railroad stated "that it is very much the business of the company to make sober, moral men of their employees, and that any money successfully expended for that end is well invested."[23]

Worried about the proper behavior of the men in their employ, railroad officials hoped to find workers who by conforming to the desired standards of manhood also validated their employers' manliness. Writing in 1903, the president of the Delaware, Lackawanna and Western Railroad, W. H. Truesdale, stated that an employer seeks to hire "the same type of man as he is himself, to serve him in all departments of industry or business."[24] Railroad managers certainly wished to safeguard and preserve values of sobriety and industriousness among their workers, because the benefits would accrue to them, both financially and culturally. I suggest that concerns with proper standards of manhood in the workplace point to railroad officials' apprehensions not only over their workers manliness, but to concerns with their own identity as gendered beings as well.

Nineteenth-century ideals of manhood seemed to validate managers' advancement in an emerging corporate economy and affirmed their model of manhood. On their way to the top, however, managers had become entangled in the contradictions of the ideal of manhood that sanctioned their occupational mobility: while a true man had nearly unlimited opportunities for advancement, manhood was tied to an ideal of the independent producer that regarded salaried nonmanual work as suspicious and not worthy of a man.[25] By the end of the nineteenth century, this elusive ideal of social harmony, based on a vision of American society as a republic of producers, which carried a promise of social mobility for all men, had come under serious strain. Labor activists, like William Sylvis, praised the dignity of industrial, manual labor, but condemned managers and other nonmanual laborers as "effeminate non-producers." Railroad managers had reaped the promises of the code of the self-made man, but as nonmanual workers, their manliness had become suspect.[26]

At stake was the employers' cultural position both as members of an entrepreneurial class and as gendered beings. The antebellum ideal of the self-made man, by grounding manhood "more exclusively in work and entrepreneurial competition," raised as many questions as it offered solutions to the predicaments of men at midcentury. As David Leverenz put it: "was manliness the independence and self-respect of the craftsman or the ability of an entrepreneur to best his competitors and exploit resources, human as well as material? Did a man's self-respect depend on a sense of being free and equal to any other man or on a struggle to be dominant?"[27]

Leverenz has sorted out three paradigms of manhood, implied in the concept of self-made manhood: the "patrician paradigm," which defined manhood through "property, patriarchy, and citizenship," the "artisan paradigm," which articulated manliness foremostly in terms of "Jeffersonian . . . autonomous self-sufficiency," and an emerging "entrepreneurial paradigm," which "made competition and power dynamics in the workplace the only source for valuing and measuring oneself."[28] The power of differentiating among these different paths and possibilities, all of them implied in the self-made man, meant the power to authorize and sanction one path toward self-made manhood, while refuting others. As "character" was quintessential to the self-made man and good public order, defining it became a key cultural battleground. The YMCA and its supporters in industry, seeking to stabilize labor relations and power in the workplace in their favor, sought to fuse what Leverenz refers to as the "patrician" and "entrepreneurial paradigms": employers were to expect deference due to them in their roles as industrial patriarchs. Thus gaining control over defining the cultural matrix that would frame the social relations of production, they would also gain power in the workplace. Through defining character and shaping their workers as men, then, industrialists and managers aspired to validate their own manhood and the social relations of production upon which it depended.

Developing manhood among workingmen represented the key to peace and progress in labor relations and was considered indispensable for in industrial productivity. Without properly developed character, as an *Association Men* editorial put it, there would be no industrial progress: "The success of any enterprise . . . depends . . . upon the character of the individual man." In turn, "the integrity of the man who runs the machine . . . is important to the efficiency of the machine, and on this success is found to turn."[29]

Since the early nineteenth century, when the term *character* made its initial appearance, employers expected their employees to cultivate all those habits that made for true character. A worker, endowed with character, executed each task willingly and cheerfully and did not expect special reward for his efforts. An employee was expected to be reliable and indispensable and recognize that what was best for his employer was ultimately best for him, always placing the employer's interest above his own. As work was widely believed to be ennobling, he took pride in a job well done regardless of the pecuniary remuneration. In exchange, however, the employer would take a paternalistic interest in the worker and provide him with guidance and opportunities for social advancement. This way, the worker would better his material condition, and, more importantly, become a better man as well. While this language of manhood validated a type of manliness that would eschew industrial strife, it also proclaimed to facilitate the workingmen's social advancement: all the qualities that the workers allegedly lacked had helped to propel railroad managers to their station in life.[30]

Character was a key quality which railroad management required of every employee, and railroad officials admonished their workers to form and built the requisite behavioral traits. Charles L. Colby, president of the Wisconsin central Railroad and chairman of the railroad committee of the Milwaukee YMCA, explaining his motives for supporting the YMCA stated that "the main object is to afford [the workers] . . . the opportunities for elevating social pleasures, for moral and religious growth and cultivation . . . and, above else, for the acquirement of sterling Christian character."[31] Railroad officials, like Colby, understood the upbuilding of character as a project that would intensify the cultural bonds between workers and management. William J. Latta, chairman of the committee of management of the Pennsylvania Railroad YMCA, argued that "a responsibility rests upon them [manager and worker] for more than mere superior and subordinate in daily work; a feeling of simple, Christian, neighborly duty; to aid in the upbuilding of character; the founding of opportunities to see the better side of life."[32] Character promised to join the humble and the powerful, bridging differences of class.

Building a bridge between social classes, true manhood eschewed erratic and irregular behavior, and instead consisted of a strong work ethic and a devotion to service, railroad managers felt. Burns Durbin Caldwell, traffic manager of the Delaware, Lackawanna and Western Railroad, and after 1906 a member of the YMCA International Department Railroad Committee wrote that "railroad employees must measure up to the best and highest standards of intelligence, activity and fidelity and all of those traits which constitute strong, self-reliant and forceful manhood." Caldwell urged that men should make the striving for manhood "an ambition, a determination which carries the man constantly forward in the development of his better self." Manhood, he wrote, "contains all the inspiration and incentive necessary to success and there is no good reason why this should not be the ideal of every railroad employee no matter how humble his position."[33] Certainly, managers romanticized the ideals to which they believed they owed their careers and offer it to others as prescription for advancement in life.

As YMCA and company officials debated how to secure the making of character, the focus shifted away from the public, entrepreneurial qualities inherent in the character ideal and toward service, self-sacrifice, and deference. While the concept of character encompassed such behavior traits, Victorian Americans associated these very same attributes also with domestic sentiment. Instead of economic acquisitiveness, entrepreneurial independence, and upward social mobility, character came to symbolize Christian values of self-denial, sacrifice, and collectivity, while retaining the emphasis on hard work, as employers and YMCA officials articulated their expectations of workingmen.[34] William Bender Wilson, vice-chairman of the governing committee of the Pennsylvania Railroad YMCA and telegraph executive for the railroad, encouraged his audience in an 1893 address to "study a true manhood, of which industry, sobriety and earnest resolve are essentials." But Wilson qualified his emphasis on manly, entrepreneurial determination by placing an equally as strong importance on self-restraint, sacrifice, and service. He argued that "the true type of manhood is not found in Achilles before the walls of Troy, Hannibal crossing the Alps, Caesar passing the Rubicon, or Bonaparte encountering the rigors of a Russian Winter." Such traits, which many contemporary middle-class men may have readily associated with the "strenuous life," Wilson identified as "perhaps a correct type of the overcoming man," but, nonetheless, "a false manhood, capable of overshadowing for a time the finer objects of man's creation, engulfing virtue, meekness and the love of others in the whirlpool of personal ambitions." Instead, Wilson asserted that "the lamb submitting itself to be shorn for the benefit of others is a more correct type of manhood than the lion devouring everything in the pathway." Wilson implored his audience that "a lowly and unpretentious life, lived self-sacrificiously and full of desire to benefit others rather than one's self, with a reverential observance of God's laws, will produce manhood, whilst efforts in any other direction will fail." The goal was, he added, to achieve the highest Christian manhood possible, and to live "the manly life on the model of the Christ man."[35] YMCA secretaries and railroad officials shifted the balance of qualities inherent in antebellum definitions of character from the entrepreneurial, acquisitive drive toward sentimental qualities of meekness, self-sacrifice, and service to others. This redefinition of character enabled employers and the YMCA to make private relations of domestic sentiment the matrix of labor relations.

The YMCA concerned itself with that very question. As an editorial in the YMCA's monthly magazine, *Association Men*, put it, "when the manufacturing business of the world was largely done by men whose employees became members of their own households, the employer found the problem of maintaining the character of his employees a comparatively simple matter."[36] YMCA officials envisioned an idealized past when household and shop formed an integral unit and work relations between employer and employee were subject to patriarchal family governance, long obliterated by the rise of the factory system. In the workshop, the YMCA saw the workingmen as integral parts of the family household, ruled by reciprocal obligations: moral and educational guidance from the master-employer in exchange for obedience and service from the worker. The YMCA believed that this system not only provided work but also ensured proper development of good character, a set of behavior traits fundamentally necessary to sustain and support a family and household economically. Whereas the antebellum merchant or artisan household may have accommodated social relations of production, framed by employer patriarchy and worker deference, modern economics of scale would not. The link between workplace and worker would have to be recast as patriarchal household.

If proprietors and managers sought to cultivate an image of themselves as caring household patriarchs, the YMCA catered to those desires and sought to open opportunities to cast the shopfloor as an extension of the employer-patriarch's household. When YMCA work at a company was sufficiently established, one official suggested, "it may be advantageous to sometimes invite ladies to sing, especially if the proprietor has a wife or a daughter gifted with a good voice and some sense." The YMCA believed that "the men like the novelty, are often moved more than by the singing of men, and the women like to do it." Moreover, this would lead to better relations with the factory owner or manager: "it wins the head of the business more than any other courtesy which can be shown and frequently encourages a reciprocity of interest between the office and the shop."[37] YMCA programs frequently were designed to uphold and reinforce an understanding of the workplace as an extension of the domestic sphere, under guidance of a proprietor-patriarch, which, by implication, made the workers his children. Employers supporting the YMCA built and expanded on that same imagery, establishing new ways of enmeshing not only the worker but workingmen's families with the workplace as patriarchal household.

Entrepreneurs sought to mold power relations in the workplace by telescoping a set of social relations of production associated with a notion of a patriarchal household onto the public realm of labor relations. Railroad official B. F. Bush of the Missouri Pacific–Iron Mountain Railway linked the obligations and duties of the railroad workers toward their employers to the workers' roles as fathers and husbands. Accordingly, he cast the relations between employers and workers akin to patriarchal family governance. Only the worker who fulfilled his duties as domestic patriarch could be of service to his employer. "No man can serve his employer faithfully," Bush stated, "and with a conscientious sense of due responsibility for the faithful performance of the duties entrusted to him, without at the same time calling into action those finer attributes . . . which render him a better man in his family affairs, and in his relations with his fellow men." He claimed that the YMCA "has been most effectual and helpful in raising the standard of manhood," which, in turn, "has been reflected in better care and attention to their families, in kindlier consideration of their fellow men, and in more faithful and efficient service in the duties assigned to them."[38] Cultivating sentiment and a sense for proper domestic relations in a worker was to be the key to making him a better man and a more diligent employee. Shorn of its ability to enable acquisitive performance in the marketplace, the new idea of character cast the worker as the dependent member of his employers' patriarchal household—a private solution to the public problem of labor strife. Thus, encouraging men to be dutiful providers to their families would not only anchor them to acquisitive market relations, but workers would serve as conduits between the company and the employees' households. The workingmen themselves were to serve as social conduits between their own households and the workplace. According to this extension of the social relations of production into the workers' households, all men, whether workers or managers, would share the role as providers and patriarchal guardians. In this enlarged household, managers and workers alike fulfilled their duties toward their charges, camouflaging class difference between them and affirming a principle of patriarchal leadership in the process.[39]

Telescoping private values of sentiment onto the workplace cast labor relations in terms of a workplace domesticity. Sentimental values, which YMCA and railroad officials now invested into the ideal of character, encapsulated an ideal of individuality and of social relations independent and autonomous from the marketplace. By deploying sentimental values as a means to shape the social relations of production, railroad executives also metaphorically removed labor relations from the nexus of capitalist exchange. Production would continue according to the rules of capitalist gain, whereas employer-employee relations, guided by values of self-denial, collectivity, and paternalistic governance, would no longer be part of the realm of the capitalist marketplace. Recasting the factory as a homelike, private realm apart from the public sphere promised to preserve the inequities inherent in the social relations of production, while the emphasis on work-ethic related forms of behavior would nonetheless affirm capitalist production. As patriarchs presiding over their companies and all its social relations, employers could expect deference and cooperation from their workers. Thus, having gained control over defining the cultural matrix of the social relations of production, these employers would also gain power and control over the workplace and assert their manhood as corporate entrepreneurs.[40] While a good worker had to have a strong work ethic, pecuniary remuneration and economic advancement were not among the dividends workers should expect.

Proof of manhood gained was its own reward at a time when character alone no longer guaranteed social and economic advancement, and in popular discourse the acquisition of character became a reward in itself, disconnected from the economic benefits. More and more men seemed to become casualties of the struggle for self-made manhood, prompting commentators like Henry Ward Beecher to emphasize that industriousness in itself, not the acquisition of wealth, was the proof of a true man.[41] Burns Durbin Caldwell agreed: "success does not necessarily mean greatness in influence or acquirement, and the failure to attain some specific distinction is not of itself an evidence of failure."[42] While character no longer guaranteed economic advancement, lack thereof remained associated with failure.

Character, as YMCA officials put it, was the reward of hard work and the wholehearted application of one's abilities. As the authors of one brochure put it, "One of the rewards of steadily and faithfully pursuing a life calling is the fibre it puts into the will," which is the "the chief element in character." Instead of expecting material rewards, men should be content with the assurance that dedication in carrying out one's duties would build character: "A duty well performed develops character. Character is not dependent on material success, and yet faithful performance of duty brings a sure reward in the development of character." Productive labor, in turn, made manhood: the "kind of toil . . . which produces something for ourselves or our fellowmen . . . makes manhood."[43] As Caldwell explained, "every step costs effort. . . . Let no man complain, . . . but rather take heart in the fact that his progress is toilsome, for it could not be progress if it were not toilsome."[44] Contemporaries could rest assured, though, since character was regarded as crucial to the struggle toward self-made manhood, the struggle was reward in itself.

The acquisition of character that essentially demanded the same kind of struggle as monetary compensation, was to be its own reward. In 1921 a front-page article in *New York Railroad Men* informed readers that "the road to character, self-respect and manliness is up precisely the same kind of hill as the steep ascent of purpose that leads to any sort of material success."[45] Character and the transformation a worker had to undergo in the process of acquiring it had become a reward in and of itself. This character resembled an internal possession of the man, impossible to take away from him. The man of character, in short, was beyond reproach. YMCA programs aimed to defuse workers' potential for labor unrest by nurturing this set of qualities, summarized as character, within them. However, by the 1910s, employers' understanding and perception of the link between manhood and shopfloor relations began to shift.

Declining support of the YMCA was tied to changes in managerial approaches to labor and personnel policies, but also to changing perceptions of manhood and class. Managerial understandings of manhood shifted from a paternalistic, mutualistic understanding of manhood and its concurrent valuation of personal ties between managers and workers, to an understanding of manhood based on class distinction. Managers abandoned a shared gender consciousness as the foundation of labor relations. David Nye has outlined the process for corporate culture at General Electric. Relying on photographs of GE shops, Nye notes that, as workers' skills were replaced by machinery in the 1880s and 1890s, the workers themselves became less and less prominent in these photographs. Correspondingly, as workers' skills lost significance, it was no longer necessary to devise means for uplifting them into the brotherhood of true men, since they could be replaced by machinery. By the 1920s, the connections made between manhood, rituals of initiation, and social mobility and promotion, became a managerial exclusive, available only by secret invitation: promising young managers and white-collar employees were selected to attend camps at company-owned locations to meet the highest officials of the corporation. Somewhat reminiscent of a campy version of fraternal initiation ceremonies, participants wore special costumes—dressing as lumberjacks, Roman soldiers, or "Lonesome Eunuchs." While not all camp activities appeared to have been conducted in such a seemingly adolescent fashion, they represented, as Nye points out, "a sanctuary where regression to premarital male bonding was actively encouraged."[46] By the 1920s, masculine homosocial company culture had evolved into a managerial prerogative in which workers no longer played a part, because management, assisted by technology, had replaced "the manager's brain under the workman's cap" in David Montgomery's words.[47]

Concerned with maintaining peace and profits in a highly competitive corporate economy, some corporate officials also embraced an ideal of manhood that reinforced their control and authority over the company and its workforce. Reared in a tradition of paternalism, they tried to extend the social relations of production beyond the economic transaction of the labor contract with the goal to shape their workers' behavior on the shopfloor and in their families and communities. Within this paternalistic exchange, the employer would provide guidance and care, which the workers were expected to reciprocate by cheerfully and selflessly giving their service to the company. Disconnecting labor relations from the financial aspect of that exchange enabled employers to proclaim the validity of ideals of manhood as commonly shared across class lines. Instilling workers with an ideal of manhood suitable to their purposes, railroad managers hoped to substitute the mutualistic workplace culture of their workers with an individualistic code of manhood and character, which would redirect the workers' loyalty and service toward another collective, the company.

This language of manhood, then, served company officials on two levels. On the level of class, this language of manhood purported the appearance of equality between men but vested power in the hands of management and submerged the realities of class difference in an ideal of manliness. On the level of masculinity, this language of manhood reevaluated new forms of dependent work, associated with a loss of manly autonomy, as providing service, which antebellum men had already considered as a mark of distinction of a true man. Providing service became disassociated from an allegedly effeminizing loss of autonomy, and instead identified with manhood. Proclaiming the supremacy of service as the measure of manhood aimed not only at lining the company's coffers but possibly also performed important cultural work by reaffirming managers' own power and manliness.

YMCA secretaries and company officials attempted to extend an emerging ideal of manhood of the corporate team player to working-class men, who would equate their own best interest with the company's interest, while the economic benefits would not accrue to them: gaining manhood through serving the company was to be its own reward. Through the redefinition of character in terms of a workplace domesticity, then, this language of manhood created subject positions for workers and their employers, bound in hierarchical relations of gender and class. What subject position would be available for YMCA secretaries remained to be seen.

"A Most Effective Ally in the Work of Labor
Advancement": Workingmen and the YMCA

❖

To a certain extent, late nineteenth-century workingmen shared this entrepreneurial ideal of manliness, which emphasized individual responsibility, self-restraint, sobriety, and hard work as the path toward social advancement and economic mobility. They believed that a man established
self-esteem and earned the respect of his fellow workers, superiors, and the
community through industry, sobriety, duty, civility, and responsibility.
Particular craftsmen embraced the ideals of a producer culture and believed
that labor and capital could share a common purpose, evident, for example,
in the Knights of Labor. In the name of social harmony and respectable
manhood, craftworkers felt that a union would have to exercise certain edifying and uplifting influences over its members. But nineteenth-century
workingmen also expected that in due time such behavior would not only
bring the respect of the community and one's peers, but that employers
would reciprocate and respect the manly independence of the craftsmen and
all that it stood for. Moreover, craftworkers' understanding of their manly
bearing included going on strike in defense of the very independence and
autonomy it entailed.[1]

YMCA programs attempted to defuse workers' potential for labor
unrest by involving them in a web of uplifting activities, all of which were
designed to make them better men and more loyal employees. Concerned about mounting discontent among workers, YMCA officials hoped
that building a higher type of manhood among them would resolve labor-

management conflict and would abet workers' allegiance to the company.[2] Working-class patrons, however, frequently brought their own interests to the halls of railroad YMCAs and attempted to infuse their own ideas and agendas about working-class leisure and its purposes into association spaces.

The nature of the YMCA as a voluntary association enabled members to obtain some influence within their respective local branches. Railroad YMCAs were usually established in response to demands initiated either by the YMCA, the workers, or company management. In many cases, a YMCA official, either a secretary of the International Committee of YMCAs of North America or the secretary of an already existing city association, established contacts with the management of a railroad company to launch an association. Occasionally workers even took the initiative without aid from the International YMCA. Customarily, association officials or workers interested in establishing an association presented their case to the railroad management to obtain a pledge of funding and permission to drum up support for the YMCA among the railroad's employees. Once a YMCA branch was established, a group of railroad employees appointed from their ranks a Committee of Management. Local association governance was vested in this committee, which hired a secretary suggested by the YMCA International Committee.[3] One railroad YMCA secretary explained, "the backing is generally from men of wealth, but the approach to men is always from the standpoint of comradeship." This YMCA official emphasized that the association belonged to the railroad workers, and not to management. He stressed that "the Association at the division points is an association of railroad men, organized by them, offered by them. The president is not a superintendent, but an engineer or a conductor."[4] This YMCA official was possibly a bit overly optimistic as to the egalitarian structure of YMCA governance, as we have seen. However, despite the heavy involvement of management, the YMCA needed some cooperation from the workers themselves.

The establishment of a YMCA industrial branch at International Paper in Rumford Falls, Maine, illustrates the extent to which the YMCA relied on approval from the workers themselves. Between 1904 and 1905 Charles C. Michener negotiated with the International Paper Company. After two conferences with the company's president, a meeting was arranged with "the influential men in different departments of the mills"— most likely the foremen. By the end of this meeting, "32 men took lists and at once began the canvass. After one day's work 13 reported 291 signatures. The other 20 [sic] had a large number of names for membership but had not finished their canvass when this report was sent." Eventually, "over 400 men" agreed to become members and "over $5,000" was "secured in subscription." In addition, the company paid an unknown sum for the building and gave $1,800 toward the maintenance expenses. By September 1905 the necessary funds were provided and the construction work began.[5] While YMCA branches frequently were under the control of management, the process of establishing an association and the structure of local governance, vested in a Committee of Management appointed from among the members, relied on some cooperation from the workers themselves. This involvement, documented best for railroad YMCAs, could potentially give workers a considerable voice in the affairs of local YMCA branches.

Railroad YMCAs drew many of their members from the office workforce, but the majority came from the ranks of the so-called running services, composed of highly skilled railroad engineers and conductors as well as semiskilled brakemen and firemen. A single surviving petition, which circulated among railroad employees in Chicago in 1908, illustrates this point. W. J. Biebesheimer, a trainman with the Baltimore and Ohio Railroad at Chicago and a YMCA activist, obtained the signatures of 360 railroad employees for the purpose of petitioning the Chicago YMCA to organize a railroad department in South Chicago. The signers promised to become members at an annual fee of $5.00. The 360 men who signed their names represented more than thirty occupations. Firemen, with 81 signatures, were followed by 71 engineers, 48 switchmen, 36 brakemen, 32 clerks, and 14 conductors. Only two of the signers identified themselves as laborers.[6]

Membership figures for other railroad YMCAs provide a similar picture. In January 1890 the Pocatello, Idaho, Railroad YMCA on the Union Pacific Railroad counted among its members 16 conductors, 61 brakemen, 33 firemen, 36 officemen, 17 engineers, 31 yardmen, 120 shopmen, and 30 "others." According to the 1905 annual report of the New York, New Haven and Hartford Railroad YMCA, the association had 806 members, consisting of 264 passenger and freight trainmen who were part of the running services, 248 enginemen, 100 officemen, and 60 shopmen. Listings of new members, available for the months from February through August and for November and December of 1905, round out that picture. During those months 204 men joined the YMCA, among them 51 brakemen, 42 firemen, 41 engineers, 18 clerks, and 11 conductors.[7]

Employees in the running services found the YMCA a convenience while on the road away from home. A freight conductor of the Boston and Maine Railroad stated that he "wanted a clean, wholesome, home-like place among Christian gentlemen, where I could stay when out on the various runs."[8] Yet the strong presence of workers in the running services among the association membership was also related to their position and goals within the railroad workforce.

Recruited from among the unskilled workers, the positions of fireman and brakeman represented stepping stones for professional and economic advancement. Firemen aspired to become engineers, and brakemen hoped to move up to the position of conductor. Firemen and brakemen tended to share the concept of manhood of the engineers and conductors, the "aristocracy of labor," because they were part of a common occupational culture, but also to further their own careers. One brakeman, who may have hoped to advance one day to the position of conductor, praised the YMCA for promoting manliness among railroad workers: "I have often wanted to tell you that the 'Y' has made me a better man. . . . You should be proud you are in the Business of Bettering Men." By joining the YMCA, workers such as this brakeman signaled their superiors that they subscribed to values that both company management and the skilled aristocracy of the railroad workforce embraced. One railroad worker gave expression to this motive for joining the YMCA: "I felt that it would be the means of making a better man of me and with the making of a better man comes the making of a better employee, a thing desired by those above you."[9]

Engineers and conductors, among the highest paid railroad employees, regarded the YMCA as a means through which they could initiate fellow workers into a craft culture that represented their values. As skilled workers, they believed that a man established self-esteem and earned the respect of his fellow workers, superiors, and the community, through industry, sobriety, duty, civility, and responsibility.[10] A conductor at the Lake Shore and Michigan Railroad in Cleveland was convinced that the YMCA could be used to direct others onto the right path. He told his brethren that "there is always a class of men who have been there a long time, and have established themselves, and are ready to draw men who are just from home into the saloon, gambling houses and the like." This conductor suggested, "to counteract this, let us get up cottage prayer meetings, and reading-room sociables." He was convinced that "if you can get young men, when they first come into railroad employ, to go into that class of society they will leave the saloon and are safe."[11] A worker at the Meadow Shops at Jersey City, New Jersey, concurred, emphasizing the YMCA as the means to turn young railroad workers into men: "when I observe the many pitfalls that are being concocted to catch the young men of today, we cannot help joining such an organization as the Y.M.C.A., which insures all a young men needs to make him a real man."[12]

"Some Members of the Gang." The YMCA hoped to impress its message that men could be tough and rugged—and YMCA members at the same time. Reprinted from *Association Men* (May 1912): 384. (Courtesy of Kautz Family YMCA Archives, University Libraries, University of Minnesota, Twin Cities, and the YMCA of the USA.)

Skilled railroad workers had several reasons to draw others into the fold. In the 1880s the Knights of Labor began to eclipse the Brotherhoods as a major force in organizing railroad labor. Brotherhood leaders, therefore, may have seen the YMCA as a potential means to draw workers into the fold, strengthening their own ranks.[13] Certainly, the Brotherhoods not only hoped to perpetuate their own craft culture, but also felt the need to guard their own reputation, afraid that they would be judged by the behavior of their less reputable fellow workers. A master mechanic at the Big Four Shops at Brightwood, Indiana, stated that "it would be a blessing if all our men could be inducted to attend the shop meetings and Bible classes, as I am sure we would all be better men for it."[14]

Some skilled railroad workers not only joined the YMCA, but volunteered to carry forward the association's message to their fellow workers. Jim Burwick, a freight conductor, usually spent six months on the railroad. The reminder of the year, including Sundays, he conducted religious meetings for his fellow railroad men for the YMCA. Similarly, Will Byers, an engineer, devoted his time between runs to conducting meetings, and Tom Pape, a boilermaker with the New York Central Railroad, took leaves of absence to do volunteer work. Pape had arrived in the United States in the

1870s and soon turned toward drink and dissipation. He became a "drunk-ard, . . . a burden to society, a menace to law and decency, and a constant source of terror to his family," according to a biographical sketch composed by YMCA secretary Ward W. Adair. One day, escaping from a policeman's club, Pape ended up in a missionary building and embraced the Christian life. Upon his conversion, Pape was able to regain his position with the New York Central Railroad and became a "Christian Gentlemen, . . . a blessing and inspiration to all who knew him." He also became active in the Rail-road Department of the YMCA, where he recounted his life story before conferences and at meetings in YMCA buildings.[15]

The YMCA, in turn, tried to enlist the skilled workers and their fami-lies in the effort of uplifting railroad workers. The secretary of the Elmira, New York, railroad association explained that they would usually ask "the conductors and their wives to give a general reception, and we will invite all the other men. In this way, we seek to bring all the men and their fami-lies into more direct connection with one another, and with the Associa-tion."[16] Skilled workers formed the organizational backbone of the YMCA along the railroads on multiple levels.

While railroad management had a hand in running railroad YMCAs, the engineers and conductors who considered the association's notion of manliness central to the individual's social, moral, and economic uplift played a considerable role in the governance of railroad YMCAs. Lists of delegates available for several YMCA railroad conferences support this point. Among the 308 delegates present at the seventh YMCA railroad con-ference in New York City in 1894 were 38 shopmen, 35 engineers, 9 fire-men, and 8 brakemen. The following year, at the eighth YMCA railroad conference at Clifton Forge, Virginia, 469 delegates were present, among them 66 engineers, 60 clerks, 52 shop men, 31 conductors, 25 firemen, and 20 brakemen. Over the years, engineers continued to send the largest num-bers of delegates to YMCA railroad conferences.[17] Thus, the YMCA and railroad Brotherhoods became closely connected.

Labor union officials, such as Peter M. Arthur of the Brotherhood of Locomotive Engineers and his successor, Warren S. Stone, frequently praised the YMCA's efforts to promote manliness among the workingmen. Arthur, Grand Chief Engineer of the Brotherhood of Locomotive Engi-neers, counted the YMCA "among the many agencies existing in our midst for the healthy training of young men." Arthur associated manliness with individual responsibility, achievement, and self-improvement. He claimed that "a person endowed with a true manly spirit finds little fault with the conditions of his life." Instead, Arthur asserted, a true man will strive for individual accomplishment and take pride in his work. Choosing words similar to those spoken by YMCA secretaries and company officials, Arthur summarized the meaning of manhood:

> Every man's first duty is to improve, to educate and elevate himself, helping forward his brethren at the same time by all reasonable methods. Each has within himself the capability of free will and free action to a large extent; and the fact is proven by the multitude of men who have successfully battled with and overcome the adverse circumstances of life in which they have been placed, and who have risen from the lowest depths of poverty and social debasement, as if to prove what an energetic man, resolute of purpose, can do for his own elevation, progress and advancement in the world.

He maintained that the YMCA's programs greatly benefited the railroad workers who, as a result, "have become more conscientious in their work and have been better workmen because they were better men." Crediting the YMCA for its efforts in ameliorating industrial conflict through moral reform, Arthur framed "manhood" in terms of interdependence between workers and company officials, crediting the YMCA for facilitating such relations. Because of the YMCA's presence, Arthur proclaimed, "there is a better feeling between the men and those over them, a better understanding of the fact that all men can meet on the common plane of religion and Bible study as well as manliness and honesty."[18] Arthur's successor, Warren Stone concurred and insisted that an important goal of any union should be the advancement of manhood among its members. At a railroad YMCA conference at St. Louis, Stone proclaimed that "the labor union which looks after the wage scale of its members and does not strive to uplift the man to a higher standard of citizenship and manliness falls short of its mission."[19] Both the Brotherhood of Locomotive Engineers and the Order of Railroad Conductors shared the YMCA's ideal of Christian manhood. In addition, they also tended to identify with the interests of management, and the rules established to regulate the behavior of their members matched the efforts of railroads to enforce strict discipline among their employees.[20]

While some labor unions shared the conservative goals of the YMCA and management, others believed that association buildings and their genteel surroundings might very well serve the interests of organized labor and stir the workers into action. Articles in the *Union Pacific Employee Magazine*, a Knights of Labor publication, pointed to the possible multiple uses

_A building. The author acknowledged that YMCAs were de-
_prevent workers from organizing but also insisted that the ameni-
_sociation buildings could serve purposes other than those of its cor-
porate sponsors. Association buildings, the article pointed out, could "be
made the most effective ally in the work of labor advancement." Exposed
to the genteel environment of the YMCA parlor, the article predicted,
workers would develop "the desire to have them all the times [sic]." They
would gain a sense "of very unjust and unnecessary conditions" and search
for remedies. Therefore, the article concluded, "labor organizations everywhere should encourage the growth of the demand of such places and see
that they are patronized. . . . If possible make the lecture rooms their assem-
bly rooms." The _Union Pacific Employee Magazine_ encouraged its readers to
explore ways in which workers could infuse YMCA facilities with meanings
of their own.[21]

In some cases the working-class patrons' determination to exercise
more control over railroad associations resulted in the complete separation
of railroad branches from the YMCA. By 1879, only two years after the inauguration of the YMCA's Railroad Department, five railroad associations
decided to separate from YMCA governance. The separation of the railroad associations of Cleveland; Indianapolis; Elmira, New York; Meads-
ville, Illinois; and Altoona, Pennsylvania; from their respective city branches
challenged the integrity of the still fledgling Railroad Department.[22]

The reasons for these separations are difficult to assess, but strictures
of YMCA governance and a feeling that affiliation with the city branches
would stifle the expansion of the railroad association movement played key
roles. Some of the separatists apparently feared that the rapidly growing
railroad work might be bogged down by the city branches who set association policy on the local level and controlled the purse strings of the railroad
branches. Henry Stager, President of the Railroad Men's Christian Association of Cleveland, explained that prior to separation railroad workers had
to become members of the city association, which then transferred funding to the railroad branch. Cleveland's separatists were convinced that their
affiliation with the city branch, which, like most city associations, was controlled by the urban business leaders, hampered their ability to attract railroad workers. By severing its ties with the Cleveland YMCA and becoming the Railroad Men's Christian Association of Cleveland, the leaders of
the railroad branch tried to gain control over the railroad branch's own
membership contributions. This, Stager claimed, would place "the association in full control of those directly interested."[23] By vesting control over

the railroad branch's affairs in the hands of the workers who represented its membership, Stager hoped to attract more workers.

Other railroad branches separated from the YMCA because of its forbidding attitude toward games, which apparently limited the association's appeal to workers. George Cobb, secretary of the separatist Indianapolis railroad association, claimed that the lack of games alienated workers and drove them into saloons. Cobb urged the introduction of "innocent" games such as checkers and parlor croquet as a strategy to keep the workers out of disreputable places. Moreover, Cobb cautioned "not to plaster the walls of our rooms with 'don't do this' and 'don't do that,' for as a result the boys don't come in." Cobb trusted that the YMCA's restrictive policy toward games and entertainment prevented more workers from entering association buildings. Cobb reported that the situation in Indianapolis had changed since the association had separated from the YMCA. Asked how the railroad men in Indianapolis responded to the independent association, Cobb replied that he occasionally encountered "R.R. boys who are a little suspicious of the Y.M.C.A." He said that he had recently asked a railroad worker to join the association, but the man responded, "'That is a Y.M.C.A. affair.'" Cobb explained the changed circumstances to this worker and was able "to remove his suspicions, and got his name as a member." He added, politely scolding his fellow delegates at Altoona, that "there have been mistakes made by the Y.M.C.A. We might as well confess that."[24] Cobb felt that prevailing YMCA policies on leisure activities within the buildings hindered the association's objective to reach out to workingmen.

Even though they were only a few, a further spread of separatist sentiments among railroad associations would have undermined the leverage of the YMCA in negotiations with railroad companies for further funding. Richard C. Morse, General Secretary of the International Committee of YMCAs, implied as much. Offering reconciliation, Morse stated that "the advantages of fellowship are mutual; we welcome and rejoice in it to-day, not only because it helps forward the Railroad work, but also all other work of the Young Men's Christian Associations." Morse said that "much of the best fibre of muscle, brain and heart, and of all that goes to make up genuine manhood in our land, is possessed by Railroad Men." Morse continued that "joyfully we welcome Railroad Men to companionship with us in the work. We need them. They are coming to our help. . . . It is a glorious work; we need in it all the elements of strength in the country."[25] Influential railroad officials, such as Cornelius Vanderbilt, urged autonomous associations, which depended on railroad contributions and used railroad property, to reunite with the YMCA. Association representatives and railroad officials also assured the workers that they would continue to have a voice in the management of railroad YMCAs. By 1883 the issue was settled in favor of the YMCA, and it appears that all separatist branches had renewed their affiliation with the respective city associations.[26] But the lesson that the YMCA had to do more to attract workers was not lost on YMCA Railroad Department officials.

In the aftermath of the separatist threat, the YMCA Railroad Department made efforts to become more attractive to the workers, but it did not abandon its primary goal of morally uplifting the railroad men. Indeed, YMCA officials believed that the games and amusements could be incorporated into the association's grand strategy of improving men by means of moral reform. In his 1883 annual report, Edwin D. Ingersoll, the International Committee's General Secretary for Railroad Work, recognized that many workers might not be interested in prayer meetings and Bible classes. But he hoped that workers attracted into YMCA buildings by activities in which they were interested would soon also "become interested in social and musical entertainments, or in illustrated newspapers and magazines." Ingersoll considered more uplifting forms of entertainment only a first step in the process of morally regenerating the workers. As railroad workers would partake in more genteel leisure activities, Ingersoll asserted that "amusements are less attractive or needful. [The worker] has learned to want and use something better. Thought is stimulated. His social instincts are satisfied with healthful associations." Ingersoll trusted that, given the chance to experience more uplifting entertainment, the workers' leisure preferences would undergo a change. As men were led to desire more genteel ways to use their leisure, Ingersoll was convinced, "beer gardens and billiard rooms are less attractive than our rooms."[27] Once exposed to the inspiring environment of a YMCA building, Ingersoll surmised, workingmen would turn their back on traditional forms of working-class culture.

This change, Ingersoll believed, would have consequences for their behavior on the job. As a result, "the man becomes a better man, a better citizen, a more intelligent and loyal servant of the corporation," Ingersoll reported in 1882.[28] Two years later, he added that the "social, literary and musical attractions . . . cheerful rooms and good influences" of the YMCA left "no excuse . . . to any employee to use stimulants or seek harmful surroundings for society, refuge and rest in leisure hours."[29] Even when the YMCA broadened its program to include games and other amusements, association officials continued to insist on instilling workers with a sense of gentility in hopes of turning them into more faithful employees.

Gradually, some railroad secretaries advocated an approach more akin to the leisure activities of railroad workers by introducing games. In 1882 Orlin R. Stockwell, of the Columbus Railroad YMCA, argued that the association should integrate entertainment into its larger program. He felt that "amusement rooms are good things in our work if properly managed." Stockwell believed that "good will result, because some men will be attracted to the room through the amusements whom you cannot reach in every other way." Games and entertainment were a controversial issue within the YMCA. Stockwell responded that games had never resulted in "what I would call direct evil; men have never gambled . . . in connection with our games." Of course, Stockwell conceded, "sometimes a man gets a little excited, and perhaps there may be a few hasty words spoken." He admitted that "there is danger in such a case; but if the secretary is wise it can be overcome."[30]

Nonetheless, games remained a controversial subject. The YMCA had begun to accept chess and checkers, but games such as billiards were identified with gambling and drinking and therefore detrimental to the association's goal of building Christian manhood. The Hartford, Connecticut, Workingmen's Exchange, in the basement of the local YMCA building, provided for an opportunity to play pool, cards, and smoke since 1893. The Workingmen's Exchange, though, was an exception, and the name suggests that it was not an official part of that association's program, but merely carried out in affiliation and under the same roof. By the early twentieth century, however, workers had forced the YMCA to make concessions and to accept billiards, smoking rooms, and bowling alleys.[31]

The initiative often came from the railroad workers themselves, who in some places overruled YMCA regulations. In 1899, for example, rank-and-file workers of the railroad association in Hoboken, New Jersey, introduced billiards. Most likely aware of the controversial nature of the subject and in lieu of the appropriate equipment, the workers introduced billiards in a rather piecemeal process. For a while, the YMCA parlor must have been an amusing sight, as the workers started playing pool on a croquet table "using cues instead of mallets; then a few adventurous undertook to play a kind of mongrel game of billiards on the croquet table, in spite of the disadvantages of the wickets." Eventually, "the wickets were taken out, a new cloth provided for the table, and billiards were played on a house-made table." Finally, the Superintendent of Construction of a local railroad "made a billiard table, which seemed to answer the purpose very well."[32] By taking the initiative into their own hands, the workers at Hoboken had taken a stand against YMCA policy.

The workers' introduction of billiards put the secretary of Hoboken's railroad branch into an awkward position. Local donations and membership dues provided for the secretary's salary. In addition, Joseph L. R. Sunderlin, the general secretary of the Hoboken Railroad YMCA and a former railroad engineer himself, may have been partial to the interests of his clientele. But the secretary was a representative of the International YMCA and as such required to uphold association policy, including the ban on billiards. Sunderlin, therefore, had to absolve himself of any responsibility for the situation. The introduction of billiards, he claimed, was "the natural result of a chain of circumstances beyond the control of the leaders in the Christian work of the Association, who were opposed to the movement." However, the secretary tried to assure his fellow YMCA officials that "he did all in his power to promote the best interests of the scheme, immediately taking precautions to surround the playing of billiards in the Association with proper safeguards." Although the secretary did not elaborate on the precautions he took, close supervision of the workers' activities surrounding the table was certainly among them.[33]

Despite the secretary's opposition, the committee of management of Hoboken's railroad YMCA welcomed the introduction of billiards. Hoboken's committee of management, composed of workers, claimed that billiards could very well aid in weaning workers away from saloons and launched a fundraising campaign among the patrons for the acquisition of a billiard table. By embracing billiards, the railroad workers espoused a rather pragmatic, and ultimately more practical, vision of the YMCA's mission. A conductor argued: "I consider billiards a good thing for the Association, as it keeps men in the building, and away from objectionable places." Railroad conductors and engineers represented the aristocracy of railroad labor, who often shared the YMCA's ideal of manhood. This conductor certainly did not think that billiards would counter the YMCA's effort of promoting higher ideals of manhood among the workers. Another railroad worker expressed similar sentiments. He urged the YMCA, "if you are going to rob the saloon of its patronage, you must rob it of its games, when they are not necessarily wrong."[34] Voices among the railroad workers at the Hoboken Railroad YMCA hoped that billiards would aid in drawing the men away from saloons and other places of ill repute and bring them under proper guidance within the YMCA.

With the support of the workers and the committee of management, billiards became a permanent feature of the Hoboken association despite the YMCA's and the secretary's opposition to the game. A month after his first report on the developments in Hoboken, the secretary wrote, "we are still studying the billiard table problem." But his reservations were already obsolete, because, he added, "there is no doubt that with us the game has come to stay."[35] While the secretary at Hoboken had definitely accepted the facts created by the association's patrons, in general, the YMCA remained uneasy about such amusements with the halls of association buildings.

Some within the association worried that billiards might damage the YMCA's Christian image. One author, signing as "your uncle," wrote that "it may be alright for a railroad Association to introduce billiards in its social room, but when an Association gets so proud of it that they issue a flashy announcement about their 'billiard and pool rooms,' it is time for something corrective." "Your uncle," as Richard Cary Morse, General Secretary of the International Committee, was known in YMCA circles, did not oppose games, such as billiards, but was afraid that a more orthodox, Christian segment of the YMCA's patrons might take offense. He counseled that "if these games are conducted in a quiet way, the same as the other games of the Association, there may be no strong objection to them." However, he continued, "a work placarded as above will not command the respect of conservative Christian people." "Your uncle" warned that "it takes wisdom to handle these games in connection with our work, and where this is lacking, it were better to do without the games."[36]

From the perspective of YMCA policy, he may have had a point, as the billiard table occasionally did become the center of association activity, much to the dismay of those who opposed such secular developments. One secretary reported in a slightly exasperated fashion: "I am alone here daytimes; because of the pool table I find it very difficult to do much outside of the building." Apologetically, he added, emphasizing the revenue gained, that "this nets $440 a year." "Your uncle" questioned the usefulness of a pool table under such circumstances and asked whether it was "worthwhile for a secretary to make himself a pool table attendant?"[37] Such discomfort with billiard tables and related recreational activities dominated debates in the YMCA for quite some time. Not everybody in the YMCA was upset about the introduction of games and other activities that to others seemed to threaten to tear down the fabric of moral manhood.

At least one YMCA secretary regarded the potentially negative moral influences, such as games and smoking, as a challenge rather than a threat. "The most encouraging feature of the work, here" a YMCA secretary at

Hagerstown, Maryland, wrote, "is that the devil is contesting every inch of the ground. Sometimes there is so much smoke and dust in the air that it is hard to tell where we are." Notwithstanding, this secretary had no doubts about the outcome of the struggle for the railroad workers' souls. He exclaimed that "the devil loves the railroad boys, and so do we. By God's help we will possess the land in Jesus' name."[38] Such exuberant optimism, however, remained the exception in YMCA circles.

Only after the turn of the century did major railroad officials embrace billiards. George A. Warburton, general secretary of the New York city railroad branch and the influential editor of *New York Railroad Men*, acknowledged that "the games and the smoking rooms have been a large factor in helping the Association to compete with the saloons for the patronage of railroad men." Games, Warburton claimed, were "a distinct help, each appealing to men with different social and intellectual tastes."[39] Warburton recognized that although games were not directly linked to the promotion of moral uplift they could nonetheless fulfill a useful role within the YMCA's strategy of moral reform. "Associations have tested billiards and pool with the best results. Men who have given the game proper attention and safeguard know that the Association is the best place in any city for the game. I am thoroughly convinced that any bad result is the fault of the management instead of the game itself. . . . The pool Association room under a strong Christian man will get as many men into Bible classes and into Church membership from this department as any other—the opportunity there is even greater."[40] In the end, the YMCA accepted billiards and other previously undesirable activities, but association officials remained convinced that they could control games and smoking rooms as part and parcel of a larger strategy that would result in better, morally reformed men.

Whatever the motives, billiards and other games drew far more workers into YMCAs than quests for religious salvation. Between January and July 1913 the Grand Trunk Railroad YMCA conducted thirty-five interviews with workers on their religious lives, but not a single worker joined the church. At the same time, however, more than 3,000 men requested games, such as chess and checkers, and more than 4,000 men played billiards. The general secretary of the Chicago and Eastern Illinois branch reported similar figures. Between February and September 1913, ninety-one patrons requested a religious interview. While no men converted or joined the church as a result of these interviews, more than 1,600 men played pool during the same time period.[41]

To be certain, this was not a uniform picture. For example, during March 1899, 547 railroad workers with the Chesapeake and Ohio Railroad

Initially, the YMCA opposed billiards as a danger to Christian manhood. Despite YMCA opposition, railroad workers successfully established billiards at many railroad YMCA branches by
the early twentieth century. Reprinted from *Railroad Men* 27 (September 1914): 12. (Courtesy
of Kautz Family YMCA Archives, University Libraries, University of Minnesota, Twin Cities,
and the YMCA of the USA.)

attended religious meetings at eight railroad associations located throughout Kentucky and Virginia, whereas only 165 workers participated in other
entertainments.[42] By and large, however, the evidence suggests that the
majority of workers did not go to the YMCA to satisfy spiritual needs.

Composition of the railroad workforce may have contributed to the
problems YMCA officials experienced with religious work. As a result of
immigration, the ethnic and religious composition of the American workforce had begun to change, and this was reflected in the membership of
railroad YMCAs. Although precise numbers are not available, according
to one source, Roman Catholics outnumbered members from all other
churches in railroad YMCAs by 1899.[43] This shift in the ethnic and religious composition of the railroad workforce might help to explain the severe objections of workers against YMCA religious work.

In general, railroad workers reacted to the religious programs of the
railroad YMCA with a sullen resentment. In East St. Louis, for example,

lack of interest led to the discontinuation of religious work in 1899. Due to space constraints, the branch's secretary had conducted gospel meetings in the association's reading room, which "resulted in driving out a number of men who were not interested" and instead "made an adjacent saloon their place of resort until the meetings were over."[44] A brakeman with the Pennsylvania Railroad expressed what many workers must have felt about the YMCA's attempts to minister to them. He complained to the YMCA's secretary: "I have been bothered with Bible-study lessons lately; I believe they came through you. . . . I wish you'd have them discontinued."[45]

The feeling of resentment frequently also extended to the question of joining the YMCA. The general secretary at the Dearborn, Chicago, station, for example, noted that whenever he asked workers to take out memberships in the YMCA, workers tended to avoid the issue by complaining about "dull times." The same secretary noted that some men, who apparently were not members, "made a convenience of the rooms in disagreeable winter weather, absent themselves as the weather is more pleasant outdoors."[46]

Among those railroad workers who joined, few considered membership in the YMCA as a long-term commitment, and membership turnover was generally high. Between 1897 and 1901 the New York Railroad YMCA gained each year between 376 (1897) and 590 (1899) new members, but also lost between 346 (1898) and 473 (1899) old members. In part, this fluctuation corresponded to workforce turnover. In each of the above years, between 149 (1897) and 238 (1899) members left the YMCA because they left the company. But also between 74 (1898) and 94 (1899) workers canceled their membership without giving a reason, and between 26 (1898) and 154 (1897) were dropped because they failed to pay their dues. The year 1904 brought new records: out of 656 members who left the YMCA, 221 were no longer employed by a railroad, 119 resigned without giving a reason, and 233 had quit paying dues.[47] Railroad workers generally refused to identify themselves with the YMCA as an institution.

Instead, railroad workers who patronized the YMCA felt that the services they rendered to the company gave them the right to use the amenities offered in YMCA buildings and indicated this through their behavior. Along the Pennsylvania Railroad, workers demonstrated their sense of entitlement by leaving the YMCA without paying their bills. To alleviate this problem, the Chicago YMCA requested railroad management to introduce a system of payroll deduction. The company, however, refused to implement it, because they felt that it was beyond their responsibility.[48]

Some YMCA officials complained about the abuse of association facili-

ties and privileges. YMCA secretary Ward Adair from Scranton, Pennsylvania, for example, protested about workers whose "idea is that the place
was built for the use and abuse of railroad men irrespective of membership." Adair particularly disapproved of the general lack of respect for etiquette among some of the workers. The "mossback," Adair complained,
"spits on the new floor as he did on the old [and] his used up quids are
thrown in the general direction of the cu[s]pidor, but he cares little where
they land." Adair alerted his fellow secretaries that "when he patronizes the
washroom, it will be well to search his side-pockets for soap before he
leaves the place. . . . [and] should he be so reckless as to take a bath, look in
his calaboose for your missing bath towel." With some disdain, Adair concluded that "he is the same old hog in new surroundings." Such concerns
may not have been without grounds: the theft of the soap dispenser at the
Pennsylvania Railroad YMCA at Jersey City prompted the secretary to
post the following "moderate and carefully restrained statement": "The
man who stole the soap dispenser from the P.R.R. Y.M.C.A. will need
something stronger than soap powder to cleanse his guilt and he will get
something stronger and hotter if he does not repent."[49] While such grous-
ing sounds amusingly petty, it also illustrates that workers paid little respect
to YMCA officials' concerns regarding standards of respectable behavior.
Violations of etiquette and theft of soap dispensers turned out to be a mi-
nor concerns, however, when compared to some more serious breaches of
good behavior.

At a railroad YMCA at East Deerfield, Massachusetts, on the Boston
and Maine railroad, a riot took place in the building in 1907. The record
does not reveal the reasons for the brawl, but during the course of events
"a party of drunken [railroad] employees got into difficulties with the night
man, knocked him down, broke dishes over his head, broke down the door
to the Secretary's office, overturned the pool table, threw burning lamps
about, smashed windows and escaped." The fact that the drunken workers
involved in this riot targeted the pool table would have served to confirm
the fears of many YMCA officials that games resulted in drunkenness
and undermined discipline. In addition to random acts of destruction, the
workers also broke into the office of the YMCA secretary. This act may
suggest that the drunken brawl was not quite as random as it may appear at
first glance, but possibly was deliberately staged to get rid of an unwanted
association representative. If this was the case, the workers succeeded:
upon request of a "better class of railroad men," the YMCA replaced the
secretary at East Deerfield, whom the petitioners "held responsible for the
outbreak because of the lax discipline." East Deerfield remained a trouble

spot, as two years later a drunken brakeman assaulted the new secretary. Joseph Mathiews Dudley of the Railroad Department, responsible for the area, noted that "this was the fourth time that such outbreaks have occurred." Evidence suggests that there was a pattern to these frequent altercations between workers and YMCA officials. Underrepresentation of railroad rank-and-file workers on the YMCA's committee of management was apparently one reason behind challenges to association authority at East Deerfield. In 1913 the local railroad Brotherhoods on the Boston and Maine Railroad at East Deerfield, Massachusetts, gained greater representation of the rank-and-file employees on local YMCA committees.[50] After the YMCA agreed to add rank-and-file workers to the committee of management, the reports of violent outbreaks disappeared from the record.

In addition to such isolated incidents, workers boycotted the YMCA in at least two locations. In Washington, D.C., trainmen of the Pennsylvania Railroad, who had free accommodations in an old train station, boycotted the YMCA and "resent[ed] being asked to join the Association to receive privileges." The boycott must have been organized, because the confidential report on the situation claimed that "a group of leaders are responsible."[51]

Not easily hoodwinked, workers quite correctly perceived the YMCA as a tool of the company and in no uncertain terms resisted the association's attempts to attract members. One company official recalled "the history of one association organized in a particularly difficult field." At that undisclosed location, the YMCA secretary "had been told that several hundred employees had signed the petition for the establishment of the Association, and that the new field was a very promising one." Upon visiting the shops, a different picture emerged. When he entered the shops to solicit members, the watchman "grabbed him by the arm with upraised club, and said, 'Get out here, lively, or I'll break your head.'" Endowed with a company pass, the secretary was allowed to proceed. However, the workers showed little enthusiasm when asked to join the YMCA: "the first man . . . said, 'No, I'll never join your charity association. It's for the poor dupes who know no better.'" Another worker responded forcefully: "'We are no heathen and don't need any missionary sent to us by the railroad company. I signed the petition on request of the foreman, but I'll never join. We all know that you are simply a tool of the company and after we have all joined your Association, they will cut our wages and send you to do missionary work elsewhere.'"[52] While the flaw in this worker's logic is easily discernible, it is also clear that workers at some locations at least perceived the association as a company tool to mollify more severe labor policies. At the same time, workers did not always reject the association in such a fashion.

Instead, in some locations workers pressed for a greater role association governance. At Ignace, along the Canadian Pacific Railw   ...e local railroad Brotherhoods of engineers and firemen appointed a committee of management to take charge of the association in September 1910. The union leaders claimed to know nothing of the already existing committee. Under rules of YMCA governance, they had violated the Evangelical Test, as they had not previously declared their allegiance to a Protestant church. The secretary in charge of the area, Joseph M. Dudley, reported two months later, though, that "a slight misunderstanding with the Brotherhoods of Engineers and Firemen about the method of appointment of the Committee of Management at Ignace on the Canadian Pacific Railway was happily settled." Dudley added that "the evangelical basis is fully understood now and approved. One other result is that a splendid engineer has joined church and accepted appointment on the Ignace Committee." Although the YMCA and the Brotherhoods arrived at an agreement, the association apparently had to make a concession, as an engineer was added to the previously appointed Committee of Management. At Russell, Kentucky, "one of our most serious Association problems," in the words of the secretary in charge of the region, a Brotherhood member called a committee to close the YMCA and evict the secretary. The attempt, though, was opposed by other Brotherhood members.[53] All of the above, however, faded in significance when compared to the problems that the YMCA had to face during a strike.

Strikes represented the most severe challenge to the relationship between YMCA secretaries and railroad workers. During labor conflicts, the YMCA tried to maintain a neutral position in an attempt to appease both employers and employees. Preserving the association's neutrality, however, was a difficult task. While companies generally insisted that their financial contributions entitled them to put up strike breakers at the YMCA, the dues-paying working-class members also demanded loyalty from the association for their cause. If a secretary rejected the demands of the employer to accommodate strike breakers, the railroad company in all likelihood cut their financial support of the association. In 1911 the secretary of the Waterloo, Illinois, Railroad YMCA refused to put up strike breakers. The Illinois Central, in turn, put plans to extend railroad YMCAs along its lines on hold. Resisting attempts by management to take control of a YMCA branch in such situations brought the workers' sympathies. During a strike along the Grand Trunk railroad in July 1910, the railroad superintendent at Niagara Falls tried to order the secretary's assistant to evict two of the strikers and refund their money. The assistant not only "refused point blank to do so," but also prevented the railroad superintendent to enter the building and oust the offending workers himself. The railroad YMCA secretary reported that "this episode was heralded all along the line and did not a little toward softening the feeling of the strikers toward the Association."[54] In the event of a strike, only a firm stand against company interference could win workers' sympathies for the YMCA.

Workers not only demanded that the YMCA refuse to support the railroad companies' interests during strikes, but on several occasions they took it into their own hands to prevent strike breakers from entering the building. In 1902 a fight broke out at the Cleburne Railroad YMCA between strikers and railroad company guards, who tried to bring an injured strike breaker into the YMCA building. At Meridian, Mississippi, local labor unions demanded that the YMCA not accept strike breakers into membership during a 1903 strike. Similarly, during a strike at East St. Louis on the Big Four Railroad in 1917, the yardmen, who had walked out in opposition to the hiring of a new foreman, "advised" the YMCA secretary of the local railroad branch not to put up strike breakers in the building.[55]

During a strike, individual loyalties of association employees could draw a railroad YMCA even further into the vortex of strike events. In 1908, during a strike of the car men at Van Buren, Mississippi, one of the strike breakers went to the YMCA building, where the man at the lunch counter, sympathetic to the strikers, refused to serve him. In another incident a YMCA secretary employed a man as a porter who had lost his job with the railroad during a recent strike. When one of the new employees of that railroad, a former strike breaker, visited the association, a group of men, led by the porter, attacked him outside. The YMCA secretary apparently tolerated the porter's actions. Although he witnessed the ensuing fight from a window, he did not fire the porter and failed to report the incident to the board of directors of that YMCA.[56]

While the instances were few, occasionally a YMCA secretary took the side of the workers. During the 1922 railroad shopmen strike, the Monon Railroad wished to put up strike breakers at the Lafayette, Indiana, Railroad YMCA. When contacted on the phone by a company official, the YMCA secretary replied, "'I am only the secretary. This building, as you know, is operated by a Committee of Management. I will make an appointment with them to meet you tomorrow.'" That committee, however, consisting of employees of the Monon Railroad, was on strike. Relying on

proper professional decorum, this YMCA secretary ap
favor of the workers.[57] Not always did YMCA secretarie
union in such an indirect way.

In one instance, a YMCA secretary outright and
union positions. In 1907 the Industrial Department beg
the Kensington branch of the Philadelphia YMCA, located
Kensington manufacturing district. By 1908 the shop meetings attracted
5,800 workers each month, the educational talks 800, and the health talks
398. One of the YMCA officials, religious work director Millard L. Robinson, held classes among ministers in Kensington to study sociological problems. Robinson deviated from general YMCA policy and supported organized labor when he invited the social gospel advocate Reverend Charles
Stelzle to speak at five meetings. Stelzle's lectures supported the eight-hour
day and the right of workers to unionize. Subsequently, Robinson came out
in favor of the union label during a strike of the International Typographi-
cal Workers Union (ITU). An ITU official explained that the union label
"stood for equal wages to men and women, against child labor, for sanitary
conditions, eight hours and the best workmen of the trade, and that it was
the proper emblem for his association to use on its printing." After the
meeting, Robinson wished "to be quoted as being in favor of the label and
will exercise his influence hereafter to have it placed on all [YMCA] printing." After initial cooperation, the relations between the Industrial Department and the Philadelphia YMCA soon turned sour and the project was
terminated.[58]

By the turn of the century, it was clear that the YMCA had not won the
hearts and minds of the majority of workers. Some considered the YMCA
as less than beneficial to the workers' cause. Herbert N. Casson wrote in
the Philadelphia *Trades Union News* that "the Y.M.C.A. is another substitute for unionism that is being pushed" besides the so-called open shop.
Casson said that at the YMCA, which he ridiculed as a "chewing gum club,"
the workers "are taught to swim, but [not] to think, to keep their nails clean,
but do not ask for fewer hours and more pay." Similarly, the *Iron Moulders
Journal* suggested that workers "dispense with Y.M.C.A.'s, and elevate
ourselves."[59] Many workingmen probably shared the opinion of a Ford
worker, commenting on the company's attempt to drum up support for the
YMCA during World War I. Resenting such attempts to reach into the
workers' pockets, he stated that "he would be damned if he would give a
damned cent and anybody is a fool to give their money to such damned
schemers."[60] We do not know whether all workers expressed their antipa-
thies in such strong language. It is certain, however, that the majority of

Tom Pape came to the United States in the 1870s and made the YMCA his lifetime calling as an employee of the New York Central Railroad. Reprinted from *Railroad Men* 12 (November 1898): 49. (Courtesy of Kautz Family YMCA Archives, University Libraries, University of Minnesota, Twin Cities, and the YMCA of the USA.)

workingmen did not easily, if at all, defer to their alleged social betters. Workers responded differently to the YMCA, often depending on the context of each specific situation.

On occasion a worker may have been seeking what the YMCA had to offer and gladly made the association's purpose his own, as the case of Tom Pape suggests. One Sunday afternoon "Roundhouse Tom" Pape attended a religious meeting at the New York Railroad Branch of the YMCA. Arriving late, he "complained of feeling faint and asked if he might lie down on the couch a few minutes." As he lay on the couch, he listened to the men singing "My Faith Looks up to Thee," to which he responded, the story goes, murmuring, "Yes, my faith looks up to Thee." Tom Pape, the account of his life suggests, knew that he had arrived at the end of his life, and only the usher "noticed immediately that the old man was passing, and even before the hymn had ended, the spirit had left the tired body and returned to God who gave it."[61]

Workers, then, both embraced and contested the YMCA's provision of leisure activities in an exclusively male environment. Despite the mostly amicable relations between YMCA secretaries and railroad workers and their unions, only a few men appeared to have taken the association's offering lock, stock, and barrel. Workingmen remade YMCA branches to reflect their leisure preferences, often in defiance of association standards of propriety and good behavior. In defying YMCA expectations about appropriate behavior in the building and by challenging company control over associations during strikes, workers contested the purpose of YMCA programs and activities that aimed to turn them into more loyal servants of the corporation. The contest over the use of YMCA facilities particularly escalated during strikes. Situated at a critical junction between workers and management, YMCAs could not escape the conflicts between them. On such occasions, railroad workers made it clear that they expected the YMCA to serve their purposes and interests. It must have been increasingly clear to YMCA officials, then, that the workingmen the association hoped to uplift could put up serious resistance. At least, they were far from being as easily swayed by the association's message as the YMCA officials had hoped. Such conflicts between the YMCA and its working-class audience abetted a shift in the role of the YMCA secretary from leader of Bible study classes and janitor more to that of a manager of personnel relations within the confines of a YMCA building.

"None of Your Milk-and-Water Sops, Flabby-Handed
and Mealy-Mouthed, for Dealing with Such Men":
The YMCA, the Secretaryship, and Professionalization

W

The growth and subsequent expansion of YMCA programs for working-men had direct consequences for the ways in which YMCA secretaries per-ceived themselves, both as professionals and as men. Initially, the YMCA effort on behalf of railroad workers had a strong missionary bent. YMCA secretaries resembled evangelists more than the hybrid of industrial wel-fare professionals and social workers they would become. As the YMCA successfully solicited funding from more and more companies, taking its message of Christian manhood to a working-class audience, the need for more and better-qualified employees arose. The YMCA had to adjust to the combined pressures of urbanization and industrialization. Both urban-ization and industrialization jointly promoted the role of experts, who in-creasingly established themselves as providers of social services or man-agers of social processes, based on the special knowledge or expertise they possessed. Subsequently, as providers of company-sponsored welfare pro-grams, the YMCA and its officials began to adopt a professional outlook that would lend credibility and substance to the association's claims of expertise.[1]

As YMCA officials began to raise questions as to the qualifications re-quired of YMCA secretaries as professionals, they also raised questions as to the kind of manliness required—a quality that YMCA sources regarded as crucial to gain the confidence of rugged workingmen and to lead them onto a path toward higher ideals of manhood. Leading YMCA officials urged their fellow secretaries to live up to the manly example set by the railroad men, while they also emphasized the more refined qualities of Christian manhood, which their role as leaders of workingmen supposedly required. In a period in which the definitions and contours of various professions still remained undefined and in flux, the YMCA relied on manhood as an anchor and foundation of expertise and professional knowledge.[2]

Gradually, YMCA officials elaborated on their ideal of manly leadership as they further defined their language of manhood in ways that generated a common set of social relations. As YMCA officials further articulated their language of manhood, they set standards that regulated their behavior, as men from a wide range of social backgrounds congealed into a professional body of men, the secretaryship of the YMCA. By the late 1880s the YMCA Railroad Department and its officials began to combine calls for manhood with calls for professional, managerial expertise as the association strove to emulate corporate management techniques, pioneered by the railroads.[3]

YMCA officials adjusted to the social pressures of their changing environment and began to transform antebellum ideals of middle-class manhood. The new ideal of manhood YMCA secretaries articulated for themselves was grounded in personality. Making its first appearance in YMCA circles in the vocabulary of the YMCA Women's Auxiliaries, where it signified female moral suasion and sentiment, male YMCA officials appropriated the concept for themselves, changing its meaning in the 1890s. In the language of YMCA secretaries, personality became associated with efficiency, dominance, "personal magnetism," and leadership. The ascent of personality alongside character in the YMCA's language of manhood would enable YMCA secretaries to articulate and enact class difference through gender.[4]

As the YMCA began to seek members among railroad and industrial workers, it was at first hardly equipped to handle this institutional expansion and staff the rapidly mushrooming associations with competent personnel capable of dealing with the new administrative challenges. YMCA officials generally acknowledged the need for salaried staff, but most associations could not afford a YMCA secretary, so the work relied heavily on volunteers.[5]

As YMCA railroad work expanded, however, so did its secretarial force. As I have described in chapter 2, with the support and contributions from the association's benefactors in industry, the YMCA was able to considerably expand the number of executive personnel in its employ. In 1889, the first year the YMCA *Yearbook* actually listed such numbers for railroad

YMCAs, the secretarial staff of the YMCA Railroad Department consisted of 2 secretaries nationally and 113 locally. With the expansion of work in the 1890s and the addition of the Industrial Department in 1903, more staff had to be added. By 1921 218 YMCA officials served workers in urban industries and 226 YMCA secretaries catered to the needs of workingmen along the nation's railroads.[6]

Most of these men entered YMCA work in their twenties and thirties, some even as young as sixteen, coming from a variety of white-collar clerical and skilled trades. The *Roster of Paid Secretaries* does not specify occupations for the years from 1880–1900, except in a very few cases, but the *Roster* is very specific for the years from 1900–1905, when 407 new secretaries entered YMCA railroad work. Among that group, seventy-two had been clerks, eighteen farmers, seventeen teachers, thirteen bookkeepers, thirteen machinists, twelve locomotive firemen, twelve salesmen, nine carpenters, seven stenographers, seven insurance salesmen, six clergy, five electricians, four foremen, and four brakemen. In addition, railroad secretaries came in smaller numbers from a wide range of occupations, such as telegraph operator, accountant, iron moulder, pharmacist, police officer, creamery worker, grocer, jeweler, and so forth. While white-collar occupations were the largest group of vocations from which the YMCA drew its personnel, if categorized by industry, the largest number of secretaries came from railroad employment.[7] The YMCA, then, functioned as a practical school, shaping men from a wide range of occupations into industrial welfare professionals. As the occupational backgrounds of these men indicate, the YMCA could not expect much previous training or experience among its recruits.

In the Gilded Age most railroad secretaries had hardly any training. In some cases applicants apparently entered the "secretaryship," as YMCA officials called their occupation, late in life. In such circumstances, the job essentially represented a retirement pension, arranged between the railroad company and the local YMCA. From the viewpoint of the association, these men often were the least qualified for the job. Other secretaries made their way up from the post of assistant secretary, a glamorized title for what was essentially a janitorial position.[8]

Expectations and guidelines for the conduct, behavior, and appearance of YMCA secretaries were formulated with this pool of recruits in mind. For example, 1874 guidelines for secretaries suggested that the secretary should "avoid anything that smacks of the cloth." Furthermore, he "should not be a snob or a coxcomb, for even to the snob himself snobbery is repulsive." Similarly, YMCA railroad secretary John F. Moore, reminiscing about the early requirements for railroad secretaries, wrote that a YMCA secretary should avoid "unkempt hair and beard, unshaven face, unblackened boots, untrimmed and uncleaned nails." Robert Wiebe has argued that the members of disparate professions to be merged into members of a new middle class initially shared little "more than a . . . salary, a set of clean clothes, and a hope that somehow they would rise in the world." It would seem that, with regard to cleanliness, the YMCA had far less to work with.[9] Such exhortations about clean clothes and proper grooming indicate the limited expectations the association had for its personnel in the early years of YMCA railroad work.

However, as YMCA railroad work expanded in the 1880s, the association upgraded its demands slowly and in a piecemeal fashion, and earlier exhortations about cleanliness and physical appearance subsided in favor of other requirements. In 1881, for example, Edwin Ingersoll, General Secretary for railroad work of the YMCA Railroad Department, suggested that the "Railroad secretary is not simply to keep a record of books drawn and returned; but knowing both the man and the books, he should be able to stimulate or help each man in his choice and use of books."[10] With the institutional expansion of the YMCA railroad work in the 1890s, the demands and expectations increased along with the workloads.

The rapid expansion of YMCA railroad work in the 1880s and 1890s, and the accompanying changes in administrative procedures, led to great increases in the workload for YMCA secretaries. Since the YMCA could not expand its workforce fast enough, the individual workload of secretaries became quite burdensome, despite an expansion in personnel. The expense account book of John F. Moore, YMCA Travelling Secretary, helps us to assess the daily life and workload of these men. Moore and his colleagues carried out a crucial function in the YMCA railroad work. By maintaining lines of communication between the national headquarters and the local branches, these YMCA officials coordinated the YMCA Railroad Department's efforts. In 1896 Moore traveled between 2,244 and 2,744 miles per month, the low and high amounts for the year, covering Maine, New York, Pennsylvania, and Massachusetts. In August 1899 he traveled 3,180 miles — the low amount for the years from 1898 to 1900. Six months later, in February 1900, he traveled 8,130 miles, the high amount in his expense account book, with his monthly travels usually ranging between 4,500 and 6,000 miles. Admittedly, the distances covered by YMCA railroad secretaries were often less than those covered by other railroad employees: sleeping car porters, for example, covered on average 11,000 miles a month, which kept them at least twenty days on the rail.[11] Nevertheless, the job of

a YMCA railroad secretary was taxing, as time spent on the road did not include time spent on visiting and consulting with local YMCA secretaries, so-
liciting funds, meeting with railroad officials, leading membership drives,
and other related matters.

The life of a somewhat more sedentary branch secretary was not easy,
either. The wife of one secretary remarked that, during the early years of
YMCA railroad work, "the secretary was the whole 'outfit,' he was the janitor as well as secretary and assistant, and physical director if he was so un-
fortunate as to have a gymnasium." [12] At major metropolitan locations, such
as New York, Chicago, Boston, or Philadelphia, the secretary may have had
a support staff. At small, more remote locations, however, the secretary may
have had to wear many hats. That way, some YMCA secretaries had the
chance to develop both domestic and managerial skills while on the job and
even had an opportunity to contribute to the welfare of the community.
That could require a considerable amount of ingenuity. At the copper mining town of Jenkins, Kentucky, rats had infested many buildings; they "even
ran across the rafters in the Association hall." Indubitably, "they were a
nuisance as well as a [source of] disease." The YMCA secretary at Jenkins
responded by holding an entertainment on the night of the "community
clean-up day." Admission: "one rat's tail." The workers responded to the
YMCA's call. On the evening of the event, 552 rat tails were cashed in. In
fact, rat hunts became quite popular days before. According to the secretary's report, "in the mining company's barn No. 204 sacks of corn were
placed in the middle of the floor, the lights were extinguished and then sud-
denly thrown on; the boys went for the rats with clubs and killed 39." The
report stated that "much was accomplished this clean-up day." [13] While
some secretaries may have handled their jobs with great ingenuity and possibly even greater success, the workloads these men had to face often became
excessive.

The pressure of the workload was further compounded by the fact that
branch secretaries could expect to be reassigned to another association
every three to four years. In extreme cases, a secretary changed positions
within less than a year. Especially during a phase of expansion of a railroad
system, a YMCA railroad secretary could expect to be frequently reassigned
to another location. The job of a YMCA secretary demanded a high degree
of mobility. [14]

Managing frequent reassignments and reconciling the time spent on
the rail or at the association building with spending time with their families was one more problem many YMCA secretaries encountered. One secretary stated that to have a satisfactory home life, he should be able to spend

"at least two evenings a week" at home with his family. This statement implied the reality many YMCA railroad secretaries had to confront: their job actually occupied them for seven days a week and most of the evenings as well, leaving mostly the weekend evenings for a home life. But even such an arrangement remained elusive for many YMCA secretaries, who had to make substantial adjustments in their expectations of a normal family life. One secretary, asked about his ideal of a normal home life, stated that "really, my views of a normal life are so vague and the possibilities so far off, that I have tried to adjust myself to the conditions and make our home life seem normal." The wife of one secretary noted that "our husbands . . . are ready to sacrifice themselves and all who belong to them." While late nineteenth-century middle-class men in general had to expect that their job would separate them for much of the day and the week from family and children, the job of a YMCA secretary appears to have required extraordinary sacrifices.[15]

Sooner or later the pressure of the job was sure to have consequences for the man's health. One secretary's wife remarked, "the character of the work demanded from the secretary of an Association has to be done at high pressure, nervous tension, and in consequence greatly reduces the vitality." She added that "the inevitable break-down, usually insomnia, nervous prostration, or heart trouble, is sure to occur sooner or later." On occasion, heavy work, possibly accompanied by the use of intoxicating substances, could even result in a missing-person case, as the case of Henry Curry demonstrates. Formerly a secretary at the railroad YMCA at Watertown, New York, Curry "left home . . . for the Association at Rochester and Buffalo" on 20 March 1903 and was "last seen at New York Central Railroad at Syracuse." As the call for information, published in the September issue of *Association Men* almost six months after Curry's initial disappearance, put it, "as loss of memory from overwork or foul play is feared, any information will be gratefully received by his wife, 212 Bronley Avenue, Scranton, Pa." Whether Curry vanished because of "overwork" or "foul play," we do not know. What we do know is that the work of a YMCA secretary was not necessarily conducive to good health: during the years from 1880–1905, forty left the YMCA because of ill health.[16]

In addition to health problems, heavy workloads, and frequent reassignment, some YMCA secretaries had problems making ends meet on the salaries they received. At least some of the secretaries who left the association did so because of financial difficulties. Some secretaries took on extra work, such as selling "books, insurance, entertainment promotion, or preaching for remuneration." At least one YMCA secretary turned to theft to improve his salary. Joseph Pawling, a former railroad employee and secretary at the railroad YMCA at Bellefontaine, Ohio, turned out to be a "clever rascal" who absconded with $500 out of the association's treasury and about an equal amount of funds from others who had endorsed his checks on local banks.[17]

Not all YMCA secretaries with financial problems turned to such extraordinary means to bolster their income, but evidence suggests that finances posed problems for a number of YMCA secretaries. YMCA railroad secretary John F. Moore quoted a "well-known businessman who has dealings with secretaries" as stating that "'next to (mentioning another class of customers), Young Men's Christian Association secretaries are our most difficult patrons when it comes to the settlement of personal accounts.'" While YMCA officials such as Moore dismissed such behavior as signs of personal failure, the work often turned out to be more demanding and financially less rewarding than many could be expected to bear. As one wife stated at a conference for secretaries' wives, a secretary "must give up independence, accept a small salary (and perhaps not get that), with little prospect of advance, and possible failure."[18] And many did fail.

Throughout the late nineteenth and early twentieth centuries, the YMCA had to cope with a high turnover rate among its secretaries. While no figures are available for specific departments—the numbers are figures on general turnover—high turnover rates were common when the YMCA railroad work went through a phase of rapid expansion in the 1880s and 1890s. Throughout the 1880s and 1890s, the total annual turnover rate was 20 percent. For some years, the number of new recruits was equal to the number of secretaries who left the profession. In 1904 470 new recruits joined the ranks of the association's secretaryship and 420 left it. Even previous training for the secretaryship did not necessarily guarantee success. Fred Baumgartner joined the YMCA in 1891 at age 24. A graduate of the YMCA's Chicago Training School, in 1894 Baumgartner resigned "discouraged" after assignments with the YMCA in Chicago, Taylorville, Illinois, and Pittsburgh, Kansas. On the *Roster*, a YMCA official added the remark "unsatisfactory."[19] Apparently, the association found it difficult not only to recruit and retain men of suitable qualifications but to retain personnel in general.

Employees quit the YMCA for a variety of reasons. Some of the men who left apparently found the YMCA an unsatisfactory vocation, for financial or spiritual reasons, judging by the fields they entered next. Of those who left, 104 entered "business," 54 entered missionary work or the ministry. Others may have seen employment in the YMCA simply as a stepping stone in their career, or a type of resume builder, as about forty-nine men pursued further education upon leaving association work. Some left YMCA employment but not the YMCA: one Ransom Liddle left the employment of the Moline, Illinois, Railroad YMCA in 1904 to open up a barbershop in the same building.[20]

Other YMCA secretaries were less successful in juggling careers than was Mr. Liddle. The YMCA secretary at the Delaware, Lackawanna and Western Railroad had decided to hold political office against the warnings and protests from colleagues. This secretary, stationed at Elmira, was elected on a reform ticket to the post of Alderman from his ward in 1913. However, on 7 October, "while investigating the Character of a place of questionable resort, in his capacity as Alderman, the place was raided by the police, the Secretary taken to the police station, resulting in an awful newspaper scandal." When the superintendent of the Delaware, Lackawanna and Western Railroad at Elmira heard of the incident, he insisted that the man be replaced.[21] If the Elmira YMCA secretary had hoped to use his YMCA credentials to launch himself into a political career, that success failed over his careless visit to "a place of questionable resort" and the attentive local newspaper.

Probably few men on their quest for a fulfilling career, though, used the YMCA as a revolving door to the extent of one G. C. Butterfield. He entered the employment of the New Haven, Connecticut, Railroad YMCA in August 1881 at age 21. In February 1882 he left after six months of service, listed as "unsuccessful." He reentered YMCA employment in Peru, Indiana, in January 1883, moved on to the New Albany, Indiana, branch in January 1884, and after another three years left in December 1886 because of "ill health." Butterfield returned to the YMCA in March 1887. This time he lasted for five years, until March 1892, when he left to go into "business." Apparently, Butterfield was not too successful, as he returned one last time in January 1893. He quit YMCA employment in May 1894, at the height of a depression, but this time, it seems, he had found his calling: Butterfield became a minister.[22] It is easy to dismiss a man like Butterfield as unstable and undecided, possibly taking advantage of the YMCA in a time of staff shortage, or simply as a source of income in times of economic hardship in the mid-1880s. Butterfield's career pattern, however, not so unlike that of some leading YMCA officials previous to entering association work, also underscores the fluidity and lack of stability in middle-class men's careers during this time. In any case, compared to some, Butterfield could consider himself fortunate.

Not every man who left YMCA employment found the happiness or satisfaction he may have been looking for. In 1889 Charles Freeman had entered YMCA railroad work later than most at age 39. He left the association after only three years to enter "business." Two years later, on 16 September 1894, at the onset of an economic depression, Freeman committed suicide in Allegheny, Pennsylvania.[23]

In the 1880s and 1890s YMCA officials, with varying degrees of success, attempted to grapple with the pressures of their jobs, and the YMCA as a whole tried to come to terms with the problems of recruiting and retaining staff. Leading YMCA officials articulated the problems and faults of individual secretaries as well as the professional standards the association expected from its staff in terms of manhood. In addition to formulating professional standards conducive to generating and maintaining institutional cohesion, YMCA officials needed to reconcile other aspects as they defined their professional identity around an ideal of manhood. Such reconciliation potentially required a YMCA secretary to perform some cultural balancing acts. First, the YMCA staff should demonstrate professional conduct and ability equaling those of its sponsors' office and managerial staff. Second, to successfully appeal to the workers, YMCA officials had to accommodate their needs and preferences, while gaining their acceptance and respect as men. Last, but not least, the very job of a YMCA branch secretary came with a gender role conflict built in. At a time, when American middle-class men worried about their manliness and expressed concerns regarding alleged threats of effeminization, the setting of a YMCA building itself resembled the domestic setting of the home more than a site of strenuous, manly pursuit. Reconciling demands for managerial conduct and for the highest Christian spirituality with the need to display a more strenuous, rugged manliness, considered necessary to gain the acceptance of the workers, all in the somewhat domestic setting of a YMCA building, YMCA secretaries had their work cut out for them. Concerns with manhood framed the internal debates YMCA officials carried on over these issues.

Eschewing all those very real problems many YMCA secretaries encountered, leading YMCA railroad officials blamed difficulties with recruitment and staff retention on the secretaries' lack of manly stamina. John Moore wrote of the "tragic" and "pathetic" stories "of good men who from great usefulness have fallen to worse than uselessness through the loss of that splendid altruism which characterized the early fruitful years of their service." At first, Moore wrote, these secretaries showed "substantial and encouraging . . . results." However, after a short while "with success came the subtle serpent of selfishness and then inordinate and unwholesome ambition supplanted conquering self-forgetfulness." The result was inevitable. Due to an apparent lack of manly endurance, "slowly at first but none the less surely, they lost that firm grip which had power in it. . . . Samson shorn of his power—strengthless, sightless, broken, standing desolate amid the ruins of his former glory." Because of "past achievements," Moore wrote, these men often held on to their positions, "but they were rotten timber in the secretarial forest and the inevitable came soon to pass." Moore identified these men as those who "drift in and out of the profession." He added with regret that "these men constitute a considerable percentage of the whole number of employed officers."[24] While speaking in the plural, Moore may have had the case of one of the founders of YMCA railroad work in Cleveland, Lang Sheaff, in mind.

In 1911 in a confidential memorandum Edwin D. Ingersoll, the first YMCA railroad secretary of the International Committee, questioned the qualifications of one of the often acclaimed founders of railroad work in Cleveland, Lang Sheaff.[25] Ingersoll reported that before becoming superintendent of the Cleveland YMCA, Sheaff had worked in a number of different positions, such as "an auctioneer, a house painter, and a clerk in a warehouse." Ingersoll's description of Sheaff resembles the prototype of a confidence man who, by superficial means, was able to obfuscate his shortcomings and insincerity and to persuade others of his good intentions. In his report Ingersoll noted that Sheaff "was an exceptionally good 'mixer,' shook hands vigorously, and with a smile and manner that made friends and admirers rapidly." Further, he wrote that Sheaff "had decided platform ability" but only "a small store of incidents which he told with his strongly emotional nature, [and] tremolo voice (some thought somewhat cultivated)." Sheaff's potential, according to Ingersoll, was limited. As he put it, "on the platform no man in Association work made a greater impression, if he did not address the same audience too many times. If he did he soon wore out the welcome and appreciation." And Sheaff wore out his welcome with the Cleveland YMCA after a very short time, indeed.

At the end of his first year in Cleveland, the YMCA regretted its decision to hire Sheaff and decided to terminate his contract. Before the three-year contract ended, the Board of Directors notified Sheaff that he could not remain on the payroll of the Association. Sheaff enlisted the support of T. P. Handy, a leading Cleveland banker and contributor to many charitable causes in the city. According to Ingersoll, Handy was "so sweet a dispositioned man that he could not believe any man really to be bad." In the ensuing negotiations, Sheaff won an extension of his contract and eventually was transferred to the railroad work. "From that hour," Ingersoll claimed, "the Railroad work [in Cleveland] declined until it was almost non-est [sic]."

Through his poor efforts and negligence, Sheaff had soon discredited the YMCA with railroad officials. E. B. Thomas, general manager of the C.C.C. & I. Railroad conducted an investigation into the Cleveland railroad work himself "and found that Sheaff kept no statistics or records, but printed monthly bulletins." These reports, Thomas noted, gave "precise figures of attendance at rooms and meetings . . . all fictitious, and sent copies to Railroad officials, and officials and supporters of the Y.M.C.A." Thomas told Ingersoll that "your work is a fraud and a humbug and I have no more money for it." Ingersoll stated in his report that the Cleveland YMCA, after conducting its own investigation, found these allegations to be true. As if this was not enough, Ingersoll accused Sheaff of violating YMCA guidelines of association governance. Ingersoll wrote that he had "never heard, seen, or found any evidence that while organizing under the direction of the International Committee [Sheaff] ever advised any meeting of railroad men proposing to organize [a YMCA], that a secretary, or the Church Membership test, or Union with the local Y.M.C.A. was necessary or desirable." Sheaff's case may have been extreme, but given the difficulties of hiring and retaining secretaries, it was probably not unique.

Right from the beginning, recruitment of suitable staff represented a problem and challenge to the very integrity of YMCA programs with railroad workers. John Moore believed that the problem lay in exercising more control over the quality of recruits and in maintaining discriminating standards even at a time of shortage of secretaries, when expansion outpaced recruitment: "for in the great demand for men hundreds have been attracted to the profession, only a small number of whom had the qualities for permanent success." With optimism, though, he noted that "this element, the chief weakness of the organization, is gradually being eliminated, and before long will disappear."[26]

As YMCA secretaries began to form a group identity around ideas of manliness, they realized that not all members of the profession reflected those ideals. Ward W. Adair, YMCA secretary at the Scranton, Pennsylvania, Railroad YMCA, complained about two types of YMCA secretaries—the busybody, who lacked the spiritual qualities of the post, and the slacker. Writing in the YMCA's newsletter, *Association Men*, where he had a regular column, Adair voiced his disapproval about "the voluntary galley-slave who is of chore-boy calibre, and who goes pattering about the building with a quick, jerky footfall that gets on everybody's nerves, as he files papers, dusts chairs, and arranges furniture." A busybody, he was "an office-boy, to

Ward Adair, secretary of the Scranton and, later, New York railroad YMCAs, where he succeeded George Warburton, helped to shape the professional standards the YMCA expected from its staff. (Courtesy of Kautz Family YMCA Archives, University Libraries, University of Minnesota, Twin Cities, and the YMCA of the USA.)

the manner born, but by some unexcusable blunder has been placed in charge of a job that is miles and acres too big for him." Whereas the "voluntary galley-slave" lacked the qualities of spiritual leadership required of a YMCA secretary, Adair's other target was the "chronic loafer, who by reason of toothache, toeache and junketing trips, manages to absent himself from duty pretty much all the year without the formality of a real vacation." The need to staff buildings caused considerable problems for the YMCA both in terms of quality of recruits and coherence of the work.[27]

Adair felt that the high demand for personnel had made it difficult to ensure the professional and personal qualifications of those recruited into the ranks of YMCA secretaries. Hard pressed to staff YMCA buildings sprouting along expanding railroad systems, local and national authorities had neglected to examine the qualifications of aspiring candidates as closely as they should have, or so Adair believed. Adair warned of a decline of the YMCA secretaryship as a profession: "the tendency of the past years has been to put the secretaryship upon too low a plane." He stated that, as a result, "men have been allowed to enter it with too little thought, and the percentage of failure has been greatly increased because of the misconceptions that workers within and without the Association have entertained." Adair did not spare older, established secretaries from criticism. He complained that "men with unworthy motives and erroneous ideas have drifted in and out of the work, encouraged oftentimes by experienced secretaries who have a meager idea of its requirements." Adair appealed to his readers that "we owe to our craft . . . the exercise of greater vigilance in relation to men who we invite into the work."[28]

In phasing out undesirable candidates, YMCA officials such as Ward Adair especially targeted former railroad workers incapacitated by injury. Adair recalled the following encounter: "He was one of those men whom we speak of as 'a secretarial aspirant.' He came swinging into the office on his crutches and sank into a chair with a sigh of relief." Adair admitted that his was a sad case, being deprived of the use of his lower limbs, but explained to him the physical requirements of the work and assured the man that he could not expect anything but failure. Having sent off the applicant, Adair closed his column on an exasperated note: "Alas, for the day when the secretaryship was flaunted as a field for men incapacitated for other employment! We have long since gotten beyond it, but how to make poor cripples and invalids understand it is as much a mystery as ever."[29] At least from Adair's point of view, the criteria applied to identifying suitable recruits required revision as much as the image of the YMCA as a place of employment. But Adair's complaint also suggests that by the early twentieth century, the YMCA had reached a turning point in terms of recruitment. As the YMCA secretaryship began to stabilize and gained professional cohesiveness, YMCA officials began to articulate their mission with increasing clarity, and the professional qualifications expected of a YMCA secretary became more precisely defined. In turn, YMCA secretaries devoted greater attention to the articulation of the standards of manhood the association expected its employees to conform to.

The YMCA programs on behalf of railroad workers and the workers' own manliness placed special requirements on the YMCA secretaries as professionals and as men. YMCA secretaries were expected to match railroad workers' virility, balanced by high moral and spiritual qualities. George A. Warburton, influential secretary of the New York Railroad YMCA branch, wrote that a YMCA secretary "must be a manly man. Abounding virility is a requisite. The preeminently masculine qualities of mind and heart must dominate his life."[30]

YMCA secretaries had to fulfill the highest standards of manliness because of the example set for them by workingmen. Workers, Warburton wrote, "live a strenuous life" and "how, in God's name, can there be any help rendered to them if the man who seeks to give it is only a bit of driftwood on the current of events?" The workers, then, set standards of manliness, to which a YMCA official had to measure up. As Warburton put it, "he will be required to meet *men*. . . . None of your milk-and-water sops, flabby-handed and mealy-mouthed, for dealing with such men" (emphasis in original). YMCA secretaries believed that they had to learn a significant lesson from their observation of workingmen.

Although the YMCA sought to encourage meekness and obedience among the workers, association officials also learned that to effectively reach workingmen, they had to find ways to be respected and accepted as men. Although the YMCA wished to convert men to Christianity, making them better men, the association actually did not always disapprove of such men defending their honor, even if it involved violence. One such converted railroad worker and YMCA Bible meeting volunteer once got embroiled in a "beer-room brawl" when "an intoxicated man" pulled a knife, cutting the converted railroad worker "on the cheek from his ear to the corner of his mouth." The assaulted worker proceeded to respond in a rather old-testamentarian, eye-for-an-eye fashion: "quicker than a flash . . . [he] drew his revolver and placed it against the forehead of his assailant and taking the open knife from his hand proceeded to cut his face in the same way that he himself had been cut." Upon completing his work, the worker gave "the knife back to the man from whom he had taken it, he put the revolver in his own pocket, shook hands, and they walked out together." While the YMCA did not encourage any form of violence, association officials nonetheless realized that such acts of masculine bravado and brinkmanship could help to further the YMCA's cause. As a YMCA secretary who witnessed the event described above commented with an admiring tone: "such a man will have a mighty influence among railroad men, as he has decided to use his voice and testimony in endeavoring to reach this class for Christ."[31] If YMCA secretaries wished to win over workingmen, they may not have had to carry guns or knives, but they had to be ready to confront the workers as men.

On occasion, that could become a hands-on task. At the South Cumberland, Maryland, railroad branch, one day "a big, overgrown, double-jointed, profane, large-mouthed and half drunken man—evidently a railroader—entered the building and destroyed everything within his reach." The assistant secretary attempted to calm down the intoxicated man and to get him out of the building, but in return the worker attempted to strike him. The assistant secretary, "who gives promise to be more than a fair middleweight pugilist," was apparently not only sober but also more apt in the use of his hands, because when the railroad worker "was able to realize where he was he lay on the ground near the building." Thus sobered up, the man got back on his feet, and offered an apology for his behavior. According to the YMCA source, "It made a different man of him."[32]

More than the physical vigilance needed to handle a drunk worker, however, a YMCA railroad secretary had to possess a Christian manliness to enable him to reach out and win over workingmen. While a YMCA secretary should be virile, he should also possess high spiritual qualities: "the manliness required does not relate so much to physical proportions as to mental and moral characteristics. Mere bulk does not always indicate manliness." Elevating manliness beyond embodied existence, Warburton saw other, nonphysical qualities of character as decisive if not more than a man's physical virility. Warburton wrote that the true type of manhood had to be of a more refined nature: "the man we need . . . must have strength made gentle." To help railroad men, Christian convictions in a man had to be equally as strong as his rugged side in the manly make-up of a secretary. A vigorous physique may have been useful but was clearly not the most important quality sought in a YMCA secretary. The qualities required were both alike and decisively different from the qualities of railroad workers. Warburton called for a "kind of manliness . . . [that] will have a mixture of elements; courage, firmness, forbearance, self-control, independence will be among them." YMCA secretaries had to develop manly qualities similar to those of the railroad workers they worked with, blending them with high spiritual qualities. The combination of virile manhood and spirituality prepared them to assert their authority. Such a combination represented the true manliness sure to attract the workers and convince them of their need for uplift. Warburton was convinced that "there is hardly any power comparable to the magnetism of manliness."[33] Whereas Warburton emphasized rugged qualities alongside more spiritual qualities, other YMCA officials leaned more toward managerial rationality in their articulations of manliness.

Clarence J. Hicks, who had modeled railroad YMCA work on the example of railroad corporations, urged his fellow secretaries to model themselves on company officials and emulate them in handling the YMCA's effort. "Command of Self and Time," "Courtesy," "Economy," "Efficiency," "Promptness," "Aggressiveness," "Foresight," "Adaptability," "Daring or Nerve or Courage," "Publicity," and "Correct Business Methods" were now foremost among the qualities secretaries should bring to their calling. Such expectations had come a long way from the advice on good grooming and clean shoes. By the turn of the century the YMCA's increasing need for professional secretaries and for buildings signaled a maturation of the movement.[34]

As the YMCA's efforts with railroad workers gathered steam, the YMCA placed increasing emphasis on executive and management skills. One YMCA official likened the qualities required of YMCA secretaries in general to those needed from a general manager of a railroad. As one YMCA secretary put it, "The secretary is virtually the manager of a million dollar corporation. The position is big enough for the best kind of business man. And its dividends are to be paid in manhood, so there must be no carelessness of operation." Any hardships in the life of a YMCA secretary would be more than offset by the "unlimited opportunity," which the position offered.[35]

Following a pattern of increasing professionalization among occupational groups in the Gilded Age, the composition and background of YMCA recruits changed as the organization expanded. Between 1880 and 1900, under "entered association work from," the *Roster* lists "school" and "college" in only 42 cases each. After 1900, secretaries no longer entered the association directly from school, and 65 new recruits came from college. YMCA officials noted with delight "the new company of young trained experts" among their ranks. One YMCA official hopefully remarked that these well-trained young men are "in reality the most significant, for these constitute the promise of the future." What distinguished YMCA secretaries as professionals from other occupational groups, however, was their ability to blend the new call for managerial expertise with the need for spreading the gospel and the ability to guide others toward salvation: "they are the men who have heard a divine call to give themselves to some great sacrificial service for human good, and are determined to prepare themselves to do it well."[36] A YMCA secretary was supposed to be the perfect blend of Christian missionary, corporate manager, fund raiser, and rugged man, who could be accepted by tough workingmen any time.

As YMCA secretaries attempted to reconcile the various aspects of their work into a whole, they confronted a conflict between Victorian ideals of sincerity and new notions of charisma. As Victorians, YMCA secretaries prized sincerity in all social relations above everything, especially because they had to set an example to others. But as urban professionals they needed to exude charisma and often assume the role of a skilled salesman as they tried to win new members, obtain funding, or attract new sponsors in industry. YMCA secretaries saw this problem clearly. Warburton stated that among the greatest threats to a man, a by-product of "our calling and our positions," was "insincerity."[37] The new social environment made it increasingly difficult to sustain the ideal of an integrated self.

YMCA secretaries experienced firsthand this fragmentation of the self into multiple roles and expressed concern about what must have seemed like the unraveling of dearly held values. George Warburton captured the problem:

> Because we must be all things to all men we are in constant danger of failing to be true to ourselves and our own convictions of duty. We must win friends for our work and so we seek to become adepts at adaptation. We would fight rather than lie, but the wisdom of the serpent is the lure that leads us on, until we blunt the keenness of our moral sense in our eagerness to secure the co-operation that we want. There is no danger more real than this. The temptations of policy are insidious, but unless we are guarded they will undermine the spirituality of our personal lives and ruin us as factors in any large and truly spiritual leadership. It would be far better to be too frank than to be crafty, better to err in the direction of frankness than to become a mere worldly flatterer of men.[38]

In the new urban environment, the need to win members and sponsors in industry forced YMCA secretaries constantly to adopt skills somewhat more akin to the archetypal nineteenth-century confidence man.

Ward Adair, always the optimist, expressed his grave concerns about the consequences of this development for the integrity of the secretaryship as a profession. Adair warned that "a very real danger of Railroad Association work to-day is an actual or apparent lack of depth and sincerity on the part of the men behind the counter." What Adair found wanting among an increasing number of YMCA secretaries was spiritual depth and sincerity. Faulting an unspecified number of his own colleagues, Adair noticed "an alarming lack of strength and sincerity in the men next to the public" in many YMCAs. Adair claimed that all too often he encountered "a forced smile, a too ready handshake, and a greeting in which effusiveness is made to take the place of downright heartiness." Adair saw the association endangered by a type of secretary he referred to as a "cheap jollier." Adair saw the old ideals of sturdy manhood giving way to an ideal that relied on forms of outward representation. Adair implored his readers not to sway from the old ways and reminded them that it was better to offer "a quiet, manly greeting, just so it be sincerely friendly, than a lot of foolish familiarity that makes a decent man discount the whole enterprize [sic]." Adair suggested "better no smile than a forced smile. Far better no handshake than an unwarranted and meaningless one." Any other path, Adair warned, led down the road of emasculation: "When our men degenerate into the habits and characteristics of hotel clerks then barrenness and impotency falls upon the

Associations."[39] Using language loaded with images bound up with the of the ability to sexually reproduce, Adair was gravely concerned about YMCA as an institution becoming not merely effeminized, but losing momentum, if its staff lacked true sincerity. Whereas a leading YMCA secretary such as Ward Adair may have perceived the presence of confidence men as a threat to the integrity of the work, the actual identity problems connected to the phenomenon went much deeper and had wider ramifications.

The problem posed by "insincerity" went much deeper than the appearance of an isolated confidence man or a "cheap jollier" in the ranks of the secretaryship. Victorian Americans expected truthfulness, or sincerity, in all walks of life from one another. This ideal of sincerity stood for a notion of the self that was independent, stable, and unchanging. The work of a YMCA secretary, however, increasingly required the ability to play different roles, depending on the circumstances. Victorian Americans associated such role playing with the deceptive arts of the "confidence man" and, therefore, a danger to sincere social relations. While YMCA secretaries were not "confidence men," the difficulty posed by cultural expectations of sincerity that conflicted with the need to play act in carrying out the duties of the position was all too real to some secretaries, going to the very core of their understanding of themselves both as professionals and as men. One YMCA secretary wrote Warburton of the difficulties posed by his position and the ease with which YMCA positions could be compromised.[40] This unnamed secretary wrote that he joined the ranks of YMCA secretaries because he "saw in it an unique opportunity to touch the lives of men in a way which seemed to me absolutely unique. I took it up almost as a passion." The reality of the job, however, turned out to be different and often disenchanting. He wrote that "my days are spent with men of large incomes who are not making sacrifices that impoverish them." This secretary constantly felt the need to compromise his own values and viewpoints to guarantee the progress of the work: "the gathering at luxurious eating places, the riding in motor cars, the intercourse with men of luxurious life, have always required fight to the bitter end to prevent me from becoming removed and cut off from the young man who is fighting his battle for his daily bread, as well as for his manhood." The experience must have been profoundly troubling for many secretaries, as the words of this YMCA official suggest. He wrote with some distress that "the ease with which I can compromise on a great question like the liquor traffic in the presence of a man who has wine on the table, or whose revenue is derived even remotely from vice, decreases the chance of my being an advocate, a special leader for the young man who is fighting those very things in the temptations of the day." While

o quoted from the above letter at a conference,
also acknowledged a key problem possibly faced
onymous secretary. He noted a "changed em-
loss of "that ring of absolute sincerity that we
ession committed to saving others from temptation.
ubled by qualities that they found useful in their work as
es—the ability to play roles and to hide, or if need be deliberately
conceal, one's true feelings, one's true self—qualities that middle-class
Americans born in the nineteenth century associated with confidence men.
More than a question of the integrity of the self, it was also a question of
the social stability of human relations and the fabric of society itself. Most
of all, the contradiction between the need to adapt and the desire for sincerity raised a profound role conflict for YMCA secretaries and challenged
Victorian ideals of manliness.

Much of the cultural strain YMCA secretaries experienced in their understanding of themselves as man had to do with the urban environment.
The demands of urban life on YMCA secretaries were quite testing, and
the urban environment posed a great challenge for them, as it did for many
other middle-class men. Warburton explained, "the old days when an official place insured respect are gone. . . . The currents of life in the big city
ebb and flow in such a fashion as to wipe out the marks of the feet of those
men who do not tread the streets as masters."[41] YMCA secretaries apparently felt they had arrived at a dividing point. For many, the need for adaptation, the need for manhood, raised the question of how to reconcile old
ideals of high moral and spiritual qualities and sincerity with new demands
for adaptability. Torn between their Victorian past and the realities of a
rapidly changing society, YMCA secretaries stood at a crucial juncture in
the transformation of notions of gender and the self, posing the question
of how to deal with the mounting pressure of change. The fact that YMCA
secretaries had to pursue their quest within a rather domestic setting,
which explicitly built on Victorian notions of the domestic sphere, added
to an already existing set of creative tensions, steering YMCA definitions
of middle-class manliness into new directions.

As men, they were assigned the public sphere as their domain by
nineteenth-century American culture. As YMCA secretaries, however,
they had to be patriarchs as well as to safeguard and perpetuate an ideal
of domestic sentiment, which Victorians associated with womanhood. In
short, they had to be men but also maintain a womanly atmosphere within
the YMCA building. This gender role-conflict was practically written into
the job description of a YMCA official. George Warburton explained that

it was precisely the morally sound, homelike atmosphere that railroad men appreciated and that brought them into the buildings. Railroad men, he wrote, "find here a place where womanhood is held in high esteem, where pure motherhood and sisterhood would be glad to have you come." More than anything else, it was the influence of women that would make good men. As Warburton's colleague David Latshaw put it, "God uses the love of a good woman, sister, wife, in His business of building manhood."[42] The secretary needed to balance rugged, strenuous manliness with more re-fined qualities, akin to domesticity and inoffensive to a good woman.

Concerned with casting the essentially domestic character of the association building as a masculine preserve, YMCA secretaries strove to limit women's role in association activities. Leading YMCA officials warned that YMCA secretaries' "domestic relations"—that is their marriages and the relation between their wives and their work—should never interfere with their job performance. John F. Moore praised the wives of the many association secretaries, "who uncomplainingly bear the taxing responsibilities of our households." Moore scorned "unwise wives," who were too ambitious for their husbands' good, too demanding on his time, or even the "good wife," who, "resentful of her husband's long hours at the Association . . . sought compensation by spending a good share of her time at the building." In one such case, Moore added, "a new secretary was soon in charge." For a secretary's wife to be supportive without transgressing her sphere played a crucial role in her husband's effectiveness. Even the wife of one secretary chimed in: "No man can do his best if his wife is always repining at the situation."[43] In short, the presence of women in other than the strict meta-phorical sense of domesticity and motherhood could beget problems.

While the homosocial culture prevalent in railroad employment and within the sacred halls of the YMCA carried the implied promise that women would remain excluded, in some instances the presence of women was not only tolerated but appreciated by both management and workers—to the chagrin of YMCA authorities. In 1901 a conflict arose at the De-catur, Illinois, Railroad YMCA. The secretary of the railroad branch of the Decatur YMCA, whose performance had been satisfactory to the railroad men, became the target of criticism from the Decatur city YMCA. Apparently, the secretary had hired a female employee for performing domestic chores, who allegedly was not "a proper person to employ in the department, owing to the unfavorable rumors . . . regarding her character." It was later claimed that "the same woman was seen permitting the embraces of rail-road men, without resentment on her part." The report further stated, "that same woman was seen dancing a jig in the corridor of the building."

The list of complaints by YMCA authorities about behavior, which had become prevalent since the woman had been hired, included the use of "profane language, cigarette smoking, flirting, and the indecent performance of the cakewalk . . . permitted without rebuke." The Decatur YMCA, after consulting with the state committee, asked the secretary to resign. However, the Wabash railroad refused to recommend the resignation of the secretary, whose salary the company paid, "in view of the favor with which his work was looked upon, both by the railroad men and the representatives of the railroad company, the only interests concerned in the conduct of the work of the Branch." The Railroad Department of the International Committee investigated the matter, which resulted in an exoneration of the secretary. But the conflicting parties could not reach an agreement, and the Decatur YMCA terminated its connection with the railroad branch.[44] Notwithstanding the question of the roles played by secretaries' wives or the problems caused by a female staff member too eager in the eyes of the YMCA to please the patrons, the ways in which an association branch resembled the domestic sphere of the home, albeit male-controlled, raised the issue of who should be in charge of YMCA branches as gendered settings.

An important feature in the work of the YMCA was the Women's Auxiliaries, which held fund raisers, organized and conducted a range of social activities at YMCA buildings, and decorated the buildings. In general, they added a feminine touch and assisted the YMCA and its officials in a variety of ways. Secretaries attempted to enlist these Auxiliaries in a supplementary role, believing that they could help in bringing wayward young men into the manly embrace of the association. YMCA secretary Cecil L. Gates suggested the YMCA could "arrange for the occasional invitation of young men, who have no homes in our cities, to the homes of our friends, the invitations coming from the lady of the house and including some Association worker as a leader of the party." At the Collinwood railroad YMCA branch in Cleveland, "the ladies have supplied . . . an excellent library, and we have sociables where the men bring their wives, and sisters, and children, once a month or every two weeks." At the meetings of the Temperance Union, which met as a part of the YMCA, "a Choir of young ladies gives us the benefit of their voices, and we have pleasant times."[45] The YMCA Women's Auxiliaries felt they made important contributions in providing a sound, morally healthful environment within the confines of a YMCA building.

While women's assistance was welcome, YMCA secretaries stressed the careful balance of the sexes in the arrangement, always sure to give patriarchal preeminence to the secretary. A well-governed YMCA had to resemble a well-ordered patriarchal household, in which the secretary, in the role of the patriarch, led the way. For this arrangement to function properly, the secretary's manliness was of the foremost importance in gaining the respect of the Auxiliary women. Cecil Gates argued that their cooperation "depends upon the estimate formed by these ladies of the man in the General Secretary." The ladies, Gates alerted his readers, "take measure of the man himself, his manliness, his honesty of purpose, his devotion to his work, his consecration; these are weighed, and hapless is the man, however accomplished or attractive, in whom they are found wanting." Only "by straightforward, frank, manly bearing we can secure and retain these ladies as our personal friends," Gates insisted.[46]

Some of the ladies concurred with that view. As one women at a Women's Auxiliary conference put it, "heaven's most precious gift to earth is the soul of a man actually sent down from the skies with God's message to us, and these are his credentials, vision, power, sympathy, sincerity, and zeal for righteousness. It is for such a soul that she lives, in such she rejoices."[47] But other women among the Women's Auxiliaries had a much broader and more ambitious vision of their ability and purpose.

YMCA Women's Auxiliaries envisioned a role for themselves that was far from the supplementary function that male secretaries attempted to assign to them. The women of the Women's Auxiliaries, too, believed that they were by nature suited to bring wayward men into the safe haven of the YMCA before others might prey upon them: "Many young men in our cities are away from home. They can speak to any man or boy whom they meet, but are prohibited from speaking to ladies, because they are strangers. They have been used to a society of mothers, sisters and friends, and how they miss it. Satan never misses a chance like this. His auxiliaries are watchful, and his rooms are always open. Auxiliary sisters, try the strength of your womanly influence against this watchful foe."[48] Women in the YMCA Women's Auxiliaries indirectly benefited from the separation of private and public spheres that had emerged in the early nineteenth century. That shift had signified female sentiment as a source of regeneration from the marketplace and assigned it to the domestic sphere of the home. In turn, women activists had redefined the private sphere of the home from a site disconnected from productive, value-creating labor, into a source of female reform activism. Able to draw on a heritage of female activism, women in the Women's Auxiliaries were at much greater ease in formulating the type of sentimental approaches needed and conducive to the domestic setting of a YMCA building.[49] In their quest for the hearts, minds, and souls of workingmen, YMCA secretaries faced competition within their own ranks, from the YMCA's Women's Auxiliaries.

The ways in which the women of the Women's Auxiliaries perceived their role as far more important than simply providing the domestic backdrop to the activities of activities of YMCA secretaries contrasted sharply with the sense of crisis articulated by male YMCA secretaries. Whereas the men often expressed grave doubts about their manliness and professional capacity, the Women's Auxiliaries expressed the utmost confidence in their ability to lead workingmen to a higher ideal of manhood. As one Women's Auxiliary leader put it, "we help to give receptions and entertainments. . . . But our real strength is not in this; all this could be done without us." More than simply assuming a supplementary role for women in the YMCA's work, she argued that "the refining influence, the homelike look, thoughts of mothers, sisters and friends, awakened in the hearts of young men, are things which only women can give." These women believed that the association of womanhood with domesticity and sentiment uniquely qualified them to lead men onto the path to moral regeneration and the manly life. But even such an outgrowth of woman's domestic duties, she emphasized, "is but the first step in our work." Due to their feminine, compassionate natures, she stated, "women are quick to see when things are wrong. The sad, troubled or reckless look is not unnoticed by them. They have tact, which enables them to give just the words which are needed without giving offense." At a time when male YMCA executives worried about their manliness and their ability to achieve their goal of reforming workingmen, the Women's Auxiliaries readily embraced the opportunity. One woman stated at a Women's Auxiliaries conference that the women of the YMCA "are ready sympathizers; kindly sympathy saves many from despair. They are not easily cast down; when all seems dark and hopeless, they are the first . . . to see the 'silver lining' to the cloud." These traits, she argued, "are God's gifts to women. In them lies our strength as helpers in this great work for young men."[50]

While Women's Auxiliary delegates shared the concerns of their male counterparts with the moral challenges and temptations the man away from home had to face, they also had a clear vision of their own role in this mission. One woman explained that "many of the great army of railroad men are away from home . . . a part or all of the time separated from its tender and restraining influences." Here, the YMCA was to step in and safeguard these men. She wrote that "the R.R. Y.M.C.A. was organized to reach these men. . . . Sobriety and purity must present more charms than debauchery and sin, and the place where these are taught must be made more attractive." However, this Women's Auxiliary delegate also made quite clear, who she thought was best equipped for the job: "who better than the Women's Auxiliary knows how to give the home touch to the headquarters."[51]

The Women's Auxiliaries saw their role not merely as supplementary to the men's, but believed that their role was the same as that of their male counterparts—building manhood. The Women's Auxiliaries regarded as their "privilege as Christian women to present an ideal of perfect manliness to them and help by our influence to attain it." For that, the Women's Auxiliaries were well equipped, because "the greatness of men is generally due to mothers" [because] "it is she who stamps the coin of character."[52]

The ability to mold others represented the key quality that distinguished the women for this task. And the women believed that they possessed the proper credentials. One Women's Auxiliary leader described this quality as women's "encouraging personality." The same official implored her audience "that the results are the greatest where we can win persons to ourselves and the cause, either by personality or contact with the Association activities." The concept of a winning personality, reflecting a higher, more pure state of spirituality, represents here what Casey Blake has referred to as a feminine ideal of "maternal union," upon the foundation of which the tensions of the ongoing social and economic transformations could be resolved. In short, the women were about to beat the men at their own game.[53] YMCA secretaries found a way out of their predicament by adopting and redefining this notion of personality.

Around the turn of the century, personality became the quality in demand among prospective candidates for the YMCA secretaryship. Finding men that fit the new mold was apparently not easy, however, and good personnel were in high demand. On one occasion, George Warburton received a letter asking him for assistance in procuring a secretary. The writer asked for "a man of fine personality . . . who has the necessary tact and ability to handle a group of two hundred railroad men." Furthermore, "he must be a good business manager, and a spiritual leader who can organize and conduct successful Bible classes." The writer rounded out his description, stating that, all in all "we want a man who will develop qualities that will fit him for larger service in the Railroad Association brotherhood to prove himself a growing man." The author of the letter closed by offering such a man "a salary of fifty dollars per month." Warburton replied, "if you find the man characterized in your letter . . . send him to me by the first train, and we will pay him a hundred."[54] Apparently, men with personality and capacity for growth were scarce and in high demand for employment with the YMCA.

This shift in emphasis toward personality in the YMCA's language of manhood reflected a change in middle-class ideals of manhood. The success literature of the time associated personality with "personal magnetism" as that "subtle form of domination that could 'move upon others, bending them as the wind sways a field of grain.' The man of magnetism thus possessed in abundance what the new success literature called 'executive ability,' the art of acting as a 'master and manager of human conduct.'" Condemned by antebellum advice literature as the art of the confidence man, personal magnetism, or personality, became the mark of a man of success.[55] And YMCA secretaries were expected to have these qualities.

Reasons for dismissal of secretaries reflected this cultural change. A substantial number of YMCA secretaries left because they had been "unsuccessful" in their work. In a number of cases the YMCA added remarks, explaining the reasons. Some "disappeared," were "intemperate," "didn't like the field," were dismissed for "incompetency" or "general inability," simply "lacked qualifications," or had shown "extravagant management." In other cases, the remark stated the man had "never intended to make a secretary" or had shown "conduct unbecoming a secretary." However, among the wide variety of reasons given, a trend emerged: in 1889. The *Roster of Paid Secretaries* gives as reason for the dismissal of one secretary "very popular on a/c [sic] of integrity but lacked ex. [sic] ability." This is the first time that a reference to executive ability appears in the *Roster*. Such mention of lacking executive ability, combined with references to lacking "personal magnetism," "spiritual character," "tact and business methods," "energy," or "leadership" become quite frequent after the turn-of-the-century. After 1900 a YMCA secretary was expected to have a combination of qualities that would befit a manager: "there are, at least, nine essential qualities that a man must have to make a good secretary:" "character, calibre, personality, faith, vision, sympathy, tact, leadership, and adaptation."[56] In turn, YMCA sources generally blamed the failure of a man as YMCA secretary on a lack of training, the refusal to continue his education while on the job, and the absence of a set of qualities that made a man able to work with and attract others: "his failure to study, his lack of the manly elements of strength, grace, tact and aggression which are necessary to attract young men."[57] Accordingly, by the early twentieth century, YMCA sources borrowed ideas and concepts from the natural and applied sciences. They combined them with their language of manhood when describing YMCA secretaries as "Man-Culturists," the YMCA as a place dents in the culture of Christian manhood," and the job tary as "Manhood Engineering."[58] While YMCA offic social pressures of their changing environment and beg ideals of middle-class manhood, they reconciled expec gender performance and occupational pressures. This process of reconciliation prepared YMCA officials to assume a well-defined occupational identity centering on the ideal of a higher type of self that found its expression in personality.

This concept of personality offered YMCA officials a way out of their troubles with defining a satisfactory identity as men and as professionals. As YMCA secretaries embraced a notion of "personality," however, they did so with overtones distinct from the ways the Women's Auxiliary women had used it previously. While the men retained the emphasis on a larger, more pure and refined spirituality, they put less emphasis on subtle moral suasion and more on the charismatic attraction they desired to project. All that had troubled secretaries only slightly earlier, now became virtues of the successful urban YMCA secretary. What was required was an "instinctive capacity for adaptation which springs out of a cosmopolitan mind and a generous spirit." George Warburton argued that "the highest efficiency comes when the secretary so impresses himself upon all of the Association life as to be dominant, while, at the same time, he subordinates himself by magnifying the importance of and constantly increasing, the intelligent activity of volunteer workers." Warburton himself emphasized that a YMCA secretary "must first and foremost be dominant in a truly unified work by sheer sympathetic touch and comprehension of the men who are associated with him." He added that "a compassionate nature assures harmony. It also assures dominance." Key to the success of the secretary of an urban association was a "dominant personality."[59] Personality had become central to the type of manliness expected of YMCA secretaries.

The growth and expansion of YMCA programs with workers in a variety of industries led to a reorientation in the self-perception of YMCA secretaries as professionals and as men. As the work expanded, due to contributions from railroads, YMCA officials began to suggest that not just any man was suitable do be a YMCA secretary, but that he had to bring specific qualities as a man to the job. YMCA officials believed that the success of the work depended on the right kind of manhood. Only a man who united the right physical and spiritual qualities could gain the workers' confidence. YMCA officials urged their fellow secretaries to strive toward a higher al of manhood, living up to the manly example set by the railroad men, but also emphasizing more refined qualities of Christian manhood, which their role as leaders of men supposedly required.

Around the turn from the nineteenth to the twentieth century, YMCA secretaries had come under pressure to reconcile older ideals of sincerity with new demands for charismatic appearance as they sought to articulate a satisfying professional identity for themselves. What may have been even more troubling was that the very success visible in the expansion of the movement and the addition of new buildings contributed to the cultural strain. Middle-class culture expected YMCA secretaries as men to be public performers, but as social service professionals, watching over YMCA buildings and their transient population, they had to reconcile the role of the manly household patriarch with that of the somewhat effeminate domestic caregiver who would exercise a culturally uplifting influence through moral suasion. YMCA secretaries certainly must have noticed that they were competing here with the women in the Women's Auxiliaries. It was a role, moreover, in which these women were far more comfortable than the men and far more certain of their potential for success, as their own rhetoric indicates. In the process, YMCA officials adjusted to the social pressures of their changing environment and began to transform ideals of middle-class manhood from old ideals that had emerged in the antebellum era to new ideals in line with new demands for professionalization and expertise.

On the level of reconfiguring a manly self, this adjustment involved embracing a notion of *personality*, a term first introduced into YMCA debates by the Women's Auxiliaries. But this notion of personality, while it offered solutions to the predicament these men confronted, raised problems as well. Although YMCA secretaries connected personality with notions of efficiency, personal magnetism, or dominance, the concept offered a somewhat androgynous notion of the male self. This concept of personality as core of a reconfigured middle-class male self appeared equally problematic when juxtaposed with the notion of *character* that employers and YMCA secretaries sought to proffer to workingmen. After all, character, as employers and YMCA secretaries had redefined it, firmly lodged the worker in a web of domestic obligations, centering on the workplace, under the benevolent guidance and surveillance of the employer.[60] YMCA secretaries, then, faced the task of defining the relation between these two notions of manhood. Interlocking the two in relations of cultural reproduction that would affirm and reproduce class difference would offer a solution to this predicament.

Personality, Character, and Self-Expression:

The YMCA and a Language of Manhood and Class

\\//

By the early twentieth century, cultural pressure from a number of directions had begun to effect a shift in YMCA secretaries' understandings of manhood. YMCA secretaries, the association's benefactors in industry, and workingmen did share certain common assumptions about the meanings of manhood. YMCA secretaries and the association's sponsors easily agreed on a prescriptive ideal of manliness and its exhortations of service, self-sacrifice, and hard work, an ideal suitable to shape workingmen according to industry's needs. Workingmen, while they shared this language of manhood to the extent that manhood was to mean civilized morality, sobriety, and independence, frequently resisted the attempts at moral uplift made on their behalf. Further, the association's institutional expansion and subsequent articulation and elaboration of professional standards for YMCA secretaries added to the cultural pressures these men experienced in their quest for satisfying careers and a suitable identity as men. Expansion of YMCA programs to urban industrial workers after the turn of the century facilitated a rearticulation of the YMCA's language of manhood.

The expansion of YMCA programs to workers in urban industries meant reaching out to a segment of the working class whose ethno-cultural profile had been changing with the influx of new immigrants since the 1880s. Like their contemporaries, YMCA officials attempted to come to terms with the effects of this transition.[1] No longer confronting exclusively the railroad Brotherhoods, which had already proven that they could be sufficiently troublesome and recalcitrant, the YMCA now had to face a segment of the working class that was increasingly immigrant, highly urbanized, and whose politics tended to be more contentious than those of the railroad Brotherhoods.

Association officials adopted an increasingly ambiguous attitude toward workingmen by the early twentieth century. Previously, YMCA officials had admired workingmen along the railroads for their physicality and occasionally even held them up as an example for YMCA secretaries to aspire to. However, descriptions of industrial workers and their relations to YMCA officials carried no such implications. Regarded as more dangerous and radical, and consequently less manly, urban industrial workers received a far more hostile review from YMCA officials than their counterparts along the railroads earlier. Considered useful for their labor power, these male workers, YMCA officials believed, lacked the self-restraint necessary to control their physical energies and direct them into channels of civilized morality and productive effort. Whereas YMCA officials had expressed concern over workingmen's manliness and the dangers of labor unrest and radicalism when dealing with railroad workers, the description of urban industrial workingmen tended to be somewhat shrill by comparison. In turn, YMCA secretaries placed increasing emphasis on their leadership and ability to shape workingmen's minds and souls, helping them on the path toward proper manliness. Native workers and immigrant workingmen alike, the YMCA felt, required supervision and guidance that would prevent upheavals and steer them on the path toward Christian, manly character. It would be up to YMCA secretaries to provide the needed guidance and leadership—much more so than with railroad workers previously.

In this context, YMCA officials further redefined their language of manhood around concepts of character and personality. Both terms, as we have seen, originally carried distinctive meanings, linking character and personality to the public-private division in American culture. Since the early nineteenth century, when framing their debates of public issues, Victorian Americans had drawn on an extensive vocabulary developed out of the initial differentiation of middle-class culture along lines of public and private realms.[2] Victorian Americans had relied on this vocabulary to deny the significance of class or class distinctions in society. By the end of World War I, YMCA secretaries' language of manhood, structured around concepts of character and personality, articulated class differences through gender.

The shift in attitudes toward workingmen alluded to above came about with the founding of the YMCA Industrial Department in 1902. According to Charles C. Michener, the first secretary of the Industrial Department, the concentration of people in cities had broken apart traditional restraints on conduct, creating a potentially volatile social mixture. The workers and their families, Michener believed, lacked nothing more than proper spiritual guidance and a positive influence in their lives. He felt that "ambition in so many of these men seems to have almost gone. They drudge along almost hopelessly as time severs [sic], having given up any idea of ever improving their conditions."[3] Michener was not without sympathies for these workers and their families. Indeed, Michener wrote in one of his early reports that he found "the whole effect of this industrial work . . . very depressing." Being "day after day and week after week in the presence of these men with their temptations, becomes a very heavy drain. The cries of the children for food; the tired and worn mothers longing for just a few of the comforts of life."[4]

Although he expressed compassion, Michener laid the blame for these circumstances not on poor wages but on the fathers' and husbands' sinful behavior—their lack of upright manliness. Michener blamed the situation on the collapse of morality among the men—a direct result of their lack in manhood. He associated the men with sin, casting the children and mothers as suffering victims: "the sinning fathers and sons, with all that these things mean, are a heavy pull on the heart strings of any man who has any sympathy in him." The churches, Michener claimed, seem "impotent in the presence of this great problem."[5] While the churches apparently had failed to address the problem and offer solutions, labor unions, in Michener's mind, seemed to have recognized the opportunity.

Where restraints on individual conduct seemed to have lost their hold on the men, labor union organizers stepped into the fold, "preying," as Michener probably would have had it, on the needs of the downtrodden and despairing workers. Michener singled out the unions' shopfloor representatives, or walking delegates, as a main source of trouble for the YMCA's work in industry: "the walking delegate has the right of way with the union men and is as a rule an unsafe agitator and leader." These union delegates, Michener asserted, "make it more difficult to deal with these men and more care must be exercised than in any other department of our work." Michener even asserted that "as long as he [the walking delegate] is in the position of power he is at present with the unions, there will always be trouble—[YMCA] association or no [YMCA] association." Decidedly differentiating between workers along railroads and in urban industries, Michener chided labor unions and their organizers for lacking "the sane leadership of the Railroad Brotherhood." As a result, he pointed out, "the men themselves are, as a rule, more ignorant and therefore more prejudiced."[6]

Driven by a strident antiradicalism, Michener harbored a strong bias against industrial labor unions. He complained that labor strife, fomented by immigrant workers, socialist agitators, and labor unions, constantly affected the Industrial Department's work. Michener wrote that "the problems seem almost insurmountable. The conditions which enter into the strife between labor and capital are always on the surface to be reckoned with." Michener directly connected labor strife to immigration and the concentration of immigrants in the cities. He asserted that "the problem of immigration is a real one, as such large numbers of these foreigners are crowded into these industrial communities," where they helped to increase the "influence of the socialists because the recruiting comes almost exclusively from laboring men—the almost universal hatred of the Church and the Christians."[7]

From Michener's point of view, the urban environment had turned into a stage on which a contest for the minds, souls, and bodies of workingmen unfolded between forces of political radicalism and Christian civilization. He explained that "it is largely in these cities that the evil social influences are at work and where extreme socialistic agitation is most actively carried on. The working men of the cities, therefore, become more of a menace and need to be more carefully looked after."[8] Socialist workingmen agitators in the nation's urban centers undermined the moral fabric:

> The socialists are unusually active at this time. . . . it will be impossible
> for anyone to go along the principal streets in the larger cities of the
> country and not hear every night in the week, many of these socialists
> delivering their attacks upon the nation and its leading men. These
> speakers are usually working men. The working men's communities
> are being flooded with tons of printed matter, attacking the fundamental
> principles of the Republic. These men do not go to church; they do but
> little general reading; there are but few corrective influences at work.[9]

Michener substituted the socialist agitator who misdirected the men by slandering the nation and its institutions for the confidence man of antebellum Victorian lore who took advantage of gullible newcomers to the city and corrupted them.[10] This perception of industrial labor unions and their officials as a source of political dissent and moral disorder, rather than as a legitimate, mitigating force in industrial relations, had consequences for the YMCA's approach toward urban workers compared to railroad workers earlier.

While in the case of YMCA railroad work the connection between the association and railroad management had always been common knowledge, Michener felt that this plan could not be followed with factory workers: "the usual plan of dealing with the railroad men cannot, at present at least, be followed with these men. The work must begin, as far as the men know, with themselves."[11] Whereas the YMCA had worked comparatively well with the railroad Brotherhoods, association officials such as Michener did not think the same level of cooperation could be reached with nontransient urban workers. He believed that the influence of these unions and, particularly, the organizers had to be broken before the YMCA could offer effective guidance to workingmen. Christianity, Michener believed, could serve as a cultural lever.

The YMCA was convinced that converting workingmen to Christianity represented the key to peaceful relations and progress in industry. Charles Michener was convinced that "the making of a Christian men [sic] is not only the ultimate object of this department, but it is the only real solution of this labor problem." He was convinced that "in the making of Christian men, it will serve as a corrective to these socialistic influences; it will change the home life of the employees." Moreover, through making the workers Christian men, the YMCA will "make out of these communities, so many of which are churchless and godless, places which will really have the right to be called a part of a Christian Republic."[12]

The YMCA considered converting the labor movement to Christ to be a supremely important part of their mission. As it was put in one YMCA publication, "The Young Men's Christian Association is fundamentally a Christian Brotherhood, seeking to built a symmetrical Christian manhood." Workingmen in the cities, the YMCA believed, because "superior in numbers, massed in the great centers, . . . are rapidly becoming the supreme force in determining the character of our civilization and the destiny of our nation." From these men, the YMCA was convinced, "the call for individual salvation and social service comes the loudest. The divine command and human wisdom unite in urging the evangelization of this group." Bringing workingmen into the fold promised great benefits, because there is "a great power for religious leadership pent up in industrial workers, and one of the superlative engineering feats in the religious world is harnessing this power to the machinery of the Kingdom."[13] YMCA leaders confidently believed they had the resources to accomplish this great

Shop Bible class meetings like this one in Dayton, served the YMCA as a critical means to spread its message among workingmen. Reprinted from *Association Men* 30 (April 1905): 313. (Courtesy of Kautz Family YMCA Archives, University Libraries, University of Minnesota, Twin Cities, and the YMCA of the USA.)

task. Guided by a cultural imperative of Christian manliness, the workers would be enveloped in an edifying, uplifting web of relations, linking the workingmen's communities and homes to shops and factories.

The YMCA relied on shop Bible classes as the means to spread this message and to draw workingmen into the fold. Shop Bible classes actually preceded the inauguration of industrial work on the national level. The Cleveland YMCA pioneered such classes in the city's shops. Its first meeting was held on 19 September 1899 in the Lake Shore Railroad Mill Room with 71 workingmen attending. When the Industrial Department was established in 1902, shop Bible classes were an already established feature in YMCA programs for workingmen.[14]

Acknowledging the important role these shop Bible classes had played in the past, the Industrial Department executive committee instructed Michener in 1902 "that the secretary of the Industrial Department push as strongly as possible the Shop Bible Class work." The YMCA considered those classes as the first step toward establishing permanent work at a company. Moreover, shop Bible classes, YMCA officials believed, could serve as an ideal tool to intervene into workers' shopfloor politics in a corrective fashion. Michener himself was convinced that "the only aggressive plan that is counteracting [the socialists'] work is the shop Bible class." Shop Bible classes represented the means by which the YMCA intended to remind workingmen of their true need: Christian manhood. Through promoting shop Bible classes as a way to reach workingmen, the Industrial Department involved an increasing number of city YMCAs in industrial work. By 1904 72 out of 483 city associations reported 2,530 shop classes and meetings. The *Yearbook* provides no figure for the total attendance at these meetings, but average attendance varied from 12 in Ansonia, Connecticut, to 462 at Brooklyn's Central Branch. By 1907 these figures had increased: out of 464 city YMCAs 158 reported 11,260 shop meetings with a total attendance of 753,723. The average attendance ranged from 7 in Bloomington, Illinois, to 400 in Norristown, Pennsylvania, with size of community and factory populations certainly having an impact on the number of workers attending.[15]

YMCA shop Bible classes usually took place on the premises of a company. In setting up a Bible class, the volunteer had to obtain management's permission, which usually meant assuring the company that the classes would not intervene with production and that the men's approval would be sought. Attendance at the shop Bible class would by no means interfere with the workers' duties: where the so-called noon hour was from 12:00 to 12:30, the Bible class should start at 12:15 and "stop promptly" at 12:28, "two minutes before the whistle blows for return to work" at 12:30. The layman conducting the class was to ensure that further meetings were held. The volunteer leader was instructed to obtain democratic legitimization by letting the men vote on the issue, but the volunteer leader should "put the vote in such a way that it cannot fail to carry"[16] to ensure a continuation of the work. The reality, however, tended to look different, as workers for political and religious reasons resisted and resented these classes. As companies sought to assert their control over work processes, they not only attempted to reshape their workers' work habits and routines, but also sought to shape the culture of shopfloor relations. Bible classes, conducted on company premises, placed the YMCA officials who conducted them at a critical juncture in the conflict between company and workingmen over control of the workplace and shopfloor culture.

The concerns of YMCA officials with the conduct of shop Bible classes and the advice offered on what to do and what to avoid provide a glimpse into the problems the YMCA encountered. The author of the Cleveland

YMCA's manual for organizing shop Bible classes warned that the workers were "sensitive . . . of any attempts made by the 'office end' of the establishment for their betterment. They prefer independence and resent any inference that they need mental, moral, physical or spiritual help." The workers were "in constant attitude of suspicion toward their employers, believing that any move has some hidden and ulterior motive which will disadvantage them." Thus, "great care is needed not to alarm or antagonize them." The volunteer leader, therefore, had to exercise great care in conducting the class and in his relations to the workers. He should "by no means allow the men to get the impression that the shop management is back of the meeting, nor make it leverage for securing Association membership or support."[17] The YMCA was all too aware of this situation.

YMCA officials expected that any attempts at moral uplift would be met with resistance from the workingmen. YMCA shop Bible class leaders had to be able to squelch politically divisive issues that might come up during a class: "a leader should know the labor problems, but not discuss them." The volunteer leader, it was recommended, "should know the theories of the socialist, but leave them alone, as well as every fad, freak-fancy and political issue." The leader had to be watchful of the possibility that attending workers might try to challenge the volunteer leader and attempt to bring up themes not tied to the teachings of Christ. Apparently based on experience with conducting shop Bible classes in Cleveland, one YMCA official stated that the Bible class leader must "be alert to meet any kind of an emergency—to turn the laugh on the interruptions of a man in the crowd who puts a 'poser.'" But the problem apparently went beyond the occasional troublemaker disrupting the Bible class. As stated in Cleveland's "Shop Bible Classes" manual, "it is worse than useless to debate controverted subjects." Moreover, "if the teacher once gives an opening for controversational [sic] discussion, nothing can save the class. All sorts of isms and schisms, facts, and fantasies of labor, religion and politics will swamp them."[18]

Such admonitions apparently did not come not without a reason. At one shop, one worker, apparently referring to the YMCA's message of Christian brotherhood and the "golden rule," said: "What do you come down here for? Why don't you go up to the office; that is where it is needed?" Similar events occurred elsewhere. "You lied last week," one worker yelled at the Bible class leader, and another told the class leader, "Get out of here, we don't want you." A third worker, apparently of strong religious convictions himself, asked, "Do you think we are heathen? We have our own churches if we want to go to [a] meeting." In another class, held in Dayton, an engineer "attempted to break up a meeting by blowing off steam."[19]

While such situations placed a heavy burden on the YMCA secretary's capacity for anticipating, handling, and defusing conflicts, the YMCA also suggested leaders downplay the religious aspect of the work and instead emphasize the work's social aspect. In winning the workers, the shop Bible class leader had to exercise care, because, according to the Cleveland manual, the workers were "naturally shy of any scheme which an outsider tries to exploit; especially if it smacks of religion." As the YMCA introduced shop Bible classes as the entrance point for the YMCA into working-class communities, association officials urged class leaders to sidestep denominational differences in their approach. According to the Cleveland manual, if the workers thought the volunteer leader looks "upon them as another class of men fit only to be 'saved' and there his interest ceases, they will show by no ceremonious courtesies their disapprobation." The manual's author emphasized that the shop Bible class leader should treat the workers in the shop "just as . . . he treats his comrades of the office or bank or counting room, like equals and friends."[20]

The YMCA emphasized the building of manhood as central to these classes. The purpose of such Bible classes was to promote what YMCA officials called "a religion of man." As one author explained, the YMCA "conceives its function to be a ministry to the complete development of the masculine life." Therefore, the man and his manhood represented the center of the YMCA's attention: "the objective is not the prayer meeting but the man. . . . and his full manhood is to be developed in relating his complete self to his task in the world, in a real consecration to human advancement." Carrying inflections of equality among all true men, the YMCA argued that manhood represented the bonds of a well-ordered "society in which pure blooded, strong manhood, is contributing its best in loyal devotion."[21] Whether the YMCA made this shift in content because they felt workingmen emphasized their manliness as being central to their standing as workers, we cannot know. We do know, however, that to foment such social bonds in the workplace, the YMCA turned to a concept of personality.

Against the radicalism and the sinfulness of the workingmen, the shop Bible class leader was expected to deploy his personality. The Cleveland YMCA's manual for organizing shop Bible classes illustrates the role of "personality" in the YMCA's work. Among the qualities necessary to make a successful shop Bible class leader, the ability to establish relations with the men was considered most important. As the manual stated, "The future success or failure depends on the tact, resourcefulness, winsomeness and manliness of the teacher—or the want of it." The decisive quality for the successful Bible class leader was "the magnetism of a strong personality. No weakling can be galvanized into usefulness by an 'outline.' It must be in the man so much that he could make himself felt if he had none of the latest models in outline schemes for Bible study." The "touch with men" was more important than biblical knowledge. A man who lacked this social ability "cannot win his way in a shop full of hard-headed, warm-hearted mechanics. To get on with them he must . . . [establish] comradeship . . . naturally that nobody will suspect he is trying to." This concept of leadership through moral suasion reflected ideas YMCA officials associated with personality. The Bible class manual's author argued that "to be master of the situation and at the same time not seem to be controlling men's minds is an act not taught by rules or helped much by suggestions. It must be indegenous [sic] to the man."[22] Personality as a set of qualities that distinguished a successful leader of shop Bible classes represented a higher state of consciousness, spiritual perfection, control over the self, and charisma. Personality was understood to be not simply an acquired ability of role play and outward adaptation, but a quality rooted in the inner, spiritual self of the man. More than a turn toward shallow self-commodification, personality represented the self in a "process of self-realization."[23] The YMCA espoused an ideal of the male self that gained validity through shaping others, nurturing spiritual qualities, building character and fostering manliness among workingmen, directing their energies into socially useful and economically productive channels. While "personality" signified a broader spirituality, eschewing denominational boundaries, it also was expected to mitigate class tensions through appeals to a shared manliness. This appeal rested on facilitating the workers' self-expression.

In the thought of YMCA officials, building this higher type of manliness centered on opening paths for self-expression and directing them toward spiritual goals—and the desire to be useful, of course. YMCA officials felt that self-expression was central to its "religion of man": "It is not that something is to be put on top of the athletics and the classes and the social life, which we shall call spiritual; but that the whole tone and temper of a man's life shall be spiritual, and that he is seeking fullest and most joyous self-expression, he shall feel himself called to be a son of God, and called to be a servant of his fellowman."[24] Self-expression was a somewhat ambiguous concept within the YMCA's language of manhood. While the notion had definite spiritual meaning, the YMCA also linked self-expression to productive effort. Productive labor, according to one YMCA source, "satisfies one of the highest needs of the soul because it gives opportunity for

self-expression." Character-building through self-expression relied on productive effort: "One of the highest forms of work is production. In making something we reproduce our ideals, material or spiritual. In production
we find real self-expression."[25] YMCA officials encouraged self-expression
among workingmen as a way to direct potentially disruptive feelings and
restore the necessary emotional balance without which good habits were
unthinkable. If workingmen would find self-expression on the level of spirituality as well as on the more mundane level of labor, this might suggest
that one was meant to condition the other. Since the YMCA promised to
deliver more content workers by proffering an ideal of manhood conducive
to industry's needs for docile workers, the capacity to elicit and facilitate
self-expression through personality became the quality without which a
YMCA secretary could be neither a successful professional nor a true man.
Facilitating self-expression through a winning personality was crucial to
the YMCA's mission of carrying the message of Christian manhood to the
working classes.[26]

Concepts of personality and self-expression had strong ties to the private sphere of the Victorian middle-class home. In the private realm of the
home, Victorian Americans expected that personality would form through
the self-expression of one's innermost thoughts, feelings, and beliefs, forming the foundation of public character. Drawing on concepts connected
with the private sphere of the home, YMCA secretaries certainly shared with
other middle-class professionals "an earnest desire to remake the world
upon their *private* models," as noted previously. However, applying private
solutions to public problems, YMCA secretaries also redefined the dynamic
of this exchange. In Victorian culture, personality, formed through self-
expression, had been associated with the private sphere. In the YMCA's
language of manhood, personality assumed public meaning, as it was to facilitate the formation of character by opening paths for self-expression to
workingmen.[27] But what may appear at first glance as an equal exchange became a means for YMCA secretaries to affirm the status of workingmen as
dependent producers and to affirm class distinction.

In 1907 the industrial work of the YMCA received a boost by changing the man at the helm. Charles R. Towson, who succeeded Charles C.
Michener as general secretary of the YMCA Industrial Department in
1907, played a key role in further shaping this language of manhood. From
1907 to 1922, Towson represented the driving force behind the association's programs for industrial workers.[28]

In Towson's mind, the image of the worker itself underwent further change, as YMCA officials, like himself, continued to grapple with the

Charles R. Towson, here close to his retirement, was a key figure in shaping YMCA Industrial Department programs and policies between 1907 and 1920. (Courtesy of Kautz Family YMCA Archives, University Libraries, University of Minnesota, Twin Cities, and the YMCA of the USA.)

meanings of gender and class.[29] Fearful of the potential for political radicalism workers seemed to represent, albeit not quite as shrill in tone as his predecessor was, he also admired them for the rugged life many of these workingmen appeared to live. In that, he shared the perspective of George Warburton, who also admired workers for their manly ruggedness. But whereas Warburton had perceived sinful behavior as the primary problem, for Towson it was political radicalism. Despite the overwhelming concerns with subduing workers' restive impulses, however, precisely this ruggedness

and the nature it represented figured as a source of spiritual and manly re-
newal in the minds of YMCA officials. Expressing a longing for an emo-
tionally more expressive domain in which one could be more true to one's
inner self, Towson was convinced that "there is something about living
with the elements and in common with other men that makes it easier to
be frank. Much easier than when one is surrounded by hard wood furniture
and rugs, with all the conventionalities that go with them." Inflecting his
own desire for a more authentic type of manliness, Towson wrote that "one
who has known men in the open is drawn in spirit at times—away from the
high building and the things that go with it, even from the goodly fellowship of the saints therein, to be with the out-of-door workers of the world."
Towson felt that the workers had retained a potential for a more vigorous
manhood, which, as he seemed to regret, was decidedly on the retreat
among middle-class men in an emerging urban, corporate social order.

The image of workingmen as a vigorous, serviceable source of labor
power went hand in hand with a notion of workers as a source of cultural an-
archy; an ambivalent image centering on their bodies. Confronting a worker
at a dam in the Northwest, Charles Towson noted how he "looked at the bulk
of bone and muscle rising six feet three and copped [sic] by a bronzed Irish
face." He added that the appearance of this worker reminded him "of gran-
ite, of cement, of strong machinery, of strong language—all elements that
go into modern out-of-door construction work." Towson later wrote that
he felt like saying, "Bully, you're a man of the open." Men working close to
nature seemed to have held on to a more pure form of masculinity.[30]

The simple life close to nature, Towson felt, made those men emo-
tionally more receptive: "Appeals for decisions of the heart come with
power to both men and boys when grouped in common near to nature." He
explained, "That is why men in the construction camps are so responsive
to the Christian appeal of a sincere man, and it reveals the reason, too, for
the response to music of the heart." Towson added, "is [it] not true that
converts who live and work in this realm of the open witness to their faith
with a peculiar force?" "It is that subtle something," Towson said, "that . . .
makes these men, as Christians, open, aggressive and outspoken in their
advocacy of Jesus Christ as a Savior from sin." While these workers could
be easily won by a sincere appeal to their Christian manliness, however,
YMCA officials like Towson also perceived them as more easily inclined
toward unrestrained and violent behavior. This more pure form of masculinity apparently also bore hidden dangers that necessitated proper chan-
neling and control. Towson warned that "for the safety of society and the
law, we do well to enlist them on the side of a religion that exalts God,

Righteousness and the Law, or they will yield to the lure of destructive self-ishness." He added that "while ardent in their faith and conduct in religious life they are also vigorous allies of the destructive if turned wrong." The workers' "vigorous manhood" could be a force for good or evil: the YMCA could direct the workers' manhood, but without proper guidance it would prove to be destructive.[31] The challenge the YMCA had to confront was there. Free from the constraints of a good home, men all too easily could and did give in to corrupting and self-degrading instincts. These instincts the YMCA wished to control, because if given free play they would destroy not only the men but the social order as a whole. Directing workers' manliness in the right direction would rely on developing self-expression among them, as we have seen.

Towson saw the YMCA's mission as providing avenues for self-expression to develop sound character among workers under the care of capable, manly leadership through personality and in the confines of a proper environment. Towson characterized the focus of the YMCA's efforts with workingmen as "developing self-expression in terms of the better self." From the YMCA's point of view, not only would character-building through self-expression direct the workers' impulses toward higher, constructive purposes, but it was also the key to industrial peace and progress. He argued that "character-making forces must be multiplied wherever workers are massed; this is essential to economic advantage and to social safety as well." Towson added that the programs and activities of the YMCA Industrial Department centered on "the forces that make for character and efficiency and to the fundamental demand for self-expression on the part of the human factor."[32]

Towson associated YMCA secretaries with personality, a mark of their superior manhood and the key to their ability to guide workingmen by providing avenues for self-expression. The YMCA was able to instill the workingmen with character because, Towson asserted, its work "center[ed] in the leadership of manly men." Such manly leadership, flowing from a man's "personality," would foster self-expression: "the Association enlists personality . . . and affords channels for safe and sane self-expression."[33] Personality, associated with leadership, had a projective, dynamic quality, including leadership and disciplining others. Towson, then, further articulated class through gender around concepts of personality and character.

In Towson's view, a successfully operating association under the guiding leadership of a trained professional could represent a model for society. In a YMCA, Towson said, "all grades from the officers of the company down actually ran that Association." As a result, "every man feels a proprietorship, not only in the Association, but in the relation of that enterprise to the community and to the business." This was accomplished, Towson argued, because the association "was genuinely democratic; but there was a trained secretary to give information and counsel." The workers received an outlet and opportunity to give voice to their inner urges, but only under the proper supervision of a YMCA secretary. The YMCA offered workers avenues for participation without actually relinquishing control. "Men want to run something," Towson asserted, "and here is a part of the community affairs which they control, the presence of an expert leader assuring safety." Given the proper balance of employee involvement and professional guidance and control, Towson said that a YMCA "is a channel of self-expression not only of those committeemen, but of the entire membership."[34] YMCA activities directed workers' creativity away from work and into leisure activities regimented by a YMCA official, by linking self-expression to character formation through the exemplary presence of a YMCA secretary and his personality. As YMCA secretaries, like Towson, set out to build character for workingmen by facilitating self-expression, they also opened a path for YMCA secretaries to construct an identity of class by offering a collective ideal to aspire to. Middle-class men could affirm their manhood and class status by providing avenues of self-expression for workingmen, thereby taming their behavior.

In numerous accounts, albeit of questionable authenticity, of their relations with workingmen YMCA secretaries represented those interactions within distinctly domestic settings or scenarios. Turning qualities that Victorian Americans had associated with the private sphere of the home—moral suasion and self-expression—toward asserting male public power required the presence of a powerless, privatized sphere, or beings—working-class men. The following narrative illustrates how, in the minds of YMCA secretaries, the worker's validation of the YMCA secretary's manliness was bound up with inflections of domesticity and sentiment. At a track layers' camp in the Northwest, the local YMCA secretary tried to win over the cook, who had strongly resented the presence of the YMCA. An opportunity for Christian work offered itself when the cook, who had told the YMCA secretary that "he was 'done with the Y.M.C.A.,'" became ill. After resisting the offer of help at first, the cook gave in. As the account went, describing the success of the YMCA secretary, "this red-blooded missionary is nothing if not masterful, and from the moment he took the bull-cook's case into his hands, he was a czar." The YMCA secretary achieved mastery over the cook by bestowing his good domestic care upon him: "I took him to my room at the association, built a fire in my stove, heated a can of water ıked his feet thoroughly; . . . greased his chest with turpentine and lard and put him in my own bed and sweat out his cold." The next morning, he gave the cook "a warm bath and a rub down." When the cook was cured three days later, he offered the YMCA official payment for services rendered. This the YMCA secretary adamantly refused by giving the cook "a tongue-lashing that made him feel small." The cook apologized and, gushing with sentiment, offered his services to the secretary in his work: "I'd feel proud to black your boots, if you'd give me a chance." The cook and the YMCA secretary arrived at a somewhat domestic arrangement, as the cook took over all janitorial work at the shack occupied by the YMCA secretary, because "the practical demonstration of Christianity had made him a willing slave."[35]

Different from what the term "slave" might suggest, YMCA officials never regarded their attempts to provide moral and spiritual guidance to the workers as manipulative; rather, they believed that they responded to the innermost needs of the workingmen. Tales of worker–YMCA secretary interaction, such as the above and those below, encapsulated the notion that "good men" looked out for exceptional, deserving workers, who would be subsequently uplifted into the ranks of the "good men." In this sense, YMCA secretaries cast themselves as mediators across social boundaries of class.[36]

In the YMCA's literature, middle-class men who hoped to reaffirm their manliness could find an outlet by giving workingmen guidance in their spiritual and moral lives. In 1908 the YMCA began work at a construction camp in Pontis, South Dakota, under the joint auspices of the Railroad and Industrial Departments.[37] At Pontis, the temptations of the environment were strong, and the YMCA secretary was engaged in a constant, strenuous struggle against human weakness. When Christmas arrived and "a good many of [the workers] got 'roaring' drunk," the YMCA secretary, William H. Morrison, stayed on top of the situation. He went to neighboring Mobridge with a rig and hauled the drunks back to the camp, putting them to bed. One of the men whom Morrison took care of "was a little Irishman who had started in to lick a fellow about twice his size, and who was making splendid progress when Morrison stopped him, loaded him into the wagon, packed him off to camp and put him to bed." Morrison made him promise to "sign a temperance pledge" the next day. After he had signed the pledge the next day, Morrison hesitated "whether to pray with him or not, as it was a little embarrassing because of the presence in the room of six or eight other men." Before he could make a decision, a "big engineer . . . walked in and told the secretary that he, too, had come to take the temperance pledge, 'For,' said he, 'I'm sick of the life I have been living.'" Then the engineer "reached his big hand across to Morrison and said: . . . 'I want to go all the way with this thing and I want you to pray for me right here.' They knelt beside one of the bunks and both of them prayed most earnestly for God's help in saving this man to the uttermost." As they had finished their prayer, "the little Irishman who had been looking on, piped up: 'Boss Morrison, ain't ye goin' to bless me off, too?' 'Certainly, I will,' said Morrison, and they got on their knees beside the bunk and prayed that Mike might be thoroughly saved and kept from his old life." Accepting the better life, YMCA officials believed, would bring peer approval: "as they arose, the six surveyors came across the room and, taking both converts by the hand, assured them of their sympathy and help in their new life." Following the example of the YMCA secretary not only prompted a turn toward the right type of manhood that eschewed class differences but also inducted the worker into a higher type of spiritual community based on homosocial bonds of gender.

YMCA accounts of uplifting rough-and-tumble workers into the homosocial community of true men also carried reminders of men's purpose as family patriarchs and providers. In these accounts, the family home was an expression of the good manly life without which a man could not find his spiritual self. The story of how Morrison won over the remaining two "D.T. men (delirium tremens)" is a case in point. One of the two was a man named Dan, "the hostler of the camp, a genial, big-souled fellow who always boozed after pay day, and never had been able to keep sober for a month at a time." Morrison looked after Dan, helping him in his recovery by bringing him "poached eggs, toast and other delicacies" fixed by Mrs. Morrison and "showing him other kindnesses in the way of personal attention." Upon Dan's recovery, the Morrison's invited him for dinner. In this account, the Morrison's home and family serves as a reminder to Dan of his true desire and purpose in life: "As they sat about the table, at sight of the two little boys, three and five years of age, and the home touch which only a woman can give, Dan was greatly impressed with his need for living a better life." After dinner, "the conversation led to his spiritual condition, with the result that before he went home he had knelt with the family and accepted Christ as a personal Saviour."

Indeed, it was the longing for family—the reminder of men's role as provider, husband, father, and family patriarch—that swayed minds and changed hearts. The next time Dan visited the Morrison's home, he brought his friend George along. Like Dan before him, George was very much impressed with the atmosphere of the Morrisons' home. When dinner began,

"George didn't begin eating but hung his head." This time it was not Morrison who initiated the process of conversion, but the recently reformed Dan. Asked if he wasn't hungry, George replied, "'Yes, but I can't eat anything, for I'm so ashamed.'" Even when Morrison appealed to George to eat something, "he only replied, 'I am too ashamed of myself.'" At that moment, Morrison thought that it "was the time to present Christ, for it was evident that this was his great need, and he urged him then and there to take Christ as a Saviour and keeper." When Morrison asked him, if he would do so, George "replied, 'Yes, I want to be like Dan.'" They immediately interrupted their meal, and "all went to their knees in prayer, and when they arose George had won the greatest victory of his life. Dan went around the table to him, and putting his arm around his neck, he said, 'Now, then, we are two of a kind.'" While the scenario is grounded in notions of domesticity and gushing with sentiment, it also significantly differs from the ways in which Victorian Americans understood and, more importantly, gendered these concepts. The domestic realm of the home was a woman's kingdom, and only women were truly capable of sentiment, so Victorian Americans thought. In this scenario, however, the men are invested with domestic sentiment—especially the workers, Dan and George—while Morrison wields women's tools of domestic sentiment, applying moral suasion to sway the workers' souls. Morrison's wife is an important, but only supporting, player in all this. She sets the stage for her husband by making a pure and pious home and thus establishing both his paternal responsibility and his patriarchal leadership.[38]

Morrison got more chances to bring his talents to good use when he followed the construction activities of the Chicago, Milwaukee and St. Paul Railroad to Taft, Montana, were "drunken men and fallen women were loitering in front of [the saloons], and through the open doors and unscreened windows one could see the public gambling games running in nearly every saloon." The YMCA tried to correct these bad influences by declaring "war . . . on the saloons harboring fallen women and operating open gambling in violation of the state law." This time, the saloon keepers fought back: "the deputy sheriff (whose salary, it was said, was paid by the saloon keepers) arrested [Morrison] for carrying a concealed weapon, although he had been granted a permit by the sheriff." Morrison "was released within minutes, his gun handed back, and an apology made by the deputy having taken such an action in order to hold his job." Morrison was not to be stopped by this and "was again arrested and locked up in the calaboose, where he was kept for ten or fifteen minutes and then released with another apology."

Ultimately, it was the spiritual unity of purpose among the workers as men, fostered by the example and advice of the YMCA secretary, that promised to make all the difference. Morrison turned to the workers for support in this contest. On his next Sunday speech, he "told how men had been ruined through the nefarious business; how murders had been committed in Taft." He also told them of his own role and the actions of the deputy sheriff. The men sided with Morrison. One of them stepped forward and said, "Morrison, you give the word and we will go down there and put the whole place so on the bum that they will never bother you again." Morrison suggested an alternative approach. He reminded the workers that the saloon owners were counting on their business: "they are expecting you all down there on Christmas day and are making special preparation for your reception by bringing in additional gamblers, women, etc. We are going to have a good time here in camp, I want every man in this room to stay here." On Christmas "scarcely a man went to Taft." The secret of success with the men, YMCA officials believed, lay in uniting them in a common purpose according to Christian values. Embracing the almost monastic, sentimental domesticity of the YMCA, the account seems to suggest, had engendered the regeneration of the workers who agreed to forgo bodily pleasures and desires for the homosocial community at the association building. By facilitating self-expression among the men, YMCA secretary Morrison had initiated this transformation.[39]

Through providing socially beneficial outlets for workers' self-expression, YMCA secretaries believed they could reform workers and contribute to the prevention of strikes. Labor unrest, it was argued in the 1916 YMCA *Handbook for Industrial Secretaries*, resulted from a "demand for greater democracy and more fraternity—more recognition and self-expression." While tensions between employers and employees could not be prevented, they should be redirected: "since industrial unrest is natural and must continue so long as men have the God-given instinct to 'subdue the earth'—to run something—it is well to remember that while unrest cannot be subdued, it may be directed." Trained YMCA secretaries could facilitate cooperation in industry and "help beget that spirit of goodwill and mutuality without which they [employers and employees] cannot cooperate."[40] The YMCA was confident that its officials could defuse tensions in industry by providing opportunities for self-expression. And if, indeed, self-expression was the means by which labor conflict could be defused, the war would offer the YMCA a vastly enlarged field of service.

New challenges arose for the YMCA when the United States entered World War I in 1917. The wartime situation seemed to have increased the

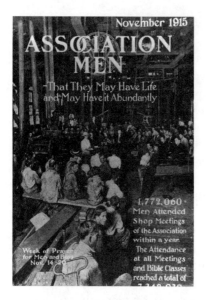

November 1915
ASSOCIATION MEN
—That They May Have Life and May Have it Abundantly

1,772,060 · Men Attended Shop Meetings of the Association within a year. The Attendance at all Meetings and Bible Classes reached a total of

Week of Prayer for Men and Boys Nov. 14-20

Facilitating workingmen's self-expression through YMCA-orchestrated programs carried the promise of not merely creating contented workers, but leading them to the path toward spiritual abundance as well. By the 1910s, YMCA officials had begun to cast its programs in consumerist terms and, by implication, workers as dependent consumers. Judging by the looks on the faces of some of the workers, their excitement remained limited. (Courtesy of Kautz Family YMCA Archives, University Libraries, University of Minnesota, Twin Cities, and the YMCA of the USA.)

potential for strife in American industry. Although the government had established maximum hours and minimum pay, labor turnover was high and the potential for social conflict increasing. This situation provoked concern among government and business leaders to stabilize labor relations and keep peace on the home front. The YMCA's industrial work expanded as a result of the war and a renewed interest among employers and the government to create a stable climate in industrial relations to guarantee uninterrupted wartime production. By January 1918 work in war industries and government arsenals had become the major focus of the YMCA. The YMCA's industrial work reached its fullest elaboration during these years.[41]

The specter of impending chaos contained the chance for true men to bring out their best abilities and recapture their manly authority by providing leadership and alerting workingmen to their responsibilities. "It is not a happy situation," a YMCA official stated, "and, while sane men must guide the way, the interim is fraught with serious possibilities." This situation, YMCA officials believed, "will demand a most careful guidance by thinking men to keep within the bounds of reason." YMCA officials assured themselves that from the ranks of their present and future personnel "will rise big men, great leaders, whose sincere earnest activities, though possibly never recorded on the country's scrolls, will count as history in the making."[42]

Offering such guidance even carried the promise of a dose of the strenuous life, as the work of a YMCA secretary required the whole man. As one

YMCA brochure described it, "the handling of men at Hog Island is no lady's job. The men sometimes are not in the mood for singing; sometimes 'roughhouse' is the uppermost thought in their minds and the form of expression of this thought is not the most gentle."[43] Usually, however, the YMCA applied more subtle approaches.

In the socially volatile climate of the war years, YMCA officials continued to rely on notions of character and personality to foster better relations in industry. The YMCA considered it its mission to "develop Christian character, through definite leadership and contagious personality."[44] YMCA officials such as Towson emphasized the need for a strong, manly spirit among the workers as the foundation for efficiency, stability, and social solidarity in wartime production. The YMCA, he wrote, was to "develop strong, manly, Christian character in the highest meaning of that term." Fostering Christian manhood among the workingmen, Towson believed, meant "begetting good-will, loyalty, fairness and efficiency, and this in turn means contented, stable and productive workers who realize their place in the nation's defense." Manly qualities, YMCA officials felt, would facilitate better relations in industry and ensure "an industrial democracy that would be safe for society."[45] Concerns over safety and solidarity led YMCA officials to link manhood to notions of unity.

Afraid that radicals, inspired by the Russian Revolution, might challenge this sense of national unity, YMCA officials joined wartime demands for political conformity. Industrial Department officials had considered workingmen a potential menace previous to the war years. But anticipating the political climate of the postwar Red Scare, YMCA officials were especially afraid that a renewed stream of immigration would bring to American shores radical doctrines fanned by the victory of Bolshevism in Russia in October 1917: "Bolshevism is the anti-thesis of Americanism and should never be tolerated in our country. It springs from discontent, disorder and disruption, the three d's that have no place in American industry." The Industrial Department felt compelled to keep America "free from this undesirable, foreign product."[46] To counteract such prospects, YMCA officials regarded it as their duty to instruct workers "in the principles underlying our democracy for which our Nation has been at war and help to counteract the destructive radicalism . . . which has proven such a menace to Europe and which now threatens America."[47]

However, the YMCA regarded radicalism in industry not as a political challenge, but primarily as an expression of youthful energies that merely required guidance and direction toward proper, productive—manly— outlets. The YMCA newsletter for industrial secretaries, *Service*, printed and approvingly commented on an address presented at a YMCA conference at Silver Bay, New York. It was argued in the address that "the I.W.W. is the naughty boy of industry. We have not given him the outlet which he must have." From the YMCA's viewpoint, however, this energy should not be suppressed. Rather, "the very energy which breaks through and makes him destructive would, if enlisted for constructive work, have made him a more useful workman than his more docile and less energetic brother." The YMCA considered it unlikely, however, that the process could be reversed. Radical workers were simply beyond redemption: "It may be too late to reclaim him now, but we can at least prevent the making of more of his kind." Casting radical workers in the roles of mischievous boys had significant implications for the ways in which the YMCA's image of workingmen changed. More menacing, the workingman remained nonetheless malleable. This perspective on workers and their behavior drew on the so-called recapitulation theory, which anthropologists and psychologists on both sides of the Atlantic had come to rely upon to establish the alleged superiority of the so-called Anglo-Saxon race and, especially, white manhood.[48]

In the early twentieth century, advocates of organized play, such as Joseph Lee, George Johnson, or the YMCA's own Luther Halsey Gulick, adapted and developed recapitulation theory. They assumed that an infant represented a psychological throwback to humanity's precivilized origins. Depicting workers as boys and political radicalism as youthful, misdirected energies placed the workers alongside boys going through previous, primitive stages of humanity's evolutionary past, and by implication, alongside the members of lesser races. Promoters of organized play, however, believed that such hedonistic, primitive mental urges, inherent in a child's mental make-up, could be constructively redirected into socially desirable behavior. This could be accomplished, they assumed, by engaging children in play activities centered around imitation and rhythmic group exercises involving music. Promoters of organized play hoped to generate feelings of social belonging and awaken the individual's moral reflexes by physically subordinating the individual to the group. Thus equipped with a suitable set of cultural instruments, YMCA officials took confidence in their ability to subdue the workers' destructive impulses and to create a cultural climate that would enable them to guide the workers' behavior and modify their political beliefs. Expertly guided group activities would help to transform disruptive and destructive emotions of adult workingmen into constructive social impulses by giving outlet to their productive energies.[49] This, YMCA officials believed, could be achieved through offering opportunities for self-expression. As one YMCA official advised his fellow secretaries,

Large shop meetings such as this served as stages on which YMCA secretaries sought to enact their superior manhood through public performance Reprinted from *Railroad Association Magazine* 6 (June 1917): 20. (Courtesy of Kautz Family YMCA Archives, University Libraries, University of Minnesota, Twin Cities, and the YMCA of the USA.)

"give men a chance for the right kind of self-expression and your battle's half won." [50]

Venting potentially disruptive emotions through self-expression would beget emotional harmony among the men, while subordinating the workers' individualities to the group. One YMCA Industrial Department official argued that "one of the underlying principles governing community mental life is imitation." Enveloped in the group, the individual man would be transformed: "it is quite clear that when men think, feel and act enmass [sic] their activities show that the emotional contact of each man has undergone a change." As a result, the worker's "individual traits have been submerged in the group, for the advancement, through cooperation of the community as a whole." [51] YMCA officials believed that the interaction of the workers in the group would lead to a modification of each individual's thought through emotional elevation. The YMCA adapted ideas of imitation and rhythmic exercises to its industrial program.

YMCA-orchestrated musical activities in factories provided the rhythm that would fuse individualities together and create a sense of emotional collectivity, turning workers into more productive employees: "born of rhythm . . . music not only increases pleasure but the rhythm of it reduces fatigue, for every exertion is succeeded by a corresponding lull." [52] As one YMCA official argued, "the introduction of music in industry is a cultural element that will permeate the life of shopmen." Making the worker interact within the group would deplete him of his dissatisfaction, because "when a man feels the interplay of his fellow workmen in musical recreation, he is no longer left stranded with his own pet irritation or complaint." Although a worker "may have had a grievance, he will find himself with an agreeable thought, lost in the singing crowd of his co-workers. His outlook on life is unquestionably of a brighter nature." Opening opportunities for moral uplift through collective emotional experience induced by music was central to the YMCA's plans for pacifying workers, while turning them into better workers as well. One YMCA official explained, "the more avenues of musical mass activities we can open up for the expression of our pent-up feelings and innermost thoughts, the greater will be our ability to attune ourselves to a higher level of thought and work." [53] Charles Towson fancied that "music in industry will help win the war and who shall say that afterward it may not put a sweeter note into industrial relationships." [54]

The YMCA believed that workers, thus assuaged, would produce with greater efficiency. YMCA officials felt that "many manual operations can be performed with more precision, speed and rapidity when accompanied with music." Musical entertainment would provide an "inspiration to the industrial worker," uplifting him to a higher level of efficiency and productivity. YMCA officials were convinced that music in industry would create harmonious relations not only between workers and management, but also between workers and their machines: "when this harmony becomes finely attuned our great industrial machine will be in perfect adjustment and literally sing." As one YMCA official described it after the war, "the Musical Director has at times swayed as many as 10,000 men in one meeting and sent them back to work on tip-toe, smiling and refreshed." [55] Certainly, through involving and guiding workers in group activities, the YMCA expected to amplify their claim to authority through public performance. YMCA-orchestrated forms of musical recreation in industry would allow the workers to participate equally, but, through the emotional outpouring in the group, their behavior would change. The experience of emotional elevation in a group would pacify the workingmen and condition them for their role in industry. [56]

Music not only provided the means to condition workers psychologically and physiologically, but also opened opportunities to instill workers with higher cultural ideals and appreciations. A YMCA official urged his fellow secretaries not to "let the groups of men reach the saturation point without being aware of their gradual improvement in tastes and their natural growth." Moreover, "plans should be made in advance to improve the cultural elements in songs."[57] YMCA musical activities aimed at furthering social homogeneity through shared emotional and cultural experience. That way YMCA officials hoped to remake the workers in their own image, without actually empowering them.

Especially group activities defused men's dangerous impulses and created a sense of emotional harmony, as the description of a factory singing at a meatpacking plant in East St. Louis illustrates. These singings, the YMCA implied, tamed potentially violent men: "girls in their white, clean aprons and caps, many men from all departments and many from the killing floors, their clothes covered with blood, their knives hanging at their sides, all join in heartily singing the songs of sentiment, love, pep, and national anthems." The brochure continued, "the songs bring smiles, deeper emotions and loftier thoughts." The images in this scenario are not only gender specific but, equally important, job specific. But the emphasis on the differences between the male and female workers is pronounced enough to draw conclusions about the ways in which the YMCA believed that activities such as singing could form gender identities: the women are associated with symbols of purity and cleanliness, whereas martial images are reserved for the men. Through participating in the singing, the men, though armed with knives, appear no more harmful than the women with whom they are united into one harmonious group. Once the workers submerged their individualities in the group, the hedonistic potential of the single workingman had lost its threat. Self-expression within the confines of the group experience implied an emotional immersion with others, creating a boundless state of union and a loss of autonomous selfhood, qualities that Victorian Americans more likely attributed to women than to men.[58]

YMCA officials created an image of workingmen that alleviated concerns over their own manliness. In 1919 a worker called on W. H. Warren, YMCA secretary at a Portland shipyard: "You don't know who the deuce I am, . . . but I know you like a book often read. I'm a cowpuncher, cattle thief, and rough rider; twice I've had a million, and I've a bad past." The worker had always believed that Warren and all others like him "were bad men." Addressing Warren, he said "ever since you first mounted a box in this yard and entertained the boys at noon, I have had my hammer out for you." The worker, "a big, raw-boned, man," had doubted Warren's manhood, but the YMCA secretaries' conduct changed his mind.

Through his conduct, Warren proved his own manhood and resolved the dormant conflict. The worker told Warren, "since you visited me when I was sick and since I have noticed the work you're doing here, I am ashamed of myself and make this public apology." Not only did the worker abandon his previous views, but he also acknowledged that the moral strength and perseverance necessary to face a crowd of hostile men was as much a manly quality as the physical toughness required to be a cowpuncher, cattle thief, and rough rider. He said, "you've been mighty white here, among the bunch, some of them not liking you at all, and have stood the gaff as a real man." And he added, "from now on, I'm your friend."[59]

Most certainly meant to entertain the readers, Warren's account also opens a window into the cultural perceptions of YMCA secretaries. Men such as Warren believed that workingmen would recognize and wished to emulate their exemplary manly conduct, thereby affirming the superior manhood of YMCA officials. Warren represents the more subtle qualities of perseverance, moral purity, and leadership as being just as authentically male as the ruggedness of the worker. He overcame the latent hostility of the shipyard worker and even won his respect by proving his own moral and spiritual purity. In acknowledging that the secretary had proven his manhood by example, the worker acknowledged Warren's superior qualities as leader. The benevolent influence of a YMCA secretary was supposedly sufficient to tame even the most suspicious and violent worker and solve conflicts in industry. Warren wanted to convince his audience, consisting mostly of YMCA officials, that their exemplary manly conduct and benevolent influence could prevail over hostility, mistrust, and class conflict. The culturally sanitized worker serves as a positive reference point from below; the worker acknowledging and deferring to the refined, superior type of manhood represented by YMCA secretaries restores social hierarchy. YMCA officials encoded the superiority of their own manhood and legitimized their attempts to exercise control over the workers through the construction of an image of workingmen as "pious consumers": won over by a YMCA secretary's personality, the workers would turn into such pious consumers, who would consume only those commodities and services that promised refinement and facilitated higher sentiment, while shirking all others. Such "pious commodities," Lori Merish has argued, "would seduce wayward individuals into [a] regenerative sociability . . . and, by inspiring purified sentiments, could draw individuals to God," and turn them into better men and more faithful, efficient workers.[60]

YMCA officials extended this representation of workers as subservient, deferential recipients of YMCA guidance and counsel to immigrant workingmen, too. That YMCA officials believed they could transform immigrants can be seen in the story of Gabriel. Dr. Edward Steiner, a writer on Americanization, who also had been involved in the Americanization program of the Pennsylvania YMCA, left us the following description of "what enlightened justice can do for the 'Roundhead.'"[61] Steiner, upon visiting the Hazleton, Pennsylvania, YMCA, "saw a man, with dust cloth and broom, walking about with the peculiarly graceful style of the mountaineer." The secretary of the Hazleton YMCA explained, "that's Gabriel—not the archangel; but an angel anyway." The secretary urged Steiner to "go from garret to cellar and you will find no dust or disorder." Impressed with the success of the efforts of the Hazleton YMCA and Gabriel's efforts, Steiner turned toward him: "'Kiss my cheek, Gabriel, and wish me well.' And Gabriel kissed my cheek and wished me well, just as he used to in his Montenegrin home, when kinsman met kinsman upon the war-path as they fought their ancient enemy, the Turk." Steiner associated the gesture of a fraternal kiss, which he traced to an expression of bonds between warriors and their honor, with goodwill and deference. With the transformation effected, Gabriel had been tamed and culturally sanitized and domesticized: "no weapons bulged from Gabriel's belt, his clothing was faultlessly American, his once furious mustachios had fallen beneath an American barber's shears, and his battlefield was this splendidly equipped building." Instead of a sword, he now wielded broom and dust cloth. But Gabriel, as Steiner explained, was not only "the janitor; but he was also the self-appointed and beneficent dictator, feared by all evil-doers and breakers of the rules, and beloved by all who could appreciate a faultlessly kept building." The Christian, manly surroundings of a YMCA building apparently had turned this immigrant workingman into a "pious consumer." At that point, Steiner's visiting tour arrived at Gabriel's own room: Gabriel "opened the door of his room with pardonable pride, for Prince Nicolas, the ruler of his country, whose bedroom I have seen and in whose throneroom I have had audience, cannot boast of an apartment so neat and clean or gorgeously decorated." He not only possessed "comfortable furniture, unrivalled in Gabriel's homeland," but "the walls were hung with pictures that reflect prevailing American tastes." Moreover, "many books and newspapers betrayed how this janitor spent his spare time." "Gabriel's face was radiant with pride," Steiner said. Steiner too was proud and asked Gabriel "for another fraternal kiss, which he gave me with a resounding smack."

More than simply pacified workers, with their physical might harnessed to a higher purpose, Steiner believed that immigrants like "Gabriel" had much to offer American society. "Archangel Gabriel, janitor . . . and self-appointed, beneficent dictator," Steiner went on, "preserves the peace by carrying out, bodily, offending or offensive visitors—a task for which he is well fitted." Apparently, Steiner was convinced that immigrants did not have to be a menace: "rightly used and wisely directed, men like Gabriel can become a power among us." Although YMCA officials feared the political radicalism of immigrant workers, they also trusted in the YMCA's ability to ward off this perceived threat. Within the YMCA's ideology of masculinity, a focus on leadership and guidance emerged. Workers, the YMCA felt, required supervision and guidance that would prevent upheavals and steer them on the path toward manly Christian character.

By 1920 the YMCA equated self-expression for workers with participation in YMCA-orchestrated leisure activities. Any creative impulses were to be transferred away from productive work and into the consumption of YMCA-run entertainment. It was argued in a YMCA brochure that "industrial workers' drive for self-expression finds satisfaction through the Y.M.C.A. industrial program which helps the workers with minstrel shows, pageants, open house and department nights." Similarly, by the 1920s, prison administrations and the American Prison Association favored the showing of films and the singing of songs because it was believed to instill the inmates with discipline.[62]

In their attempt to redefine middle-class ideals of manhood, YMCA officials articulated a definition of manhood that suited their position in the marketplace. Alarmed by mounting labor unrest and signs of political radicalism among workingmen, YMCA officials attempted to beget a sense of unity across lines of class. Doing so, however, they sacrificed the very unity they had longed for. As YMCA officials strove to reconcile traditional ideals of community and service with the new demands of the marketplace, they forged an ideal of manhood for themselves that embraced elements of the strenuous life, individualism, and service. YMCA secretaries would prove their manhood by taming the potentially violent workingmen. By exercising leadership through personality, YMCA secretaries were convinced that they would offer a valuable service to society. Workingmen, on the other hand, would demonstrate their manhood through serving industry and their employers as faithful and good willed workers. Despite the YMCA's emphasis on uniting all men in service for the common good, association officials encoded class in their language of manhood and clearly aimed at shaping men for unequal roles in society. By the end of World War I, class differences became increasingly pronounced in the YMCA's language of manhood, pointing toward an emerging middle-class consciousness among YMCA officials. They forged an ideal of manhood that reflected their position in a marketplace in which production lost meaning to social forces of expertise and consumption.

CONCLUSION

❦

The Gilded Age and the Progressive Era represented a critical phase in the transition from proprietorial to corporate capitalism and the formation of a new, professional, managerial middle class as part of a larger "reterritorialization" of capitalism. Capitalism, as a set of processes of "deterritorialization" and "reterritorialization" is constantly at work replacing and reconstructing cultural codes and boundaries. Class and gender as expressions of relations of production and reproduction are critical to such processes.[1] The YMCA contributed to both projects.

Seeking to apply itself to some of the pressing problems of the day, the YMCA decided to extend its efforts to workingmen along the nation's sprawling railroad network in 1877. Generously funded by several major railroads, the YMCA's new Railroad Department underwent a rapid expansion in the 1880s and 1890s. Opening new branches for railroad workers, the YMCA hoped to carry its message of Christian manhood to the railroad workers. The institutional expansion that followed the YMCA's outreach programs with workingmen raised the issue of YMCA secretaries' qualifications. Initially, hiring of new secretaries for the fledgling YMCA railroad work appears to have been somewhat random, with the result that the secretarial material often was below expectations. Under the leadership of Clarence J. Hicks, the YMCA Railroad Department began to fashion its governance on the corporate management structures railroads had introduced. Coinciding with the restructuring and expansion of YMCA railroad k, Railroad Department officials, such as Hicks, George Warburton, and Ward W. Adair, began to combine calls for a better type of manhood for workingmen with calls for professional, managerial expertise for themselves. Encouraged by the results of the YMCA Railroad Department's work, the association added an Industrial Department in 1902 to extend its programs to include urban, industrial workers, seen as more radical and socially more volatile than their fellow workers along the railroads.

Both the YMCA's benefactors in industry and the workers the association claimed to serve played important roles in the implementation of these efforts. Entrepreneurs and managers—interested not only in controlling their workers through reinforcing loyalty to the company, but also in validating their own brand of corporate, entrepreneurial manliness—supported the YMCA and helped shape a language of manhood. Workingmen, while they shared some of the underlying assumptions of this language of manhood, responded in a variety of ways, at once embracing and contesting the control of the spaces offered. Workers' response to the YMCA depended as much on the location and social setting as on momentary circumstances. By and large, however, workingmen seem to have rejected, and whenever possible undermined, the political program behind the shop Bible classes, reading rooms, evening socials, billiards, restaurants, wash rooms, and dormitory facilities: the molding of workers into serviceable sources of labor power.

But YMCA officials not only wanted to convert, control and uplift the workingmen for the betterment of society; they also felt an acute need to give themselves a purpose in the emerging corporate industrial order. In the course of their work, YMCA officials used ideas about manhood not only to define themselves but also to mold others who did not share their cultural sensibilities. The YMCA's attempt to carry its message to workingmen had further consequences beyond the ways in which YMCA officials saw themselves as professionals and how they perceived both themselves and the workers they served as men.

Reared in antebellum traditions of manliness, anchored in ideals of evangelical piety and of work as a contribution to both personal fulfillment and the well-being of the community, YMCA secretaries played an active role in recasting white, middle-class manhood in the Gilded Age and the Progressive Era. As the YMCA created new programs for workingmen, YMCA officials adjusted to the social pressures of a changing social and cultural environment and began to transform ideals of middle-class manhood as they had emerged in the antebellum era.

Coinciding with the market revolution, an ideal of manhood had

emerged that urged men to develop character—a blend of qu
individual acquisitiveness and entrepreneurial drive, balanced by a
honor and duty. By the late nineteenth century this ideal of chara
its validity for middle-class men, as fewer and fewer were able to realize its
implicit promise of economic independence through hard work. Confronted with changing social realities, middle-class men in the YMCA rethought concepts of manhood. Reconciling expectations toward their gender performance with their changing social and occupational reality, YMCA
officials assumed an identity centering on the ideal of a higher type of self
that found its expression in personality.

YMCA officials conceived this ideal of personality in relation to notions of gender and class. First used by members of the YMCA Women's
Auxiliaries in connection with notions of domestic sentiment and moral
suasion, around the turn of the century the men began to adopt it with a
stronger emphasis on charismatic leadership and dominating others. Like
the members of the Women's Auxiliaries, the men believed that personality shaped character. But more than facilitating moral, spiritual uplift by
nurturing character, YMCA officials relied on *personality* and *character* as
concepts of manhood to define class difference.

In the YMCA's language of manhood, *personality* came to signify power,
manliness, and dominance over others, whereas *character* came to symbolize faithful, productive work. Once associated with entrepreneurial acquisitiveness, character became the quality that any faithful worker should
strive for. The YMCA's language of manhood connected the two concepts
of the self in cultural relations of production and consumption: YMCA
officials proffered their own example for workers to emulate; the workers,
receiving the YMCA's guidance, offered their deference in exchange, validating YMCA secretaries' superior manliness. By inscribing the male self
into such cultural patterns of production and consumption, the YMCA
secretaries' language of manhood represented not so much a "fragmentation of the self" into "a series of manipulatable social masks,"[2] but a tacti-
cal relocation of its center. This new male self, as defined by YMCA secretaries, was grounded through language in intersecting identities of gender
and class.

Historians of the Gilded Age and the Progressive Era have begun to
explore the connections and intersections between the emergence of a new,
professional, managerial middle class and changing cultural constructions
of gender. Robert Wiebe himself, pointing to private concerns and cultural
impulses as the foundations for the ways in which members of this new
middle class framed the debates of public policy issues, has implied such a

connection. More recently, Robyn Muncy has suggested that this new middle class as it constituted itself also became an active participant in remapping the gender matrix of U.S. culture during that period.[3]

Gender played a critical role in the emergence of a "new" middle class. As exponents of this new, professional managerial middle class had to culturally negotiate territory within a changing social matrix, they reconstructed patterns of gender as well. YMCA officials, trying to define an identity and subject position for themselves as professionals and as men, played a significant role in processes of middle-class formation, rearticulating ideals of manhood, and reshaping gender patterns through renegotiating boundaries of private and public.

Like their female counterparts, who were engaged and involved in a variety of (often more progressive) reform causes, YMCA secretaries contributed to permeating and breaking down public-private distinctions in U.S. middle-class culture.[4] In the process of structuring their language of manhood around concepts of character and personality, YMCA officials effectively reconfigured the ways in which Victorian culture had lined up these concepts with public and private realms within middle-class culture. While both character, once denoting acquisitive individualism, and personality, associated with the private sphere of the home, acquired somewhat androgynous qualities, character became associated with a form of workplace domesticity and sentiment, whereas personality crossed the barrier from the private into the public realm. The facilitation of self-expression among workingmen through the YMCA secretary's exemplary personality became the juncture at which previously clear-cut boundaries of private and public became permeable. The YMCA's language of manhood, by deploying character and personality to shape workers' manliness and affirm the manhood of YMCA secretaries, effectively folded "private" on top of "public," merging a private vocabulary of gender with an emerging public vocabulary of class. A private vocabulary of gender, used by middle-class Americans to deny the significance of class, had turned into a means to delineate and manage such distinctions.

YMCA officials took part in articulating new definitions of manhood. They helped create an ideal of the service-oriented "corporate man" and "team player" when the standard of upward social mobility as a primary means of affirmation of the male self became an increasingly elusive quest and salaried, white-collar work became the major occupational domain for middle-class men.[5] In the course of events, YMCA secretaries refashioned themselves as cultural brokers of gender and class, contributing to a "reterritorialization" of capitalism by creating cultural codes and boundaries that would sustain capitalist relations of production and reproduction.

The question remains as to how effective the YMCA was in its endeavors. Certainly, in its immediate and self-declared purposes, the YMCA had failed by 1920. By and large, the YMCA had lost the battle for the hearts and minds of the workingmen it had hoped to reach out to. Furthermore, by 1920 the YMCA began to lose the battle for the pocketbooks of entrepreneurs interested in developing new approaches to handling their workforces as well. As an agency shaping welfare capitalism and industrial welfare policies and programs around notions of Christian benevolence, the YMCA failed to carve out a domain for itself. After 1920 several industries decreased their financial support of the YMCA. Partially because of the postwar economic downturn, which lasted through 1922, but more importantly as a result of the ways in which many companies reconfigured their personnel policies after World War I, the YMCA no longer served as the primary channel for companies' industrial welfare policies. Companies increasingly relied on trained industrial relations experts, and some YMCA officials, such as Charles Towson and Clarence Hicks, successfully transferred into that profession. The YMCA, in turn, had to reduce staff in a number of places and give up work entirely in others.

In 1921 John D. Rockefeller, in a letter to John R. Mott, General Secretary of the International Committee and successor to Richard Cary Morse, suggested a study of the YMCA's operations. Certainly, Rockefeller must have had the effective expenditure of the funds his family had contributed and continued to contribute on his mind. In 1922 Mott and the International Committee agreed to the proposed survey of the YMCA's operations. As a result of the study, in communities of more than 25,000 inhabitants, industrial work became solely the responsibility of the city association. Railroad work remained a more vital part of the YMCA's organization, albeit funding was reduced there as well, and by the onset of the Great Depression the number of association branches along railroads had been cut in half. The YMCA Industrial Department was dissolved in 1929.[6] While the YMCA failed to defend its territory as an agency delivering social services to industrial workers as part of company welfare policies, the association had made an impact on middle-class culture and capitalist cultural development in the Gilded Age and the Progressive Era more generally.

Chapter 1

1. This interpretation of the Gilded Age and the Progressive Era as a "crisis of masculinity" was initially forwarded by Joe Dubbert, "Progressivism and the Masculinity Crisis," in *The American Man*, ed. Elizabeth H. Pleck and Joseph H. Pleck (Englewood Cliffs, N.J.: Prentice Hall, 1980), 307. For a critique of this "crisis" thesis, see Clyde Griffen, "Reconstructing Masculinity from the Evangelical Revival to the Waning of Progressivism: A Speculative Synthesis," in *Meanings for Manhood: Constructions of Masculinity in Victorian America*, ed. Mark C. Carnes and Clyde Griffen (Chicago: University of Chicago Press, 1990), 183–84.

Select examples of this growing field of scholarly inquiry include Peter N. Stearns, *Be A Man! Males in Modern Society*, 2d rev. ed. (New York: Holmes & Meier, 1990); Joe Dubbert, *Men's Places: Masculinity in Transition* (Englewood Cliffs, N.J.: Prentice Hall, 1979); Peter G. Filene, *Him/Her/Self: Sex Roles in Modern America* (Baltimore: Johns Hopkins University Press, 1986); Harry Brod, ed., *The Making of Masculinities: The New Men's Studies* (Boston: Allen & Unwin, 1987); Pleck and Pleck, eds., *American Man*; and a seminal article by Charles E. Rosenberg, "Sexuality, Class, and Role in Nineteenth-Century America," *American Quarterly* 25 (May 1973): 131–53. Also highly influential have been, among many others, Mary P. Ryan, *The Cradle of the Middle Class: The Family in Oneida County, New York, 1790–1865* (Cambridge: Cambridge University Press, 1981), esp. 145–85; Graham J. Barker-Benfield, *The Horrors of the Half-Known Life: Male Attitudes toward Women and Sexuality in Nineteenth-Century America* (New York: Harper & Row, 1976). George M. Fredrickson's "The Strenuous Life," chap. 6 of *The Inner Civil War: Northern Intellectuals and the Crisis of the Union* (New York: Harper & Row, 1965), 166–82, is to the best of my knowledge the first examination of this phenomenon, usually associated with Theodore Roosevelt, by a historian. See, however, Gerald Franklin Roberts, "The Strenuous Life: The Cult of Masculinity in the Era of Theodore Roosevelt," Ph.D. dissertation, Michigan State University, 1970.

Scholarship on the history of men and masculinities has proliferated since the 1980s. Examples of major monographs and essay collections include Elliot J. Gorn, *The Manly Art: Bare-Knuckle Prize Fighting in America* (Ithaca, N.Y.: Cornell University Press, 1986); Mark C. Carnes, *Secret Ritual and Manhood in Victorian America* (New Haven, Conn.: Yale University Press, 1990); Carnes and Griffen, eds., *Meanings for Manhood;* Ava Baron, ed. *Work Engendered: Toward a New History of American Labor* (Ithaca, N.Y.: Cornell University Press, 1991); E. Anthony Rotundo, *American Manhood: Transformations in Masculinity from the Revolution to the Modern Era* (New York: Basic Books, 1993); Kevin White, *The First Sexual Revolution: The Emergence of Male Heterosexuality in Modern America* (New York: New York University Press, 1993); Robert Griswold, *Fatherhood in America: A History* (New York: Basic Books, 1993); George Chauncey, *Gay New York: Gender, Urban Culture, and the Making of the Gay Male World, 1890–1940* (New York: Basic Books, 1994); Kim Townsend, *Manhood at Harvard: William James and Others* (New York: Norton, 1996); Kristin L. Hoganson, *Fighting for American Manhood: How Gender Politics Provoked the Spanish-American and Philippine-American Wars* (New Haven, Conn.: Yale University Press, 1998); John Gustav-Wrathall, *Take the Young Stranger by the Hand: Same-Sex Relations and the YMCA* (Chicago: University of Chicago Press, 1998); Mark E. Kann, *A Republic of Men: The American Founders, Gendered Language, and Patriarchal Politics* (New York: New York University Press, 1998). For an essay collection that seeks to integrate the histories of men and women, see Laura McCall and Donald Yacovone, eds., *A Shared Experience: Men, Women, and the History of Gender* (New York: New York University Press, 1998). Studies that bring a comparative perspective to the examination of historical constructions of manliness include Michael Anton Budd, *The Sculpture Machine: Physical Culture and Body Politics in the Age of Empire* (New York: New York University Press, 1997); Angus McLaren, *The Trials of Masculinity: Policing Sexual Boundaries, 1870–1930* (Chicago: University of Chicago Press, 1997).

For a recent, highly critical assessment of the emergence of men's history and men's studies, see Bryce Traister, "Academic Viagra: The Rise of American Masculinity Studies," *American Quarterly* 52 (June 2000): 274–304. Traister claims that the "new" masculinity studies implicitly "shift Americanist cultural criticism, once again, into the dominant study of [heterosexual] malekind" (276). I am far more affirmative on the need to study men as gendered beings, just like women, and less pessimistic about the impact such scholarly pursuits have on larger paradigms of American history and cultural criticism. However, scholars in the field should keep in mind Traister's arguments.

For surveys of the Gilded Age and the Progressive Era, see, for example, Samuel P. Hays, *The Response to Industrialism, 1885–1914* (Chicago: University of Chicago Press, 1957); Robert Wiebe, *The Search for Order, 1877–1920* (New York: Hill & Wang, 1967); Ray Ginger, *The Age of Excess: The United States from 1877–1914,* 2d ed. (New York: Macmillan, 1975); Sean Dennis Cashman, *America in the Gilded Age: From the Death of Lincoln to the Rise of Theodore Roosevelt,* 3d ed. (New York: New York University Press, 1993); Cashman, *America in the Age of the Titans: The Progressive Era and World War I* (New York: New York University Press, 1988); Nell Irvin Painter, *Standing at Armageddon: The United States, 1877–1919* (New York: Norton, 1987); Mark Whalgren Summers, *The Gilded Age, or the Hazard of New Functions* (Upper Saddle River, N.J.: Prentice Hall, 1997); Steven J. Diner, *A Very Different Age: Americans of the Progressive Era* (New York: Hill & Wang, 1998).

2. Studies that have touched on the connections between cultural constructions of

manhood and class include Nancy K. Bristow, *Making Men Moral: Social Engineering during the Great War* (New York: New York University Press, 1996); Mary Ann Clawson, *Constructing Brotherhood: Class, Gender, and Fraternalism* (Princeton, N.J.: Princeton University Press, 1989). Gail Bederman's *Manliness and Civilization: A Cultural History of Gender and Race in the United States, 1880–1917* (Chicago: University of Chicago Press, 1995) briefly refers to the relations between manhood and class without, however, exploring the connection further (see 11, 14, 17, 30–31). For a more detailed discussion of Bederman's treatment of class, see below.

3. On the expansion of cities, urban elites, and the formation of a new middle class, see Wiebe, *Search for Order*, 12, 13, 113, and, more generally, 44–75, 111–32. See also Hays, *Response to Industrialism*, 94–115; Alan Trachtenberg, *The Incorporation of America: Culture and Society in the Gilded Age* (New York: Hill & Wang, 1982), 101–39; Stuart M. Blumin, *The Emergence of the Middle Class: Social Experience in the American City, 1760–1900* (Cambridge: Cambridge University Press, 1989), 192–229; Paul Boyer, *Urban Masses and Moral Order, 1820–1920* (Cambridge, Mass.: Harvard University Press, 1978); Allan Stanley Horlick, *Country Boys and Merchant Princes: The Social Control of Young Men in New York* (Lewisburg, Pa.: Bucknell University Press, 1975). On YMCA buildings and the Gilded Age and Progressive Era urban landscape, see Paula Lupkin, "Manhood Factories: Architecture, Business, and the Evolving Urban Role of the YMCA, 1865–1925," in *Men and Women Adrift: The YMCA and the YWCA in the City*, ed. Nina Mjagkij and Margaret Spratt (New York: New York University Press, 1997), 40–64.

On the relationship between bourgeois culture, and public spaces and voluntary associations, see Jürgen Habermas, *The Structural Transformation of the Public Sphere: An Inquiry into a Category of Bourgeois Society* (Cambridge, Mass.: MIT Press, 1989). On the usefulness of Habermas's work to historians, see Geoff Eley, "Nations, Publics, and Political Cultures: Placing Habermas in the Nineteenth Century," in *Culture/Power/History: A Reader in Contemporary Social Theory*, ed. Nicholas B. Dirks, Geoff Eley, and Sherry B. Ortner (Princeton, N.J.: Princeton University Press, 1993), 297–335. For applications of Habermas's concepts to the U.S. setting, see, for example, Kathryn J. Oberdeck, "Religion, Culture, and the Politics of Class: Alexander Irvine's Mission to Turn-of-the-Century New Haven," *American Quarterly* 47 (June 1995): 236–79; Michael Schudson, "Was There Ever a Public Sphere? If So, When? Reflections on the American Case," in *Habermas and the Public Sphere*, ed. Craig Calhoun (Cambridge, Mass.: MIT Press, 1992); and David Scobey, "Anatomy of the Promenade: The Politics of Bourgeois Sociability in Nineteenth-Century New York," *Social History* 17 (May 1992): 203–27.

4. C. Howard Hopkins, *History of the Y.M.C.A. in North America* (New York: Association Press, 1951), 16–17, 20–21, 148–78. Evangelical Christianity was a major strand in Gilded Age and Progressive Era reform, manifest in the so-called Social Gospel. See Henry F. May, *Protestant Churches and Industrial America* (New York: Harper & Row, 1949); Jean Quandt, *From the Small Town to the Great Community: The Social Thought of Progressive Individuals* (New Brunswick, N.J.: Rutgers University Press, 1970); Paul A. Carter, *The Spiritual Crisis of the Gilded Age* (DeKalb: Northern Illinois University Press, 1971); Donald K. Gorrell, *The Age of Responsibility: The Social Gospel in the Progressive Era, 1900–1920* (Macon: Mercer University Press, 1988); Robert M. Crunden, *Ministers of Reform: The Progressives' Achievement in American Civilization, 1889–1920* (New York: Basic Books, 1982); and Susan Curtis, *A Consuming Faith: The Social Gospel and Modern American Culture* (Baltimore: Johns Hopkins University Press, 1991). On the role of Protes-

tantism within the Gilded Age labor movement, see Herbert George Gutman, "Protestantism and the American Labor Movement: The Christian Spirit in the Gilded Age," *American Historical Review* 72 (October 1966): 74–101. On conflicts between workers and reformers over the relation between Christianity and labor issues, see Kenneth Fones-Wolf, *Trade-Union Gospel: Christianity and Labor in Industrial Philadelphia, 1865–1915* (Philadelphia: Temple University Press, 1989).

On labor activism during the late nineteenth and early twentieth century, see David Montgomery, *The Fall of the House of Labor: The Workplace, the State, and American Labor Activism, 1865–1925* (Cambridge: Cambridge University Press, 1987); Montgomery, *Citizen Worker: The Experience of Workers in the United States with Democracy and the Free Market during the Nineteenth Century* (Cambridge: Cambridge University Press, 1993); Bruce Laurie, *Artisans into Workers: Labor in Nineteenth-Century America* (New York: Noonday Press, 1989).

5. For a brief treatment of YMCA industrial work, see Paul McBride, *Culture Clash: Immigrants and Reformers, 1880–1920* (San Francisco: R & E Research Associates, 1975). See also Hopkins, *History of the Y.M.C.A. in North America*, 3–8, 15–53, 227–39, 390–91, 475–79, 504, 507, 570. Contemporary accounts include John F. Moore, *The Story of the Railroad "Y"* (New York: Association Press, 1930); Richard C. Morse, *My Life with Young Men: Fifty Years in the Young Men's Christian Association* (New York: Association Press, 1918), 391–95; Richard C. Morse, *History of the North American Young Men's Christian Associations* (New York: Association Press, 1919), 207–16; Gustav Theodor Schwenning, "A History of the Industrial Work of the Young Men's Christian Association," Ph.D. dissertation, Clark University, 1925; and Clarence J. Hicks, *My Life in Industrial Relations: Fifty Years in the Growth of a Profession* (New York: Harper & Brothers, 1941), 18–40.

6. See, for example, Montgomery, *Fall of the House of Labor;* Martin J. Sklar, *The Corporate Reconstruction of American Capitalism, 1890–1916: The Market, the Law, and Politics* (Cambridge: Cambridge University Press, 1988).

7. My understanding of welfare capitalism as an attempt to discipline both the shopfloor and workers' homes and communities owes much to Bruno Ramirez's work. See Ramirez, *When Workers Fight: The Politics of Industrial Relations in the Progressive Era, 1898–1916* (Westport, Conn.: Greenwood Press, 1978), 153. Gender has recently become the focus of historical investigations of welfare capitalism. See Andrea Tone, *The Business of Benevolence: Industrial Paternalism in Progressive America* (Ithaca, N.Y.: Cornell University Press, 1997), esp. 140–81. For a recent survey of the literature and the debates, see Howard Gitelman, "Welfare Capitalism Reconsidered," *Labor History* 33 (Winter 1992): 5–31.

Major studies of welfare capitalism include Robert Ozanne, *A Century of Labor-Management Relations at McCormick and International Harvester* (Madison: University of Wisconsin Press, 1967); Stephen J. Scheinberg, *Employees and Reformers: The Development of Corporation Labor Policy, 1900–1940* (New York: Garland Publishing, 1986); Oscar Nestor, *A History of Personnel Administration, 1890–1910* (New York: Garland Publishing, 1986); Daniel Nelson, *Managers and Workers: Origins of the New Factory System in the United States, 1880–1920* (Madison: University of Wisconsin Press, 1975); Stuart D. Brandes, *American Welfare Capitalism, 1880–1940* (Chicago: University of Chicago Press, 1976); Sarah Lyons Watts, *Order against Chaos: Business Culture and Labor Ideology in America, 1880–1915* (Westport, Conn.: Greenwood Press, 1991); Gerald Zahavi, *Workers,*

Managers, and Welfare Capitalism: The Shoeworkers and Tanners of Endicott Johnson, 1890–1950 (Urbana: University of Illinois Press, 1987).

8. For an overview of activities the YMCA offered to the workers in the early twentieth century, see *Among Industrial Workers (Ways and Means): A Handbook for Associations in Industrial Fields* (New York City: International Committee of YMCAs,1916).

9. On middle-class uses of institutions as a means to establish their cultural authority, see Wiebe, *Search for Order*, 111–32. See also David I. McLeod, *Building Character in the American Boy: The Boy Scouts, YMCA, and Their Forerunners* (Madison: University of Wisconsin Press, 1983); Blumin, *The Emergence of the Middle Class*, 192–229; Clawson, *Constructing Brotherhood*; Gregory H. Singleton, "Protestant Voluntary Organizations and the Shaping of Victorian America," *American Quarterly* 27 (Winter 1975): 549–60.

10. See Bederman, *Manliness and Civilization*, 17–18, 19, 27, 77–120, 170–216. Clyde Griffen has coined the term "hyper masculinity" to describe this phenomenon. See Griffen, "Reconstructing Masculinity," 200. See also Gorn, *The Manly Art*, 179–206; Rotundo, *American Manhood*, 167–68, 176, 222–46; Michael S. Kimmel, *Manhood in America: A Cultural History* (New York: Free Press, 1996), 81–188; Budd, *The Sculpture Machine*; Stearns, *Be A Man!* 108–53, 157–59; Carnes, *Secret Ritual and Manhood*; Peter Gay, *The Bourgeois Experience: Victoria to Freud: The Cultivation of Hatred* (New York: Norton, 1990), 95–116; Filene, *Him/Her/Self*, 68–93; John Higham, *Writing American History: Essays on Modern Scholarship* (Bloomington: Indiana University Press, 1970), 73–102.

On the aspect of therapeutic release, see T. J. Jackson Lears, "From Salvation to Self-Realization: Advertising and the Roots of the Consumer Culture, 1880–1930," in *The Culture of Consumption: Critical Essays in American History, 1880–1980*, ed. Richard Wightman Fox and T. J. Jackson Lears (New York: Pantheon Books, 1983), 1–38.

11. For discussions of social class and the reform impulse, see Boyer, *Urban Masses and Moral Order*; Frederic Cople Jaher, *Doubters and Dissenters: Cataclysmic Thought in America* (London: Free Press of Glencoe, 1964); Quandt, *From the Small Town to the Great Community*; Raymond Jackson Wilson, *In Quest of Community: Social Philosophy in the United States, 1860–1920* (New York: Oxford University Press, 1968). On "muscular Christianity," see also Clifford Wallace Putney, *Muscular Christianity: Manhood and Sports in Protestant America, 1880–1920* (Cambridge: Harvard University Press, 2001). On the YMCA's attempts to "remasculinize" Protestant churches, see Gail Bederman, "'The Women Have Had Charge of the Church Work Long Enough': The Men and Religion Forward Movement of 1911–1912 and the Masculinization of Middle-Class Protestantism," *American Quarterly* 41 (September 1989): 432–65.

12. On the public/private split and gender in nineteenth-century U.S. culture, see, for example, Mark E. Kann, *On the Man Question: Gender and Civic Virtue in America* (Philadelphia: Temple University Press, 1991), 245–69; and Ryan, *Cradle of the Middle-Class*, 146–55. On the gendered role of sentiment in American middle-class culture in the nineteenth century, see Karen Halttunen, *Confidence Men and Painted Women: A Study of Middle-Class Culture in America, 1830–1870* (New Haven, Conn.: Yale University Press, 1982).

13. My understanding of the connections between gender and class is influenced by the work of Pierre Bourdieu on what he refers to as the "habitus," which grounds identity in the social relations of production. Bourdieu argues that the habitus is derived from common social and economic dispositions, resulting in coherent practices: "the singular

habitus of members of the same class are united in a relation . . . of diversity within homogeneity reflecting the diversity within homogeneity characteristic of their social conditions of production." See Bourdieu, *The Logic of Practice* (Stanford, Calif.: Stanford University Press, 1990), 52–67, 80–97. The quote is from p. 60. My understanding of language here relies on the work of Joan Scott and Pierre Bourdieu, and the definition of language I am using here is a close paraphrase of Joan Scott's. See Joan Wallach Scott, "Deconstructing Equality-Versus-Difference: or, The Uses of Poststructuralist Theory for Feminism," *Feminist Studies* 14 (Spring 1988): 34; and the essays in Pierre Bourdieu, *Language and Symbolic Power*, ed. John B. Thompson (Cambridge, Mass.: Harvard University Press, 1991).

My interest in language, and my attempt here to uncover the linkages between language and the social processes its speakers—YMCA secretaries—are part of and attempt to intervene in, owes much to the work of Bryan D. Palmer. See Palmer, *Descent into Discourse: The Reification of Language and the Writing of Social History* (Philadelphia: Temple University Press, 1990), 120–86. I have attempted to follow his call, maybe somewhat disguised among pointed attacks on poststructural theory and its followers, for more methodological balance between concerns with language and discourse on the one hand, and more concrete historical materialist "structures of determination" (xiv).

On the relation between class and consciousness during this period in U.S. history, see also Martin J. Sklar, *Corporate Reconstruction of American Capitalism*, 5–7, 12. Relevant for my argument, in particular, is Sklar's argument that the transformation of class relations in the transition from proprietorial capitalism to corporate capitalism takes place not only between, but also within classes (12).

My understanding of this language of manhood is further influenced by Michel Foucault, *History of Sexuality*, vol. 1, *An Introduction* (New York: Vintage, 1980); Judith Butler, *Gender Trouble: Feminism and the Subversion of Identity* (New York: Routledge, 1990), 1–6; Joan W. Scott, "Gender: A Useful Category of Historical Analysis," *American Historical Review* 91 (December 1986): 1053–75.

14. Antebellum middle-class culture was a significant source of YMCA officials' understanding of manhood. On antebellum culture and manhood, see Rotundo, *American Manhood*, 10–31; Kimmel, *Manhood in America*, 13–43; Stearns, *Be A Man!* 111–32. On the link between ideals of Northern middle-class masculinity and religious beliefs, see, for example, Curtis, *A Consuming Faith*.

15. The cultural intersections between gender and class ideologies date back to the midnineteenth century, and transformations of gender ideologies have been closely bound up with the transformation of class ideologies. See David Leverenz, *Manhood and the American Renaissance* (Ithaca, N.Y.: Cornell University Press, 1989).

16. On the relations between gender and class formation in U.S. society in the nineteenth century, see Ryan, *Cradle of the Middle Class;* Leonore Davidoff and Catherine Hall, *Family Fortunes: Men and Women of the Middle Class, 1760–1850* (Chicago: University of Chicago Press, 1987). For the class implications of the way masculinity is socially constructed between men, see Clawson, *Constructing Brotherhood;* Michael Moon, "The Gentle Boy from the Dangerous Classes": Pederasty, Domesticity, and Capitalism in Horatio Alger," *Representations* 19 (1987): 87–110. Jürgen Kocka has argued that between the turn of the century and World War I, white-collar professionals expressed their occupational consciousness in increasingly divisive language when relating to blue-collar work-

ers. See Kocka, *White Collar Workers in America, 1890–1940: A Social-Political History in International Perspective* (London: Sage, 1980), 90.

For more detailed discussions of the social construction of class that have influenced my position, see E. P. Thompson, *The Making of the English Working Class* (London: Penguin, 1980), 8–9; Adam Przeworski *Capitalism and Social Democracy* (Cambridge: Cambridge University Press, 1985), 69–70; Ernesto Laclau, *Political Ideology in Marxist Theory* (London: Verso, 1979), 160–61; Marc W. Steinberg, "The Dialogue of Struggle: The Contest over Ideological Boundaries in the Case of the London Silk Weavers in the Early Nineteenth Century," *Social Science History* 18 (Winter 1994): 505–42.

For a discussion of how the denial of class differences can be an intricate part of the process of articulating such hierarchies, see Anthony Giddens, *The Class Structure of the Advanced Societies* (New York: Harper & Row, 1975). Giddens has created a concept of "class awareness," which he differentiates from "class consciousness." He argues that class awareness "does not involve a recognition that these attitudes and beliefs signify a particular class affiliation, or the recognition that there exist other classes, characterized by different attitudes, beliefs, and styles of life." It follows then, Giddens suggests that the "difference between class awareness and class consciousness is [that] . . . class awareness may take the form of a denial of the existence or reality of classes" (111).

17. Clawson, *Constructing Brotherhood*; Bristow, *Making Men Moral*.

18. Bederman, *Manliness and Civilization*, 11, 14, 17, 30–31.

19. McLaren, *Trials of Masculinity*, 3.

20. Barbara Melosh, introduction to *Gender and American History since 1890*, ed. Melosh (London: Routledge, 1993), 5. This point also has been reinforced by Gerda Lerner. See Lerner, *The Creation of Patriarchy* (New York: Oxford University Press, 1986), 239.

21. See Stephanie Coontz, *The Social Origins of Private Life: A History of American Families, 1600–1900* (London: Verso, 1988), 176–80.

22. On the fluidity of the boundaries between public and private as constantly under construction and the cultural consequences of that process, see Eve Kosofsky Sedgwick, *Epistemology of the Closet* (Berkeley: University of California Press, 1990), 110. See also Coontz, *Social Origins of Private Life*, 169–80, 330–54.

23. Wiebe, *Search for Order*, 113; my emphasis. See also Halttunen, *Confidence Men and Painted Women*, 195.

24. On *character*, see *Oxford English Dictionary*, vol. 2 (Oxford: Clarendon Press, Oxford University Press 1933), 280–81; *Supplement to the Oxford English Dictionary*, vol. 4, (Oxford: Clarendon Press, Oxford University Press, 1982), 396–97. On *personality*, see *Oxford English Dictionary*, vol. 7, 727; *Supplement to the Oxford English Dictionary*, vol. 3, 396–97.

25. I realize that the comment I am making here, insinuating a shift in the meaning of *personality* that coincided with the formation of a bourgeoisie in the Atlantic world is more tantalizing than satisfying. As there appears to be no historical study of personality, I cannot be more precise. However, I feel the diachronic relation is worth noting. For a study on changing notions of the self in relation to altering currents in philosophical and religious thought, see Charles Taylor, *Sources of the Self: The Making of the Modern Identity* (Cambridge, Mass.: Harvard University Press, 1989). Taylor's study, however, makes no

explicit mention of personality or, for that matter, character. For dated, but comprehensive, classic surveys of the period, see Christopher Hill, *A Century of Revolution, 1603–1714*, rev. ed. (New York: Norton, 1980); Robert Roswell Palmer, *The Age of Democratic Revolutions: A Political History of Europe and America, 1760–1800*, 2 vols. (Princeton, N.J.: Princeton University Press, 1959–1964); Eric J. Hobsbawm, *The Age of Revolution, 1789–1848* (London: Weidenfeld & Nicholson, 1962).

26. Warren I. Susman, *Culture as History: The Transformation of American Society in the Twentieth Century* (New York: Pantheon Books, 1984), 271–85; Lears, "From Salvation to Self-Realization," 1–38; Richard Wightman Fox, "The Culture of Liberal Protestant Progressivism," *Journal of Interdisciplinary History* 23 (Winter 1993): 639–60; Joan Shelley Rubin, *The Making of Middle-Brow Culture* (Chapel Hill: University of North Carolina Press, 1992); Casey Nelson Blake, *Beloved Community: The Cultural Criticism of Randolph Bourne, Van Wyck Brooks, Waldo Frank, and Lewis Mumford* (Chapel Hill: University of North Carolina Press, 1990), 1–9, 50–79. The character-personality shift is also mentioned by White, *First Sexual Revolution*, 17. On the link between salesmanship and personality, see also Angel Kwolek-Folland, *Engendering Business: Men and Women in the Corporate Office, 1870–1930* (Baltimore: Johns Hopkins University Press, 1994), 88–89. More generally on a "fragmentation of the self," see T. J. Jackson Lears, *No Place of Grace: Antimodernism and the Transformation of American Culture, 1880–1920* (New York: Pantheon Books, 1982), esp. 32–47.

27. Karen Lystra, *Searching the Heart: Women, Men, and Romantic Love in Nineteenth-Century America* (New York: Oxford University Press, 1989), 42, 37–38, 39.

28. Ibid., 42, 40, 38–39.

29. The concept of workplace domesticity I am introducing here resembles what Angel Kwolek-Folland has called "corporate domesticity" (*Engendering Business*, 129–64). As Kwolek-Folland has shown for financial industries, my evidence suggests that railroads and urban industries relied on the "nineteenth-century middle-class family [as] an important model" (129). Indeed, Kwolek-Folland adds that "domestic imagery contributed as much to the development of . . . organizational structures of the railroads." However, Kwolek-Folland's analysis focuses on the social and gender structures of corporate offices, whereas my analysis suggests that railroads sought to tie all workers, and not only white-collar office workers, to the company as an enlarged, patriarchal household. Simply as a matter of emphasis, then, I prefer to speak here of a workplace domesticity.

30. While *personality*, as YMCA secretaries used the term, certainly stood for a more performative concept of the self, it also suggested spiritual wholeness, self-actualization, and integration of the self, instead of a "fragmentation of the self" as Lears has argued. See Lears, *No Place of Grace*, 35. My argument about the meaning of personality is particularly influenced by studies by Steven C. Rockefeller and Casey Nelson Blake. See Rockefeller, *John Dewey: Religious Faith and Democratic Humanism* (New York: Columbia University Press, 1991), 49, 74, 99, 121, 142, 213, 353–56, 578–79 n. 67. Although Dewey was not necessarily representative for all American middle-class men of his time, the YMCA's understanding and use of the concept parallels Dewey's quite closely. Casey Nelson Blake has pointed to the multiple meanings inherent in the notion of personality. See Blake, *Beloved Community*, 1–9.

31. On metonymy and class, see Wai Chee Dimock, "Class, Gender, and a History of Metonymy," in *Rethinking Class: Literary Studies and Social Formations*, ed. Wai Chee

Dimock and Michael T. Gilmore (New York: Columbia University Press, 1994), 57–104. The distinction between character, while reflecting reputation, as a concept of the self to be shaped and operated upon, and personality as a notion of the self that signifies wholeness, an "internalized . . . possession, . . . something which can be displayed or interpreted," is also made by Raymond Williams. See Williams, "Personality," in *Keywords: A Vocabulary of Culture and Society*, rev. ed. (New York: Oxford University Press, 1983), 232–35. The quote is from p. 235.

32. The concept of the "other" as a marker of identity and difference has been introduced into academic canons by Edward Said. See Said, *Orientalism* (New York: Pantheon, 1978).

33. Klaus Theweleit, *Male Fantasies*, vol. 1, *Women, Floods, Bodies, History*, trans. Stephen Conway (Minneapolis: University of Minnesota Press, 1987), 270. The argument that capitalism, as a historical process, generates the classes it needs when it needs them, also has been made by Karl Polanyi. See Polanyi, *The Great Transformation: The Political and Economic Origins of Our Time* (Boston: Beacon Press, 1957), 155–56.

Chapter 2

1. For the term "marketplace man," see Michael S. Kimmel, "The Feminization of American Culture and the Recreation of the Male Body, 1832–1920," *Michigan Quarterly Review* 33 (Winter 1994): 9. See also Daniel Walker Howe, *Making the American Self: Jonathan Edwards to Abraham Lincoln* (Cambridge, Mass.: Harvard University Press, 1997), 107–8; E. Anthony Rotundo, *American Manhood: Transformations in Masculinity from the Revolution to the Modern Era* (New York: Basic Books, 1990), 10–30.

2. See Karen Halttunen, *Confidence Men and Painted Women*, 25. See also Rotundo, *American Manhood*, 10–25; Kimmel, *Manhood in America*, 13–50.

3. Kimmel, *Manhood in America*, 23; Wilfred M. McClay, *The Masterless: Self and Society in Modern America* (Chapel Hill: University of North Carolina Press, 1994), 61.

4. Susman, *Culture as History*, 213–14, 220; Judy Hilkey, *Character Is Capital: Success Manuals and Manhood in Gilded Age America* (Chapel Hill; University of North Carolina Press, 1997), 126–41; Howe, *Making the American Self*, 6, 9. On manhood and civic virtue, see Kann, *On the Man Question*, 187–88, 303–4, 308–9.

5. See Halttunen, *Confidence Men and Painted Women*, 33–55.

6. On the concept of a "civilizing process," see Norbert Elias, *The Civilizing Process* (1939; Oxford: Blackwell, 1994). On the relations between sincerity, character, and market economics, see Stephanie Coontz, *Social Origins of Private Life*, 176–80, 212, 213; Halttunen, *Confidence Men and Painted Women*, 25–29, 47, 50, 53–54.

7. Halttunen, *Confidence Men and Painted Women*, 49–50.

8. On the Second Great Awakening, see Charles G. Sellers, *The Market Revolution: Jacksonian America, 1815–1846* (New York: Oxford University Press, 1991), 202–36. The quote is from 214.

9. See Donald Yacovone, "Abolitionists and the 'Language of Fraternal Love,'" in *Meanings for Manhood*, ed. Carnes and Griffen, 85–95; Yacovone, "'Surpassing the Love of Women': Victorian Manhood and the Language of Fraternal Love," in *A Shared Experience: Men, Women, and the History of Gender*, ed. Laura McCall and Donald Yacovone (New York: New York University Press, 1998), 195–221.

10. Hopkins, *History of the Y.M.C.A. in North America*, 4–7. See also Anne C. Rose, *Voices of the Marketplace: American Thought and Culture, 1830–1860* (New York: Twayne, 1995), 2–3; Kathleen McCarthy, *Noblesse Oblige* (Chicago: University of Chicago Press, 1982), 59.

11. Howe, *Making the American Self*, 110. See also Mark E. Kann, *A Republic of Men*, 167.

12. Sellers, *Market Revolution*, 246.

13. As Daniel Walker Howe has recently pointed out, concerns with self-improvement and self-reinvention quite naturally carried over into attempts at improving and uplifting others. See Howe, *Making the American Self*, 155.

14. Regarding the following discussion of the lives and social backgrounds of George Warburton, Henry O. Williams, George Davis McDill, Charles R. Towson, Edwin Lorenzo Hamilton, John Ferguson Moore, Frederic Burton Shipp, Aaron G. Knebel, see YMCA Biographical Files, Kautz Family YMCA Archives, University Libraries, University of Minnesota, Minneapolis [hereafter YMCA Archives]. On Williams, Hicks, Joseph M. Dudley, William Day, Hamilton, Moore, and Knebel, see also H. S. Ninde, "Sketch of Railroad Y.M.C.A. Work with Sketches of International Department Railroad Secretaries," Historical Summaries Railroad Work, 1882–1909, box 1, YMCA Railroad/Transportation Department Records, YMCA Archives [hereafter YMCA Railroad Records].

In addition, I have been able to draw on other sources. On Williams, see U.S. Census Office, Eighth Census, 1860, reel 762, New York, Jefferson County (part). On Hicks, see U.S. Census Office, Eighth Census, 1860, reel 1437, Wisconsin, Winnebago and Woud Counties; Hicks, *My Life in Industrial Relations*. On Towson, see U.S. Census Office, Eighth Census, 1860, reel 460, Maryland, Baltimore; U.S. Census Office, Ninth Census, 1870, reel 460, Maryland, Baltimore; *Woods Baltimore City Directory* (n.p.: John H. Woods, 1860); "General Secretary Towson," *Pennsylvania Railroad Men's News* 10 (March 1898): 108; "Charles R. Towson," *Railroad Men* 11 (February 1898): 151. On Hamilton, see U.S. Census Office, Eighth Census, 1860, reel 727, New York, Cayuga County, City of Auburn. On Moore, see "John F. Moore," *Railroad Men* 19 (February 1906): 188. On Adair, see Ward Greene, "A Boy from the Backcountry," *Association Men* (January 1926): 219–20, 257–58; Ward W. Adair, *The Road to New York* (New York: Association Press, 1936); U.S. Census Office, Tenth Census, 1880, Population, reel 835, New York, Fulton (part) and Genesee Counties. On Knebel, see Aaron G. Knebel, *Four Decades with Men and Boys* (New York: Association Press, 1936).

Only Edwin Ingersoll (born in 1836), the first YMCA railroad secretary for the International Committee, and Peter Roberts (born in 1859), who would lead the Americanization programs for the industrial department from 1907 to 1921, do not quite belong to that generation. On Ingersoll, see H. S. Ninde, "Sketch of Railroad Y.M.C.A.," Historical Summaries Railroad Work, 1882–1909, box 1, YMCA Railroad Records. On Roberts, see "Rev. Dr. Roberts of Y.M.C.A. Dead," *New York Times*, 4 December 1932, 32; *Who Was Who among North American Authors, 1921–1939*, vol. 2 (Detroit: Gale Research Company, 1976), s.v. "Roberts, Peter"; *Who Was Who in America*, vol. 1, 1897–1942 (Chicago: Marquis Who's Who, 1943), s.v. "Roberts, Peter"; W. Stewart Wallace, ed., *A Dictionary of North American Authors Deceased Before 1950* (Toronto: Ryerson Press,

1968), s.v. "Roberts, Peter"; "The Outreach to Industrial Men," *Association Men* 32 (July 1907): 428.

15. Finney's influence on the YMCA both in England and in America may also help to explain why YMCA records speak so little to the theological aspects of the work, or why YMCA officials rarely identify their denominational background: antebellum revivalistic religion crossed and often purposefully defied denominational boundaries. On antebellum revivals and the burned-over district, see the somewhat dated but quite comprehensive account by Whitney R. Cross, *The Burned-Over District: The Social and Intellectual History of Enthusiastic Religion in Western New York, 1800–1850* (Ithaca, N.Y.: Cornell University Press, 1950). On these revivals, see also Charles Grandison Finney, *Memoirs of Rev. Charles G. Finney, Written by Himself* (New York: Fleming H. Revell, 1876). On the Great Awakening in an urban context, see Terry D. Bilhartz, *Urban Religion and the Second Great Awakening: Church and Society in Early National Baltimore* (Rutherford, N.J.: Farleigh Dickinson University Press, 1986).

The above mentioned similarities between YMCA secretaries and their families as a group may extend even further: Hamilton's father, George E. Hamilton, was born in Lee, Massachusetts, on 24 January 1830, his mother, Sarah, in Morovia, New York, on 13 September 1829. McDill's father, James, was born on 5 February 1833 in Crawford County, Pennsylvania, and Towson's mother, Sarah Richards, was born in Preston City, Connecticut, 18 November 1830. See n. 14 above. That places them squarely in the context of migration patterns spanning from Massachusetts, Connecticut, eastern New York and Pennsylvania to northwestern New York: the settling of northwestern New York was the result of migration from eastern New York, Pennsylvania, and, most of all, from New England. Settlers from Connecticut, Vermont, and Massachusetts migrated often as whole neighborhoods and communities and brought with them their religious heritage and their revivalistic tradition. See Cross, *Burned-Over District*, 3–13.

16. *Roster of Paid Secretaries*, vol. 1, *1880–1900*, YMCA Archives. By far the vast majority are listed with exact birthplaces. Grouping certain states by region or country was my choice. On Finney's revivals, see Sellers, *Market Revolution*, 231.

17. The two-volume *Roster of Paid Secretaries* (vol. 1, *1880–1900*, vol. 2, *1900–1905*, YMCA Archives) confirms this. On the evangelical background of many YMCA secretaries' families, see John Donald Gustav-Wrathall, *Take the Young Stranger by the Hand*, 9–15.

18. Anne C. Rose, *Victorian America and the Civil War* (Cambridge: Cambridge University Press, 1992), 166. Warburton's father was a blacksmith, his mother a dressmaker. Williams's father, Henry Gladwin, was a painter of modest means. Hamilton's father, George, was a lawyer. See n. 14 above.

19. Fredrickson, *Inner Civil War*, 166–82. On the masculinization of benevolence, see Lori D. Ginzberg, *Women and the Work of Benevolence: Morality, Politics, and Class in the Nineteenth-Century United States* (New Haven, Conn.: Yale University Press, 1990), 173.

20. See Rose, *Victorian Americans and the Civil War*, 67–71.

21. Olivier Zunz, *Making America Corporate, 1870–1920* (Chicago: University of Chicago Press, 1990), 176–83, 196–97.

22. See, in the following order, "Henry Orison Williams," YMCA Biographical

Files; "Edwin Lorenzo Hamilton," YMCA Biographical Files; "Charles R. Towson," YMCA Biographical Files. Among YMCA officials who held positions of leadership in the railroad and industrial departments, these are the only surveys available.

23. On the notion of the "liminal men," see Halttunen, *Confidence Men and Painted Women*, 29–30.

24. See "Henry Orison Williams," YMCA Biographical Files.

25. See Charles R. Towson, "The Power of Friendliness," *Association Men* 36 (September 1911): 523.

26. See "General Secretary Towson," *Pennsylvania Railroad Men's News* 10 (March 1898): 108; "Charles R. Towson," *Railroad Men* 11 (February 1898): 151.

27. This is a recurrent theme in the historiography on men. For a more detailed discussion, see Kimmel, *Manhood in America*, 81–156.

28. See Kimmel, *Manhood in America*, 59; Gail Bederman, "'The Women Have Had Charge of the Church Work Long Enough.'" For studies of the ways in which women politicized the so-called cult of domesticity, see, for example, Barbara Epstein, *The Politics of Domesticity: Women, Evangelism, and Temperance in Nineteenth-Century America* (Middletown, Conn.: Wesleyan University Press, 1981); Nancy A. Hewitt, *Women's Activism and Social Change: Rochester, New York, 1822–1872* (Ithaca, N.Y.: Cornell University Press, 1984); Ginzberg, *Women and the Work of Benevolence*. On the cult of domesticity itself, see Nancy Cott, *The Bonds of Womanhood: "Woman's Sphere" in New England, 1788–1835* (New Haven, Conn.: Yale University Press, 1977).

Chapter 3

1. For the data on strikes, see David Montgomery, *Workers Control in America: Studies in the History of Work, Technology, and Labor Struggles* (New York: Cambridge University Press, 1979), 20. Gilded Age industrial unrest reflected the attempts of workers to resist wage cuts and managerial encroachments on their traditional prerogatives and control over work processes. See Shelton Stromquist, *A Generation of Boomers: The Pattern of Railroad Labor Conflict in Nineteenth-Century America* (Urbana: University of Illinois Press, 1987), 20–47. For a recent discussion of industrial unrest in its larger context, see Walter Licht, *Industrializing America: The Nineteenth Century* (Baltimore: Johns Hopkins University Press, 1995), 133–96.

2. The classic study of the transformation from proprietorial to corporate capitalism is Alfred DuPont Chandler, *The Visible Hand* (Cambridge, Mass.: Belknap Press, Harvard University Press, 1977). See also Chandler, ed., *The Railroads: The Nation's First Big Business* (New York: Harcourt, Brace & World, 1965); Walter Licht, *Working for the Railroad: The Organization of Work in the Nineteenth Century* (Princeton, N.J.: Princeton University Press, 1983); Stromquist, *Generation of Boomers*, 100–141; Montgomery, *Fall of the House of Labor*, 54–55, 208–10. On welfare capitalism, generally, see Stuart D. Brandes, *American Welfare Capitalism, 1880–1940*.

3. Quoted in Hopkins, *History of the Y.M.C.A. in North America*, 114, 150.

4. Herbert E. Brown, "The History of the Railroad Young Men's Christian Association," graduation thesis, Institute and Training School of Young Men's Christian Associations, Chicago, Illinois, 25 May 1905, 24. On the origins of the Cleveland YMCA's

railroad work in Cleveland, see R. F. Smith, "The Beginnings of the First Railroad Branch" *New York Railroad Men* 11 (December 1897): 74.

5. Hopkins, *History of the Y.M.C.A. in North America*, 228–29; *Proceedings of the Twenty-second Annual Convention of the Young Men's Christian Associations of the United States and British Provinces, Held at Louisville, Ky., June 6–10, 1877* (New York: Executive Committee, 1877), xix [hereafter *Louisville Proceedings*]. Many railroads developed interest in industrial welfare programs after the 1877 strike and increasingly after the 1886 strikes. Studies that mention the YMCA's efforts include Brandes, *American Welfare Capitalism*, 14–15, 24–25, 67, 72; and Sanford Jacoby, *Employing Bureaucracy: Managers, Unions, and the Transformation of Work in American Industry, 1900–1945* (New York: Columbia University Press, 1985), 56–60. For contemporary studies of the YMCA's programs and activities in industrial relations, see Brown, "History of the Railroad Young Men's Christian Association"; Charles T. Rea, "The History of the Railroad Young Men's Christian Association," thesis, International Young Men's Christian Association Training School, Springfield, Mass., 1904; Fred Hamilton Rindge, Jr., "The Young Men's Christian Association and Industrial Betterment," M.A. thesis, Columbia University, 1909; Schwenning, *"History of the Industrial Work of the Young Men's Christian Association,"* 139–73; and Moore, *Story of the Railroad "Y."*

6. J. W. Walton, "The Work among Railroad Men Entrusted to the International Committee," *Louisville Proceedings*, 41–42.

7. *Proceedings of the First International Conference of the Railroad Young Men's Christian Associations of the United States and British Provinces, Held at Cleveland, Ohio, October 25–28, 1877* (New York: Executive Committee of YMCAs of the United States and British Provinces, 1877), 10, box 5, Railroad Convention Proceedings, YMCA Railroad Records.

8. Moore, *Story of the Railroad "Y,"* 76; Morse, *My Life with Young Men*, 393–94; Morse, *History of the North American Young Men's Christian Associations*, 212; Hopkins, *History of the Y.M.C.A. in North America*, 235–36.

9. Morse, *My Life with Young Men*, 393–94; Moore, *Story of the Railroad "Y,"* 76; Hopkins, *History of the Y.M.C.A. in North America*, 235–36. On railroad system-building, see Chandler, *Visible Hand*, 145–87.

10. Stromquist, *Generation of Boomers*, 248. To be certain, not all railroad officials who took an interest in industrial welfare work chose to channel their support through the YMCA. The Chicago, Burlington & Quincy Railroad, for example, consistently refused to fund the YMCA. See Vincent Black, "The Development of Management Personnel Policies on the Burlington Railroad, 1860–1900," Ph.D. dissertation, University of Wisconsin–Madison, 1982, 353. For examples, see T. J. Potter to H. Hitchcock, 6 September 1879, Potter Out-letters, series 3, subseries P6.1, vol. 16; C. E. Perkins to T. J. Potter, 14 February 1882, T. J. Potter, In-letters from C. E. Perkins, January–September 1882, series 3, subseries P6.36, no. 2; Memorandum, 15 June 1882, T. J. Potter, In-letters from C. E. Perkins, January–September 1882, series 3, subseries P6.36, no. 2; all from the Chicago, Burlington & Quincy Railroad Company Archives, The Newberry Library, Chicago.

11. C. M. Hobbs, "The Railroad Department: Its Field, Opportunity, and Purposes," *Railroad Men* 14 (December 1900): 120.

12. Hopkins, *History*, 237–38. The quote is on p. 237.

13. George Warburton, "How to Reach Young Mechanics," *Watchman*, 15 May 1881, 129.

14. Hopkins, *History of the Y.M.C.A. in North America*, 237–38.

15. *Pennsylvania Association News* 3 (April 1899): 23, Pennsylvania Association News, 1899–1905, box 42, YMCA State and Regional Records, YMCA Archives. See also Morse, *My Life with Young Men*, 394–96; H. M. J. Klein, *The Pennsylvania Young Men's Christian Association: A History, 1854–1950* (Kennett Square, Pa.: Kennett News and Advertiser Press, 1950), 59, 61, 62, 68. On the UMW, see Bruno Ramirez, *When Workers Fight*, 33.

16. H. S. Ninde, J. T. Bowne, and Erskine Uhl, eds., *A Handbook of the History, Organization, and Methods of Work of the Young Men's Christian Association* (New York: International Committee of YMCAs, 1892), 379–80.

17. Ninde, Bowne, and Uhl, eds., *Handbook*, 380–81.

18. Hopkins, *History of the Y.M.C.A. in North America*, 477; Report, September 1905, box 11, Monthly Reports, 1903–1911, Departmental Reports, 1903–1911, YMCA Industrial Department Records, 1889–1980, YMCA Archives [hereafter YMCA Industrial Records]. The quote is from Minutes of Industrial Committee Meeting, 1903, Industrial Department Minutes, 1903–1908, Industrial Committee Minutes, 1903–1908, YMCA Industrial Records.

19. Extract from International Committee Minutes, 8 October 1903, box 11, Monthly Reports, 1903–1911, Departmental Reports, 1902–1911, YMCA Industrial Records; *Yearbook of Young Men's Christian Associations of North America for the Year 1 May 1903 to 30 April 1904* (New York: International Committee of YMCAs, 1904), 20. *Yearbook 1905–1906*, 245.
The YMCA practiced racial segregation in its work, and the Buxton association was actually handled directly by African American secretaries, operating directly under the supervision of the YMCA International Committee. A YMCA Colored Work Department—coordinating YMCA programs for African Americans—was not formed until 1923. For a study of African American YMCAs, see Nina Mjagkij, *Light in the Darkness: African Americans and the YMCA, 1852–1946* (Lexington: University of Kentucky Press, 1994). Mjagkij's study focuses on African American branches in an urban context. Because of the limited efforts of the YMCA with black workers, source material on which to build a discussion of such efforts is scarce.

20. "For Alaskan Miners," *Association Men* 28 (April 1903): 316.

21. See "For Cotton Mill Workers," *Association Men* 29 (May 1904): 362; *Interstate Notes* 8 (March 1912): 2, box 36, Interstate Notes, 1905–1912, YMCA State and Regional Records. On YMCA activities in cotton mill villages, see also Harriet L. Herring, *Welfare Work in Mill Villages: The Story of Extra-Mill Activities in North Carolina* (Montclair, N.J.: Patterson Smith, 1968), 73, 106, 117, 140, 285.

22. Hopkins, *History of the Y.M.C.A. in North America*, 479; Morse, *History of the North American Young Men's Christian Associations*, 216.

23. Report, May 1907, box 11, Monthly Reports, Departmental Reports, 1903–1918, YMCA Industrial Records; *Yearbook 1906–1907*, 19.

24. For the following data on membership, see *Yearbook of the Young Men's Christian*

Associations of the United States and the Dominion of Canada for the Year 1891 (New York: International Committee of YMCAs, 1891), 155; *Yearbook 1905–1906*, 245; *Yearbook 1910–1911*, 191; *Yearbook 1917–1918*, 104; *Yearbook 1918–1919*, 126; *Yearbook 1920–1921*, 208, 216; Memorandum Report, 16 December 1912, YMCA Industrial Department Minutes, 1912–1918, Industrial Committee Minutes, box 11, YMCA Industrial Records; Morse, *History of the North American Young Men's Christian Associations*, 214.

25. *Louisville Proceedings, 1877*, xix; Morse, *My Life with Young Men*, 391. Railroads became the first corporate sponsors of the association. On company donations to the YMCA, see Pierce Williams and Frederick E. Croxton, *Corporation Contributions to Organized Community Welfare Service* (New York: National Bureau of Economic Research, 1930), 13, 228–29; F. Emerson Andrews, *Corporation Giving* (New York: Russell Sage Foundation, 1952), 25–26, 28; Scott M. Cutlip, *Fund Raising in the United States: Its Role in American Philanthropy* (New Brunswick, N.J.: Rutgers University Press, 1965), 38–47.

26. *New York Railroad Men* 11 (November 1897): 37.

27. Richard C. Morse to John D. Rockefeller, Jr., 18 November 1902, and Morse to Rockefeller, 3 December 1902, both folder 9, box 30, Welfare Interests/Youth, Record Group II, Office of the Messrs. Rockefeller, Rockefeller Family Archives, North Tarrytown, New York [hereafter Rockefeller Family Archives]. At least one adviser to John D. Rockefeller suggested that the Industrial Department was part of a fund-raising scheme designed by the YMCA to extract money from the association's benefactors in industry. This was insinuated in a memorandum prepared for John D. Rockefeller, Jr.: "observe the extraordinary skill, persistency, and success with which Mr. Morse and his friends have, from small beginnings, crowded these annual contributions up sometimes by one 'emergency,' . . . *and here a new 'department,'* until . . . vast sums of money have been secured" ("Memorandum on Mr. Morse's Letter of December 14th," folder 9, box 30, Welfare Interests/Youth, Record Group II, Rockefeller Family Archives; emphasis added).

28. "Report of Edwin D. Ingersoll," *Yearbook 1880–1881*, 24–25.

29. For the following data on numbers of secretaries and associations, see *Yearbook 1891*, 155; *Yearbook 1905–1906*, 245; *Yearbook 1910–1911*, 191; *Yearbook 1917–1918*, 104; *Yearbook 1918–1919*, 126; *Yearbook 1919–1920*, 208, 216; Morse, *History of the North American Young Men's Christian Associations*, 214.

30. Rea, "History of the Railroad Young Men's Christian Association," 33, 56; Edwin L. Hamilton, "The Evolution of an Association," *Railroad Association Magazine* 4 (May 1915): 6–7.

31. Lang Sheaff to J. T. Bowne, Secretary Y.M.C.A., Newburgh, New York, 18 March 1882, box 1, Railroad Work Historical Summaries, 1882–1909, YMCA Railroad Records; Hopkins, *History of the Y.M.C.A. in North America*, 228–29; *Annual Report of the Young Men's Christian Association of Cleveland, O., May 1, 1873* (Cleveland: Fairbanks, Benedict & Co., 1873), 18, box 15, folder 1, Annual Reports, 1859, 1870–74, YMCA of Cleveland Records, Western Reserve Historical Society, Cleveland, Ohio [hereafter YMCA of Cleveland].

32. George A. Warburton, "James Stokes and the Association Work among Railroad Men," in *James Stokes: Pioneer of Young Men's Christian Associations*, ed. Frank W. Ober (New York: Association Press, 1921), 50–51. See also Hopkins, *History of the Y.M.C.A. in North America*, 229; Moore, *Story of the Railroad "Y,"* 44; Terry Donaghue,

An Event on Mercer Street: A Brief History of the YMCA of the City of New York (New York: n.p., 1952), 51.

33. George A. Warburton, "Cornelius Vanderbilt's Contribution to the Association," *Association Men* 25 (October 1899): 1; Hopkins, *History of the Y.M.C.A. in North America*, 233.

34. *Yearbook of the Young Men's Christian Associations of the United States and the Dominion of Canada for the Year 1889* (New York: International Committee of YMCAs, 1889), 138; *Yearbook 1912–1913*, 189; Hopkins, *History of the Y.M.C.A. in North America*, 233.

35. On Westinghouse Airbrake, see Report of C. C. Michener, September 1905; on Monaghan Mills, see Report of Industrial Department, 10 March 1904, both box 11, Monthly Reports, 1903–1911, Departmental Reports, 1903–1911, YMCA Industrial Records.

36. W. C. Brown, "Character as an Asset," *Railroads and Railroaders: The Story of a Remarkable Gathering of Railroad Men* (New York: Young Men's Christian Association Press, 1909), 12, box 6, YMCA Railroad Records. The monthly reports of the Industrial Department for these years regularly detail companies underwriting such funds. See Memorandum for Executive Committee, 1903, box 11, Industrial Department, Minutes, 1903–1908, Departmental Reports, 1903–1911, YMCA Industrial Records; Report of the Executive Committee on the Industrial Work, [1903], YMCA Industrial Records. For the estimate on the cost for a YMCA building, see Lucien C. Warner, "Industrial Young Men's Christian Associations," brochure (New York: International Committee of the YMCAs, 1905), 10, box 1, Departmental Materials, 1899–1932, YMCA Industrial Records.

37. "Historical Sketch of the Railroad Branch Young Men's Christian Association, New York City," *Railroad Men* 27 (July 1914): 230; Warburton, "James Stokes," 41–42.

38. Paul Super, *Formative Ideas in the YMCA* (New York: Association Press, 1929), 174. However, a U.S. Department of Labor survey of industrial welfare work revealed that, in a number of cases in which companies had outside agencies, such as the YMCA, conduct their welfare work for them, "the financial connection is kept secret, since the employers consider that the working force would view it with suspicion" (U.S. Department of Labor, Bureau of Labor Statistics, *Welfare Work for Employees in Industrial Establishments in the United States, Bulletin of the United States Bureau of Labor Statistics*, no. 250 [Washington, D.C.: Government Printing Office, 1919], 122. Most likely, YMCA officials feared that once the connection was known, labor unions and radicals would build opposition against the YMCA among the workers.

39. For a synopsis of the events, see Howard M. Gitelman, *Legacy of the Ludlow Massacre: A Chapter in American Industrial Relations* (Philadelphia: University of Pennsylvania Press, 1988), 1–30, 155–56. On Rockefeller's relation to C.F. & I. and the events in Colorado, see Graham Adams, Jr., *Age of Industrial Violence, 1910–15: The Activities and Findings of the United States Commission on Industrial Relations* (New York: Columbia University Press, 1966), 146–75. On the intended public relations effect of industrial welfare work, see Morrell Heald, *The Social Responsibilities of Business: Company and Community, 1900–1960*, 2d ed. (New Brunswick, N.J.: Transaction Books, 1987), 40–41.

40. Walter S. Hopkins to John D. Rockefeller, Jr., 12 July 1915, folder 156, box 18, Colorado, Fuel & Iron, Business Interests, Record Group III 2 c, Rockefeller Family Archives; Peter Roberts, Walter S. Hopkins, and John A. Goodell, "Report upon the Possible

Service of the Young Men's Christian Association in the Mining Communities of the Colorado Fuel and Iron Company," folder 156, box 18, C.F. & I., Rockefeller Family Archives; Clarence J. Hicks to John D. Rockefeller, Jr., 11 December 1915, Rockefeller Family Archives; Report, 13 October 1915, box 11, Monthly Reports, Departmental Reports, 1912–1918, YMCA Industrial Records; Report, 15 December 1915, YMCA Industrial Records; "Expert Aid for C.F. & I. Clubs," *Colorado Fuel & Iron Industrial Bulletin*, 22 December 1915, box 2, YMCA Industrial Records; "Y.M.C.A. Extends Its Activities," *Colorado Fuel & Iron Industrial Bulletin*, 26 April 1916, 13; Report, 8 October 1914, box 11, Monthly Reports, Departmental Reports, 1912–1918, YMCA Industrial Records; Minutes of Luncheon Conference Industrial Service Committee and Guests, 1 October 1915, Minutes, Industrial Committee Minutes, 1909–1918, YMCA Industrial Records.

41. On Standard Steel Works, see Report of Industrial Department, [October 1905], YMCA Industrial Records. U.S. Department of Labor, *Welfare Work for Employees in Industrial Establishments in the United States*, 75; Victor H. Olmsted, "The Betterment of Industrial Conditions," *Bulletin of the Department of Labor* 5 (November 1900): 1156; Morse, *History of the North American Young Men's Christian Associations*, 214–15.

42. Rea, "History of the Railroad Young Men's Christian Association," 43; "The Railroad Department of the Y.M.C.A.," *Men* 24 (October 1898): 21; Morse, *My Life with Young Men*, 390–91; Warburton, "James Stokes," 46–48; Warburton, "Cornelius Vanderbilt's Contribution to the Association," *Association Men* 25 (October 1899): 1; "The Expanding Industrial Department," *Association Men* 33 (March 1908): 267; Irvin G. Wyllie, *The Self-Made Man in America: The Myth of Rags to Riches* (New York: Free Press, 1966), 12, 72–74, 87–93.

43. W. F. Hunting, "Shop Bible Classes," *Iowa State Notes* 22 (July 1908): 9, box 7, YMCA State and Regional Records.

44. For the following description and quotes, see John A. Fitch, "Steel and Steel Workers—and the Labor Policies of Unrestricted Capital," *United Mine Workers Journal*, 25 April 1912, 2. The incident is also cited in David Brody, *Steelworkers in America: The Non-Union Era* (Cambridge: Harvard University Press, 1960), 117–18.

45. There are no precise figures available for that specific, albeit unnamed, YMCA. However, the membership demographics hinted at by this YMCA official may have been representative for YMCAs more generally. In 1890 the Brooklyn YMCA drew 19 percent of its members from the ranks of mechanics, 3 percent from the ranks of laborers, while clerks made up a full 57 percent of the membership, with the remaining 21 percent coming from other ranks of society. See E. Clark Worman, *History of the Brooklyn and Queens Young Men's Christian Association, 1853–1949* (New York: Association Press, 1952), 82–83.

46. William Z. Foster, *The Great Steel Strike and Its Lessons* (New York: B. W. Huebsch, 1920), 188–89.

47. *Report of the International Committee of the Young Men's Christian Associations to the Thirty-ninth International Convention at Cleveland, Ohio, May 12–16, 1916* (New York: Association Press, 1917), 44.

48. *Among Industrial Workers*, 26.

49. See Charles DeLano Hine, *Letters from an Old Railway Official to His Son, a Division Superintendent* (Chicago: Railway Age, 1904), 164. I am indebted to Venitra DeGraffenreid for bringing this source to my attention.

50. See, for example, Samuel Latta, *Rest Houses for Railroad Men: The Pennsylvania's Provision for the Welfare of its Conductors, Engineers, Firemen and Trainmen—How the Railroad Men Regard Such Convenience—A Model Hospital Car* (New York: National Civic Federation Welfare Department, 1906), 15, 22-23. On the NCF, see James R. Green, *The World of the Worker: Labor in Twentieth-Century America* (New York: Hill and Wang, 1980), 53, 54, 56. See also Marguerite Green, *The National Civic Federation and the American Labor Movement, 1900-1925* (Westport, Conn.: Greenwood Press, 1973); Ramirez, *When Workers Fight*, 65-84; James Weinstein, *The Corporate Ideal in the Liberal State, 1900-1918* (Boston: Beacon Press, 1968), 3-39; Tone, *Business of Benevolence*, 45-52.

51. *Conference on Welfare Work, Held at the Waldorf-Astoria, New York City, March 16, 1904, under the Auspices of the Welfare Department of the National Civic Federation* (New York: Andrew H. Kellogg, 1904), 84-85, 89-91.

52. On the shift in personnel management techniques and the shift from the "old" to the "new" welfare work, see Jacoby, *Employing Bureaucracy*, 192-99. On the timing of this shift, see Ronald Schaeffer, *America in the Great War: The Rise of the War Welfare State* (New York: Oxford University Press, 1991), 37-39. Tone also emphasizes financial benefits as central to Progressive Era welfare capitalism (*Business of Benevolence*, 6, 8, 11-12, 14). I discuss Tone's argument in the next chapter.

Chapter 4

1. On the concept of cultural hegemony, see T. J. Jackson Lears, "The Concept of Cultural Hegemony: Problems and Possibilities," *American Historical Review* 90 (June 1985): 567-93.

On the self-perception of entrepreneurs and their understanding of labor relations in the first half of the nineteenth century, see Paul Johnson, *A Shopkeeper's Millennium: Society and Revivals in Rochester, New York, 1815-1837* (New York: Hill & Wang, 1978), 43-48; Licht, *Working for the Railroad*; Anthony F. C. Wallace, *Rockdale: The Growth of an American Village in the Early Industrial Revolution* (New York: Alfred A. Knopf, 1980), 326-37; Philip Scranton, *Proprietary Capitalism: The Textile Manufacturer at Philadelphia, 1800-1885* (Philadelphia: Temple University Press, 1983), 247-51.

On the role of manhood in artisanal craft culture, see Nick Salvatore, *Eugene V. Debs: Citizen and Socialist* (Urbana: University of Illinois Press, 1982), 22-30; David Montgomery, "Workers' Control of Machine Production in the Nineteenth Century," *Labor History* 17 (Fall 1976): 491; David Bensman, *The Practice of Solidarity: American Hat Finishers in the Nineteenth* Century (Urbana: University of Illinois Press, 1985), 68-88; Patricia A. Cooper, *Once A Cigar Maker: Men, Women, and Work Culture in American Cigar Factories, 1900-1919* (Urbana: University of Illinois Press, 1987), 75-89, 123-52, 322-23; Ava Baron, "Questions of Gender: Deskilling and Demasculinization in the U.S. Printing Industry, 1830-1915," *Gender and History* 1 (Summer 1989): 178-99; Baron, "An 'Other' Side of Gender Antagonism at Work: Men, Boys, and the Remasculinization of Printers' Work, 1830-1920," in *Work Engendered*, ed. Baron, 47-69. On nineteenth-century discourses on class and its meanings, see Martin J. Burke, *The Conundrum of Class: Public Discourse on the Social Order in America* (Chicago: University of Chicago Press, 1995), 76-132.

2. On middle-class ideals of masculinity, see Rotundo, *American Manhood*; Griffen, "Reconstructing Masculinity," 183-204; Stearns, *Be A Man!* 111-32; Kimmel, *Manhood in America*, 13-43; and Hilkey, *Character Is Capital*, esp. 142-65.

3. William L. Barney, *The Passage of the Republic: An Interdisciplinary History of Nineteenth-Century America* (Lexington, Mass.: D. C. Heath, 1987), 89, 96; Ryan, *Cradle of the Middle-Class*, 146–55; Lystra, *Searching the Heart*, 37–38; and Halttunen, *Confidence Men and Painted Women*, 50. YMCA and company officials attempted to prescribe to the workers the ideal of a balanced manhood, drawing selectively on ideals referred to by Charles Rosenberg as the "Masculine Achiever," or self-made man, and the "Christian Gentleman" ("Sexuality, Class, and Role in Nineteenth-Century America," 131–53).

4. See Halttunen, *Confidence Men and Painted Women*, 206–7.

5. My understanding of the cultural dynamics of male-male relations in capitalist society has benefited from Luce Irigaray, *This Sex Which Is Not One* (Ithaca, N.Y.: Cornell University Press, 1985), 82–83, 192–97; Eve Kosofsky Sedgwick, *Between Men: English Literature and Male Homosocial Desire* (New York: Columbia University Press, 1985), 86; and Moon, "'The Gentle Boy from the Dangerous Classes,'" 87–110.

6. Few historians have explored how notions of manhood have influenced managers' approach to labor relations and their attempts to shape workers' behavior. For exceptions, see Judith A. McGaw, *Most Wonderful Machine: Mechanization and Social Change in Berkshire Paper Making, 1801–1885* (Princeton, N.J.: Princeton University Press, 1987), 256–69, 322–24; Kwolek-Folland, *Engendering Business*, 7, 45–51, 94–164; Tone, *Business of Benevolence*, ch. 4, "Gender and Welfare Work," esp. 165–71; Lisa M. Fine, "'Our Big Factory Family': Masculinity and Paternalism at the REO Car Company of Lansing, Michigan," *Labor History* 34 (Spring-Summer 1993): 274–91.

7. See Tone, *Business of Benevolence*, 7, 168–69.

8. See Jacoby, *Employing Bureaucracy*; Montgomery, *Fall of the House of Labor*.

9. Gitelman, "Welfare Capitalism Reconsidered," 26. See also David Brody, "The Rise and Decline of American Welfare Capitalism," in *Change and Continuity in Twentieth-Century America: The 1920s*, ed. John Braeman, Robert H. Bremner, and David Brody (Columbus: Ohio State University Press, 1968), 147–78.

10. For a synopsis of the strike events, see Foster Rhea Dulles and Melvyn Dubofsky, *Labor in America: A History*, 5th ed. (Wheeling, Ill.: Harlan Davidson, 1993), 108–19. On labor practices of railroads in the Gilded Age and the 1877 railroad strikes, see Licht, *Working for the Railroad*, 79–124; 164–212; and Stromquist, *Generation of Boomers*, 21–47.

11. For a summary of the strike events in Cleveland, see Robert V. Bruce, *1877: Year of Violence* (Indianapolis: Bobbs-Merrill, 1959), 204. See also the more dated account by J. A. Dacus, *Annals of the Great Strikes of the United States: A Reliable History and Graphic Description of the Causes and Thrilling Events of Labor Strikes and Riots of 1877* (New York: Burt Franklin, 1877), 276–77.

12. James H. Deveraux, "Christianity versus Communism," box 1, Speeches and Promotional Materials, 1879–1895, YMCA Railroad Records. To some extent, manhood suggested itself as a shared bond across lines of class between employers and workers. Within the railroads, key areas such as the train service were staffed exclusively by men, and less than 1 percent of the total number of employees consisted of women. See Department of Commerce and Labor, *Statistical Abstract of the United States, 1910* (Washington, D.C.: Government Printing Office, 1911), 226; Department of Commerce, *Statistical Abstract of the United States, 1920* (Washington, D.C.: Government Printing Office, 1921), 279.

13. See "The Great Strike," *Cleveland Plain Dealer*, 23 July 1877, 4; "The Great Strike," *Cleveland Plain Dealer*, 24 July 1877, 4; "The Great Strike," *Cleveland Plain Dealer*, 25 July 1877, 4; "The Great Strike," *Cleveland Plain Dealer*, 4 August 1877, 4.

14. "The Effect of Railroad Work on Character," *Railroad Men* 22 (October 1908): 5. The classic work on Social Darwinism in American social thought is, of course, Richard Hofstadter, *Social Darwinism in American Thought*, rev. ed. (Boston: Beacon Press, 1955). For later studies of the subject, updating and complementing Hofstadter's analysis, see Cynthia Eagle Russett, *Darwin in America: The Intellectual Response, 1865–1912* (San Francisco: W. H. Freeman, 1976), 89–96, 96–102, 119–20.

15. "The Effect of Railroad Work on Character," *Railroad Men* 22 (October 1908): 7.

16. George A. Warburton, "A Study of the Success of the Railroad Work of the Young Men's Christian Association from the Standpoint of the Men," *Railroad Men* 18 (March 1904): 225.

17. Warburton, "James Stokes," 42–43. On the relations between frontier mythology and the ways American propertied classes increasingly saw workers in comparison to Native Americans and "savages" coming to America's shores from other countries, see Richard Slotkin, *The Fatal Environment: The Myth of the Frontier in the Age of Industrialization, 1800–1890* (New York: Atheneum, 1985), 480–89, 497–98.

18. For a similar argument, see Gunther Peck, "Manly Gambles: The Politics of Risk on the Comstock Lode, 1860–1880," *Journal of Social History* 26 (Summer 1993): 701–23. On changing perceptions of gambling and risk-taking in nineteenth-century American culture, see also Ann Fabian, *Card Sharps, Dream Books, and Bucket Shops: Gambling in Nineteenth-Century America* (Ithaca, N.Y.: Cornell University Press, 1990).

19. See Barker-Benfield, *Horrors of the Half-Known Life*, 181–82; Cynthia Eagle Russett, *Sexual Science: The Victorian Construction of Womanhood* (Cambridge, Massachusetts: Harvard University Press, 1989), 112–16; John S. Haller, Jr. and Robin M. Haller, *The Physician and Sexuality in Victorian America* (Urbana: University of Illinois Press, 1974), 191–234. For a classic examination of Victorian attitudes toward manhood and male sexuality, see Rosenberg, "Sexuality, Class, and Role in Nineteenth-Century America," *American Quarterly* 25 (May 1973): 131–53.

20. Warburton, "James Stokes," 43.

21. See McCarthy, *Noblesse Oblige*, 53, 67, 72, 75.

22. "The Railroad Department of the Young Men's Christian Associations," undated brochure, box 1, Promotional Materials, 1880–1899, YMCA Railroad Records.

23. Leaflet, box 1, Promotional Materials, 1880–1899, YMCA Railroad Records.

24. W. H. Truesdale, "The Good and the Bad in Labor Unions," *Railroad Men* 16 (March 1903): 216, 218.

25. The list of literature on ideals of success and the self-made man in nineteenth-century America is long. See John G. Cawelti, *Apostles of the Self-Made Man* (Chicago: University of Chicago Press, 1965); Wyllie, *Self-Made Man in America*; Richard Weiss, *The American Myth of Success: From Horatio Alger to Norman Vincent Peale* (New York: Basic Books, 1969); Richard M. Huber, *The American Myth of Success* (New York: McGraw-Hill, 1971); Rex Burns, *Success in America: The Yeoman Dream and the Industrial Revolution* (Amherst: University of Massachusetts Press, 1976).

26. Quoted in Trachtenberg, *Incorporation of America*, 77. On the relation between

NOTES TO PAGES 56-62

work, gender identity, and the charges of salaried white-collar work as effeminate, see also Kimmel, *Manhood in America*, 103. On the connections between changes in work patterns and middle-class male identity in late nineteenth-century America, see Rotundo, *American Manhood*, 167–93, 176, 222–93; Peter Gabriel Filene, *Him/Her/Self*, 68–93.

27. Leverenz, *Manhood and the American Renaissance*, 74, 78.

28. Ibid., 78, 85.

29. "The Employer and the Man," *Association Men* 29 (November 1903): 72.

30. Hilkey, *Character Is Capital*, 99, 127–29; Halttunen, *Confidence Men and Painted Women*, 25–29; Wyllie, *Self-Made Man*, 22–24, 34–54.

31. *Proceedings of the Twenty-fifth International Convention of Young Men's Christian Associations, Held at Milwaukee, Wis., May 16–20, 1883* (New York: International Committee of YMCAs, 1883), 59–60.

32. William Bender Wilson, *History of the Pennsylvania Railroad Department of the Young Men's Christian Association* (Philadelphia: Stephen Greene, 1911), 89.

33. Burns Durbin Caldwell, "The Railroad Employee as a Man," *Proceedings of the Tenth International Conference of the Railroad Department of Young Men's Christian Associations of North America, Philadelphia, Pa., October 11–14, 1900* (New York: International Committee of YMCAs, 1900), 40, 41, 42 [hereafter *Philadelphia Proceedings*], box 6, Railroad Convention Proceedings, YMCA Railroad Records.

34. On domesticity and sentiment in Victorian culture, see, for example, Halttunen, *Confidence Men and Painted Women*, 58–59.

35. Wilson, *History of the Pennsylvania Railroad Department of the Young Men's Christian Association*, 52, 66.

36. "The Employer and the Man," *Association Men* 29 (November 1903): 72.

37. "Shop Bible Classes" (Cleveland: YMCA, 1901), 18, pamphlet, box 2, folder 29, Miscellaneous Publications and Reports, 1900–1901, YMCA of Cleveland Records, series II, Western Reserve Historical Society, Cleveland, Ohio [hereafter YMCA of Cleveland II].

38. B. F. Bush, "Raising the Standard," *Railroad Association Magazine* 3 (September 1914): 1.

39. On the domestic qualities of newly emerging corporate work spaces, see Kwolek-Folland, *Engendering Business*, 94–164. Nineteenth-century American Victorians believed that a married man was more deserving of trust, because he had to provide for dependents who had no other means of survival. See Coontz, *Social Origins of Private Life*, 213.

40. This notion of sentiment played a central part in nineteenth-century middle-class culture. See Halttunen, *Confidence Men and Painted Women*. See also Coontz, *Social Origins of Private Life*, 212, 213, 210–86; Gillian Brown, *Domestic Individualism: Imagining Self in Nineteenth-Century America* (Berkeley: University of California Press, 1990), 3.

41. Kimmel, *Manhood in America*, 101–2.

42. Caldwell, "Railroad Employee as a Man," *Philadelphia Proceedings*, 42, box 6, Railroad Convention Proceedings, YMCA Railroad Records. On ideals of frugality and thrift, see also David Shi, *The Simple Life: Plain Living and High Thinking in American Culture* (New York: Oxford University Press, 1985), 175–214.

43. L. L. Doggett, W. H. Ball, H. M. Burr, W. K. Cooper, *Life Problems: Studies in the Native Interests of Young Men* (New York: International Committee of YMCAs, 1905), 11, 4, YMCA International Committee Pamphlet Collection, YMCA Archives.

44. Caldwell, "Railroad Employee as a Man," *Philadelphia Proceedings*, 45, box 6, Railroad Convention Proceedings, YMCA Railroad Records. See also Hilkey, *Character Is Capital*, 138; Rotundo, *American Manhood*, 178-79.

45. Dr. Frank Crane, "No Milksops Need Apply," *Railroad Men* 34 (March-April 1921): 1.

46. David E. Nye, *Image Worlds: Corporate Identities at General Electric, 1890-1930* (Cambridge, Mass.: MIT Press, 1985), 100. See also 72, 74, 75, 96-111.

47. See Montgomery, *Fall of the House of Labor*.

Chapter 5

1. For a summary of craftworkers' culture, see Salvatore, *Eugene V. Debs*, 22-30. For a recent study of the Knights' culture, see Robert M. Weir, *Beyond Labor's Veil: The Culture of the Knights of Labor* (University Park: Pennsylvania State University Press, 1996). For discussions of workers' notions of manhood, see also Montgomery, "Workers' Control of Machine Production in the Nineteenth Century," 491; Bensman, *Practice of Solidarity*, 68-88; Cooper, *Once A Cigar Maker*, 75-89, 123-52, 322-23; Baron, "Questions of Gender"; and Baron, "An 'Other' Side of Gender Antagonism at Work."

2. On the values emphasized by corporations, reflected in their personnel and hiring policies, see Olivier Zunz, *Making America Corporate*, 125-48. On labor activism during the late nineteenth and early twentieth century, see Montgomery, *Fall of the House of Labor*; Stromquist, *Generation of Boomers*; Paul K. Edwards, *Strikes in the United States, 1881-1974* (New York: St. Martin's Press, 1981).

3. The description of how a railroad YMCA was established is a composite, drawing on the following works: David L. Lightner, *Labor on the Illinois Central Railroad, 1852-1900: The Evolution of an Industrial Environment* (New York: Arno Press, 1977), 275-78; Hicks, *My Life in Industrial Relations*, 18-28; Moore, *Story of the Railroad "Y,"* 16-20. Because of a delay in the promised visit of YMCA international railroad secretary, Edwin D. Ingersoll, railroad workers at Parkersburg, West Virginia, took it upon themselves to organize a railroad YMCA. See *Proceedings of the Second International Conference of the Railroad Young Men's Christian Associations of the United States and British Provinces, Held at Altoona, Pennsylvania, September 18-21, 1879* (New York: Executive Committee of YMCAs of the United States and British Provinces, 1879), 32 [hereafter *Altoona Proceedings*], box 5, Railroad Convention Proceedings, YMCA Railroad Records.

4. Theodore Gerald Soares, *A Vocation with a Future: An Estimate of the Professional Leadership of the Young Men's Christian Association* (n.p.: Institute and Training School of YMCAs, 1909), 16, box 2, Conference Papers, YMCA Professional Secretaries Records, YMCA Archives.

5. See Report of the Industrial Department, n.d., 8, box 11, Monthly Reports, 1903-1908, Departmental Reports, 1903-1908, YMCA Industrial Records; Report of C. C. Michener, Secretary, Industrial Department, September 1905, YMCA Industrial Records. The quotes are from Report of the Industrial Department, 15 June 1904, and Report of Industrial Department, n.d., 11, box 11, Monthly Reports, 1903-1908, Departmental Reports, 1903-1908, YMCA Industrial Records.

6. Biebesheimer Petition, 1908, South Chicago Railroad Department, Petitions, box 17, folders 16–18, Series II, Board of Trustees, 1861–1975, Subseries 3, Vault Materials, 1861–1966, YMCA of Metropolitan Chicago Papers, Chicago Historical Society, Chicago, Illinois [hereafter YMCA of Chicago].

7. "Pocatello," *Rocky Mountain Messenger* 1 (January 1890): 3, box 3, *Rocky Mountain Messenger* YMCA Railroad Records. For membership data of the New York, New Haven, & Hartford Railroad Department, see "Annual Report of the New York, New Haven, & Hartford Railroad Department, Young Men's Christian Association, New Haven, Conn.," *New York, New Haven, & Hartford Railroad News* vol. 8, February 1905, 74; and the "New Members" column of the *New York, New Haven, & Hartford Railroad News* vol. 8 (February 1905): 83; (March 1905): 107; (April 1905): 130; (May 1905): 154; (June 1905): 178–79; (July 1905): 200; (August 1905): 221; vol. 9 (November 1905): 8–9; (December 1905): 32. See also "Classification of Membership," *New York Railroad Men*, vol. 4 (February 1891): 94–95; vol. 10 (October 1896): 170; vol. 11 (February 1898): 153; vol. 12 (February 1899): 194; vol. 13 (February 1900): 200; vol. 14 (February 1901): 220; vol. 15 (February 1902): 202; vol. 18 (February 1905): 188.

8. "Why I Joined," *Railroad Association Magazine* 5 (November 1916): 8.

9. "The Railroad Men of a Continent," *Association Men* 36 (March 1911): 271; "Why I Joined," *Railroad Association Magazine* 5 (November 1916): 8.

10. Salvatore, *Eugene V. Debs*, 22–30.

11. E. C. Dixon, "How Can Christian Railroad Men Furnish to Their Comrades the Antidote and the Substitute for the Tippling," in *Proceedings of the First International Conference of the Railroad Young Men's Christian Associations of the United States and British Provinces, held at Cleveland, Ohio, October 25–28, 1877* (New York: Executive Committee of YMCAs of the United States and British Provinces, 1877), 27, box 5, Railroad Convention Proceedings, 1877–1894, YMCA Railroad Records. See also A. M. Watt, "The Relation of the Railroad Department to the Spiritual Life of Railroad Men," *Proceedings of the Ninth International Conference of the Railroad Department of Young Men's Christian Associations of North America, Held at Fort Wayne, Indiana, October 20–23, 1898* (New York: International Committee of YMCAs, 1898), 32, box 6, Railroad Convention Proceedings, 1895–1905, YMCA Railroad Records.

12. "Why I Joined," *Railroad Association Magazine* 5 (November 1916): 8. See also "As They See It," *Railroad Association Magazine* 4 (November 1915): 13.

13. W. Thomas White, "Race, Ethnicity, and Gender in the Railroad Work Force: The Case of the Far Northwest, 1883–1918," *Western Historical Quarterly* 16 (July 1985): 265–83.

14. "The Railroad Department," *Railroad Association Magazine* 29 (March 1904): 274.

15. Ward W. Adair, *The Lure of the Iron Trail* (New York: Association Press, 1912), 137. See also "Three Railroad Workers," *Men* 25 (February 1899): 91.

16. *Proceedings of the Twenty-sixth International Convention of Young Men's Christian Associations of the United States and British Provinces, Held in Atlanta, Ga., May 13–17, 1885* (New York: International Committee, 1885), 52.

17. *Proceedings of the Seventh International Conference of the Railroad Department of Young Men's Christian Associations of North America, Held in New York City, March 29 to April 1, 1894* (New York: International Committee of YMCAs, n.d.), 14, box 5, Railroad

Convention Proceedings, 1877–1894, YMCA Railroad Records; *Proceedings of the Eighth International Conference of the Railroad Department of Young Men's Christian Associations of North America, Held in Clifton Forge, Virginia, September 13–15, 1895* (New York: International Committee of YMCAs, n.d.), 16, box 6, Railroad Convention Proceedings, 1895–1905, YMCA Railroad Records. For further examples, see the proceedings of the following conventions: *Proceedings of the Ninth International Conference of the Railroad Department of Young Men's Christian Associations of North America, Held in Fort Wayne, Indiana, October 20–23, 1898* (New York: International Committee of YMCAs, n.d.), 20, YMCA Railroad Records; *Proceedings of the Tenth International Conference of the Railroad Department of Young Men's Christian Associations of North America, Held in Philadelphia, Pa., October 11 to 14, 1900* (New York: International Committee of YMCAs, n.d.), 30, YMCA Railroad Records; *Proceedings of the Eleventh International Conference of the Railroad Department of Young Men's Christian Associations of North America, Held at Topeka, Kansas, April 30–May 3, 1903* (New York: International Committee of YMCAs, n.d.), 35–36, YMCA Railroad Records; *Proceedings of the Twelfth International Conference of the Railroad Department of Young Men's Christian Associations of North America, Held at Detroit, Michigan, September 28–October 1, 1905* (New York: International Committee of YMCAs, n.d.), 31–32, YMCA Railroad Records.

18. Peter M. Arthur, "A Labor Leader's Views of the Christian Association, Delivered at the Dedication of the John M. Toucey Memorial Building, Mott Haven Department, New York, 19 January 1902," *Railroad Association Magazine* 15 (February 1902): 171–74.

19. Quoted in "Christian Brotherliness the Great Conference Theme of Railroad Men of All Ranks at St. Louis," *Association Men* 34 (July 1909): 453.

20. Stromquist, *Generation of Boomers*, 106–7. On the attempts made by railroad companies during the nineteenth century to reshape their workforce through the introduction of new, elaborate rules that were designed to regulate workers' conduct, see Licht, *Working for the Railroad*, 79–124.

21. "Railroad Branches Y.M.C.A.," *Union Pacific Employee Magazine* 5 (August 1890): 196–98.

22. In 1879, thirty-two railroad branches were affiliated with the YMCA, whereas five had chosen to separate. At twenty-seven other locations, the YMCA or railroad men themselves had begun work for railroad men. If these twenty-seven had decided against affiliation with the YMCA, the number of separate railroad associations would have risen to thirty-two, equal to the number of YMCA-affiliated branches. See *Altoona Proceedings*, 12, box 5, Railroad Convention Proceedings, 1877–1894, YMCA Railroad Records. On the separatist movement, see Moore, *Story of the Railroad "Y,"* 47–48, 51–63; and Hopkins, *History of the Y.M.C.A. in North America*, 230–31.

23. "First Annual Report of the Railroad Men's Christian Association, Cleveland, Ohio, 1878–9" (Cleveland: J. S. Savage, 1879), 3, box 38, folder 1, Collinwood Branch, Annual and Monthly Reports, 1872–1886, YMCA of Cleveland. See also "Railway Branch Young Men's Christian Association, Monthly Report for May 1878," box 38, folder 1, Collinwood Branch, Annual and Monthly Reports, 1872–1886, YMCA of Cleveland. On the social and institutional conservatism of city branches, see Owen Pence, *The Y.M.C.A. and Social Need: A Study of Institutional Adaptation* (New York: Association Press, 1939),

246–47. On the governance issues that may have contributed to the separation of railroad associations from the YMCA, see also Moore, *Story of the Railroad "Y,"* 58.

24. George W. Cobb, "Conversation and Amusement Rooms," *Altoona Proceedings*, 44, box 5, Railroad Convention Proceedings, 1877–1894, YMCA Railroad Records.

25. Ibid., 27.

26. Moore, *Story of the Railroad "Y,"* 47–48, 51–63.; Hopkins, *History of the Y.M.C.A. in North America*, 230–31; and "Work of Edwin D. Ingersoll," *Yearbook of the Young Men's Christian Associations of the United States and the Dominion of Canada for the Year 1882* (New York: International Committee of YMCAs, 1883), 25–26; Cornelius C. Vanderbilt to Cephas Brainerd, 15 September 1879, box 1, Correspondence, 1879–91, YMCA Railroad Records. See also *Altoona Proceedings, 1879*, 29–30, box 5, Railroad Convention Proceedings, 1877–1894, YMCA Railroad Records; Brown, "History of the Railroad Young Men's Christian Association," 35.

27. "Work of Edwin D. Ingersoll," *Yearbook 1882*, 26.

28. Ibid.

29. "Report of Edwin D. Ingersoll," *Yearbook 1884–1885*, 75.

30. *Proceedings of the Third International Conference of the Railroad Young Men's Christian Associations of the United States and the Dominion of Canada, Held in Two Sections: I. St. Thomas, Ont., May 18–21, 1882. II. Springfield, Mass., May 25–28, 1882* (New York: International Committee of YMCAs, 1882), 33, box 5, Railroad Convention Proceedings, YMCA Railroad Records. See also Hopkins, *History of the Y.M.C.A. in North America*, 381–82.

31. Rea, "History of the Railroad Young Men's Christian Associations," 66–67, 78. On the Hartford YMCA "Workingmen's Exchange," see Hopkins, *History of the Y.M.C.A. in North America*, 382.

32. "Billiards Pro and Con," *Railroad Association Magazine* 12 (May 1899): 343.

33. Ibid., 343–44. On Sunderlin's background, see *Roster of Paid Secretaries*, vol. 1, 295. Games were a controversial issue in the YMCA. See Hopkins, *History of the Y.M.C.A. in North America*, 381–82. A 1916 guidebook urged YMCA secretaries to look out for "unwholesome competition or gambling" (*Among Industrial Workers*, 38). Such evidence suggests that, despite all efforts, the YMCA was unable to prevent gambling around games.

34. "Billiards Pro and Con," *Railroad Association Magazine* 12 (May 1899): 344–45.

35. "Hoboken, N.J." *Railroad Association Magazine* 12 (June 1899): 384. Not everywhere did railroad workers succeed in overruling the YMCA's policy. At the Mechanicville, New York, Railroad YMCA, the YMCA of New York State Committee effectively opposed the installation of a billiard table. See Moore, *Story of the Railroad "Y,"* 161. Whether billiards made it into the rooms of a local YMCA apparently depended to a large degree on the local circumstances and especially on the ability of the local committee of management to resist interference from state and national authorities.

36. Your Uncle, "About Railroaders," *Association Men* 26 (October 1900): 13.

37. Your Uncle, "Men of the Rail Roads," *Association Men* 32 (April 1907): 316.

38. "Hagerstown, Md.," *Railroad Men* 12 (June 1899): 388.

39. George A. Warburton, "A Study of the Success of the Railroad Work of the

Young Men's Christian Association from the Standpoint of the Men," *New York Railroad Men* 18 (March 1904): 226.

40. H. C. Snead, "The Good in Billiards," *Association Men* 39 (September 1914): 671.

41. Grand Trunk, 1913, box 9, folder 6, Series I, Historical Records, 1853–1973, Subseries I, Indexed Records, 1853–1962, YMCA of Chicago; Monthly Reports, February to September 1913, box 9, folder 5, Chicago and Eastern Illinois, 1913, YMCA of Chicago.

42. "Comparative Statement of the Chesapeake & Ohio R.R. Departments, Y.M.C.A. for the Month Ending March 31st, 1899," *New York Railroad Men* 12 (May 1899): 307.

43. Hopkins, *History of the Y.M.C.A. in North America*, 375; *Association Men* 24 (September 1899): 469.

44. "18th Annual Report of the Railroad Branch, Young Men's Christian Association, East St. Louis, Ill.," enclosure from G. Parker to Hamilton Fish, 24 February 1899, Fish, In-letters, vol. 243, Illinois Central, Series 1, Subseries F 2.2, Illinois Central Railroad Company Archives, The Newberry Library, Chicago. For a similar illustration of the problem, see also Minutes of the Committee of Management, 11 November 1895, box 35, vol. 2, Collinwood Branch, Board of Managers, Minutes, 1887–1894, YMCA of Cleveland.

45. "A Pennsylvania Railroad Combine," *Association Men* 31 (October 1906): 20.

46. Monthly Report, February 1889, box 9, folder 8, Dearborn Station, 1889–90, 1917, Series I, Subseries I, YMCA of Chicago; Monthly Report, March 1889, box 9, folder 8, Dearborn Station, 1889–90, 1917, YMCA of Chicago.

47. "The Result for 1897 in Figures," *Railroad Men* 11 (February 1899): 152; "The Result for 1898 in Figures," *Railroad Men* 12 (February 1899): 193; "The Result for 1899 in Figures," *Railroad Men* 13 (February 1900): 199; "The Result for 1900 in Figures," *Railroad Men* 14 (February 1901): 219; "The Result for 1901 in Figures," *Railroad Men* 15 (February 1902): 201; "Partial Report of the Railroad Branch of the Young Men's Christian Association of New York City for 1904," *Railroad Men* 18 (February 1905): 187. The corresponding breakdown of numbers for 1902 and 1903 is not available.

48. Holcomb to James McCrea, 25 May 1900, Pennsylvania Lines, 1897–1900, box 9, folder 4, Series I, Subseries I, YMCA of Chicago.

49. Ward W. Adair, "About Railroaders," *Association Men* 29 (March 1904): 275; "The Meanest Man," *Railroad Association Magazine* 6 (April 1917): 7.

50. On the East Deerfield Railroad YMCA, see Report of J. M. Dudley, December 1907, box 4, Reports, Railroad Secretaries International Committee Railroad Department, 1901–07, YMCA Railroad Records; Report of J. M. Dudley, February 1909, box 4, Reports, Railroad Secretaries International Committee Railroad Department, 1908–12, YMCA Railroad Records; Report of J. M. Dudley, December 1913, box 4, Reports, Railroad Secretaries International Committee Railroad Department, 1913–20, YMCA Railroad Records. For a similar development on the Grand Trunk Railroad, see Report, C. R. Parsons, January 1921, box 4, Reports, Transportation Department Secretaries YMCA, 1921–24, YMCA Railroad Records.

51. Confidential Report. Visit of A. G. Knebel to Washington (Terminal Railroad Department), 12–14 January 1907, box 4, Reports, Railroad Secretaries International

Committee Railroad Department, 1908–12, YMCA Railroad Records. At Waycross, Georgia, on the Atlantic Coast Railway, labor unions boycotted the local YMCA for several years. See Report of G. K. Roper, Jr., December 1917, box 4, Reports, Railroad Secretaries International Committee Railroad Department, 1913–20, YMCA Railroad Records.

52. C. M. Hobbs, "The Railroad Department: Its Field, Opportunity, and Purposes.—Concluded," *Railroad Men* 14 (January 1901): 169.

53. On Ignace, see Report of J. M. Dudley, September 1910, and Report of J. M. Dudley, November 1910, box 4, Reports, Railroad Secretaries International Committee Railroad Department, 1908–12, YMCA Railroad Records. On Russell, Kentucky, see Report of G. K. Roper, Jr., April 1919, and Report of G. K. Roper, Jr., March 1920, box 3, Reports, Railroad Secretaries International Committee Railroad Department, 1913–20, YMCA Railroad Records.

54. On the Waterloo, Illinois, Railroad YMCA, see Report, A. G. Knebel, October 1911; on the events on the Grand Trunk line, see Report of J. M. Dudley, July 1910, both box 4, Reports, Railroad Secretaries International Committee Railroad Department, 1908–12, YMCA Railroad Records. On the general problems of railroad YMCAs in such situations, see Hopkins, *History of the Y.M.C.A. in North America*, 478; Moore, *Story of the Railroad "Y,"* 164–73.

55. Monthly Report of George D. McDill, September 1902, box 4 Reports, Railroad Secretaries International Committee Railroad Department, 1901–07, YMCA Railroad Records.

56. On the Van Buren incident, see Report of Edwin L. Hamilton, July 1908, box 4, Reports, Railroad Secretaries International Committee Railroad Department, 1908–12, YMCA Railroad Records. On the incident at an undisclosed location, see "An Unusual Incident," *Railroad Association Magazine* 1 (May 1912): 6. For a similar occurrence, see Report of Arthur G. Knebel, April 1912, box 4, Reports, Railroad Secretaries International Committee Railroad Department, 1908–12, YMCA Railroad Records.

57. Report of F. M. M. Richardson, August 1922, box 4, Reports, Transportation Department Secretaries International Committee YMCA, 1921–24, YMCA Railroad Records.

58. Robinson is quoted in "Boosting the Label," *Eastern Laborer*, 19 October 1907, 2. The episode is described in Fones-Wolf, *Trade Union Gospel*, 135–36. On the Kensington experiment, see Industrial Department Report for the Month of January 1907, box 11, Industrial Department Monthly Reports to the YMCA International Committee, 1903–1911, Departmental Reports, 1903–1911, YMCA Industrial Records; Minutes, 22 January 1907, and Minutes, 23 January 1907, box 11, Minutes, 1903–1911, YMCA Industrial Records; Report, 14 November 1907, box 11, Monthly Reports, Departmental Records, 1903–1911, YMCA Industrial Records; "Industrial Department Briefs," *Association Men* 33 (July 1908): 492; "Rev. Stelzle Here To-morrow," *Eastern Laborer*, 12 October 1907, 2; "'Labor's Champion,'" *Eastern Laborer*, 19 October 1907, 4, 8.

The YMCA itself experienced problems with employees' demands for better pay: in the early twentieth century, the San Francisco YMCA maintained an antiunion hiring policy, declaring it as an opportunity for the unemployed. Also, the YMCA pointed to its dependence on voluntary donations, arguing that this made it impossible to pay union wages. Finally, the San Francisco YMCA asserted that YMCA members had preference in employment, and the association did not feel justified to ask them to join a union as a condition for employment. Only after World War II did the YMCA move toward a reconciliation with labor unions. See Clifford M. Drury, *San Francisco Y.M.C.A.: 100 Years by the Golden Gate, 1853–1953* (Glendale, Calif.: Arthur H. Clark, 1963), 139–40; Hopkins, *History of the Y.M.C.A. in North America*, 724.

59. Herbert N. Casson, "Get Together for the Coming Conflict—Harmless Benefit Societies and Chewing Gum Clubs Will Not Do," *Trades Union News*, 9 March 1905, 2; "Our Character," *Iron Moulders Journal*, 10 February 1876, 583.

60. Quoted in Stephen Meyer III, *The Five Dollar Day: Labor Management and Social Control in the Ford Motor Company, 1908–1921* (Albany: State University of New York Press, 1981), 180.

61. The exact year of Tom Pape's death is not given. See Adair, *Lure of the Iron Trail*, 136.

Chapter 6

1. For an overview of the emergence of professions and professionalization in the late nineteenth century, see Samuel Haber, *The Quest for Authority and Honor in the American Professions, 1750–1900* (Chicago: University of Chicago Press, 1991), 193–205. Focusing on lawyers, clergy, professors, engineers, and doctors, Haber does not discuss other white-collar professionals, such as industrial relations experts. The drive toward professionalization as a social force in American history in the Gilded Age and the Progressive Era has been emphasized in particular by Wiebe, *Search for Order*, esp. 111–32.

2. On the state of the development of the professions by the 1880s, see Wiebe, *Search for Order*, 3.

3. See George A. Warburton, "The Railroad Secretaryship, Its Demands and Opportunities," *Railroad Men* 14 (June 1901): 393–403. Further, see Hopkins, *History of the Y.M.C.A. in North America*, 231; "Annual Report of Clarence J. Hicks," *Yearbook 1893*, 27. Corporate restructuring in the late nineteenth century is discussed by Chandler, *Visible Hand*, 84–187; Zunz, *Making America Corporate*.

4. On personality as a notion of the self, see Williams, *Keywords*; Susman, *Culture as History*, 271–85; Lears, *No Place of Grace*; Lears, "From Salvation to Self-Realization"; Lystra, *Searching the Heart*, 37–42; Fox, "Culture of Liberal Protestant Progressivism"; Blake, *Beloved Community*, 10–76, 124–38, 229–65; Rubin, *Making of Middle-Brow Culture*, 1–34. For "personality" as associated with white-collar workers whose occupation required charisma, see also Daniel T. Rodgers, *The Work Ethic in Industrial America, 1850–1920* (Chicago: University of Chicago Press, 1978), 38.

5. Moore, *Story of the Railroad "Y,"* 121, 135.

6. Morse, *History of the North American Young Men's Christian Associations*, 214; YMCA Industrial Department, 16 December 1912, Memorandum Report, box 11, YMCA Industrial Department Minutes, 1912–1918, Industrial Committee Minutes, YMCA Industrial Records; *Yearbook 1917–1918*, 104; *Yearbook 1918–1919*, 126; *Yearbook 1920–1921*, 216, 208.

7. *Roster of Paid Secretaries*, vol. 2.

8. Hopkins, *History of the Y.M.C.A. in North America*, 162, 233–34; Report of

F. M. M. Richardson for May 1919, box 4, Reports, Railroad Secretaries International Committee Railroad Department, 1913–1920, YMCA Railroad Records.

9. Moore, *Story of the Railroad "Y,"* 137–38; Wiebe, *Search for Order*, 14.

10. "Biennial Report of Edwin D. Ingersoll," *Proceedings of the Twenty-fourth International Convention of Young Men's Christian Associations, Held at Cleveland, O., May 28–29, 1881* (New York: International Committee of YMCAs, 1881), xxx.

11. Expense Account Book, John Ferguson Moore, YMCA Biographical Files. On the distances traveled by sleeping car porters, see Melinda Chateauvert, *Marching Together: Women of the Brotherhood of Sleeping Car Porters* (Urbana: University of Illinois Press, 1998), 33. The increase of workloads for YMCA secretaries is mentioned in George A. Warburton, "The Railroad Secretaryship, Its Demands and Opportunities," *Railroad Men* 14 (June 1901): 393–402.

12. *Proceedings of the First Conference of Wives of Secretaries of the Young Men's Christian Associations of North America, Thousand Island Park, New York, June 7–9, 1900* (n.p.: n.p., 1900), 16, box 1, Conference Papers, YMCA Professional Secretaries Records.

13. "In the World of Labor," *Association Men* 38 (September 1913): 630.

14. John F. Moore, "A Study of His Failures and Successes," in *The Increase of Efficiency: Papers Presented at the Main Sessions of the Thirty-third Conference of the Association of Employed Officers of the Young Men's Christian Associations of North America, Held in Indianapolis, Indiana, June 1–5, 1906* (n.p.: Executive Committee of the Association, n.d.), 10, box 2, Conference Papers, YMCA Professional Secretaries Records.

15. The statement of a YMCA secretary on his family life is quoted in George W. Mehaffey, "A Study of What Constitutes a Normal Home Life," in *Increase of Efficiency*, 19, 20, box 2, Conference Papers, YMCA Professional Secretaries Records. The statement from the spouse of a YMCA secretary is quoted in *Proceedings of the First Conference of Wives of Secretaries of the Young Men's Christian Associations of North America, Thousand Island Park, New York, June 7–9, 1900* (n.p.: n.p., 1900), 17, box 1, Conference Papers, YMCA Professional Secretaries Records. For a similar depiction of the family and marital life of YMCA secretaries, See John Donald Gustav-Wrathall, *Take the Young Stranger by the Hand*, 100–106. On turn-of-the-century middle-class fatherhood and breadwinning, see Griswold, *Fatherhood in America*, 13–17.

16. See *Proceedings of the First Conference of Wives of Secretaries of the Young Men's Christian Associations of North America, Thousand Island Park, New York, June 7–9, 1900* (n.p.: n.p., 1900), 14, box 1, Conference Papers, YMCA Professional Secretaries Records. For the case of Henry Curry, see "The Railroad Department," *Association Men* 28 (September 1903): 566. On health problems as a persistent reason for YMCA secretaries to resign, see *Roster of Paid Secretaries*, 2 vols.

17. Monthly Report of E. L. Hamilton, June, 1902, box 4, Reports, Railroad Secretaries International Committee Railroad Department, 1901–1907, YMCA Railroad Records.

18. For the assessment of the financial problems many YMCA secretaries apparently suffered, see Moore, "Study of His Failures and Successes," in *Increase of Efficiency*, 12, box 2, Conference Papers, YMCA Professional Secretaries Records. The spouse of a YMCA secretary is quoted in *Proceedings of the First Conference of Wives of Secretaries of*

the Young Men's Christian Associations of North America, Thousand Island Park, New York, June 7–9, 1900 (n.p.: n.p., 1900), 16, box 1, Conference Papers, YMCA Professional Secretaries Records.

19. On turnover rates, see Hopkins, *History of the Y.M.C.A. in North America*, 167–68, 172–73; "Report of E. L. Hamilton," *Yearbook 1899*, 41; George W. Mehaffey, "A Study of What Constitutes a Normal Home Life," in *Increase of Efficiency*, 18, 23, box 2, Conference Papers, YMCA Professional Secretaries Records. For the case of Fred Baumgartner, see *Roster of Paid Secretaries*, vol. 2, 3.

20. On reasons for quitting, see *Roster of Paid Secretaries*, 2 vols. On Ransom Liddle, see *Roster of Paid Secretaries*, vol. 2, 200.

21. E. L. Hamilton, Report for October 1914, box 4, Reports, Railroad Secretaries International Committee Railroad Department, 1913–1920, YMCA Railroad Records.

22. *Roster of Paid Secretaries*, vol. 1, 35.

23. *Roster of Paid Secretaries*, vol. 1.

24. Moore, "Study of His Failures and Successes," in *Increase of Efficiency*, 9, box 2, Conference Papers, YMCA Professional Secretaries Records.

25. For the following summary of that episode and all quotes, see "Edwin D. Ingersoll to Brown, Personal and Confidential," 27 November 1911, box 1, Railroad Department Reports, 1900–1928, YMCA Railroad Records.

26. Moore, "Study of His Failures and Successes," in *Increase of Efficiency*, 9, box 2, Conference Papers, YMCA Professional Secretaries Records.

27. Adair, "The Railroad Department: Current Comment," *Association Men* 32 (August 1907): 497. See also Gustav-Wrathall, *Take the Young Stranger by the Hand*, 83.

28. Adair, "The Secretaryship as a Profession," *Railroad Men* 26 (October 1912): 11–12.

29. Adair, "The Railroad Department" *Association Men* 29 (March 1904): 275.

30. The following quotes, unless noted differently, are taken from George A. Warburton, "The Railroad Secretaryship: Its Demands and Opportunities," *Railroad Men* 14 (June 1901): 393–402.

31. "The Railroad Department: Old-Time Religion," *Association Men* 33 (June 1908): 443.

32. "Railroad Men," *Association Men* 38 (July 1913): 538.

33. George A. Warburton, "The Railroad Secretaryship: Its Demands and Opportunities," *Railroad Men* 14 (June 1901): 393–402.

34. Clarence J. Hicks, "Lessons from the Administrative Experience of Business Corporations," in *Increase of Efficiency*, 75–78, box 2, Conference Papers, YMCA Professional Secretaries Records. See also Hopkins, *History of the Y.M.C.A. in North America*, 149.

35. Soares, *Vocation with a Future*, 24, 26, box 2, Conference Papers, YMCA Professional Secretaries Records. See also Hopkins, *History of the Y.M.C.A. in North America*, 162, 165, 167.

36. The quotes are from Soares, *Vocation with a Future*, 21–22, box 2, Conference Papers, YMCA Professional Secretaries Records. On changing qualification of YMCA secretaries, see *Roster of Paid Secretaries*, 2 vols.

37. George A. Warburton, "The Secretary's Self Culture," in *Second Conference of*

Metropolitan General Secretaries, December 6–9, 1912, Niagara Falls, New York, 44, box 3, Conference Papers, YMCA Professional Secretaries Records.

38. Ibid., 45.

39. Adair, "The Railroad Department: Current Comment," *Association Men* 33 (February 1908): 248.

40. For the following, including the quotes from the YMCA secretary's letter to Warburton, see Warburton, "Secretary's Self Culture," in *Second Conference of Metropolitan General Secretaries, December 6–9, 1912, Niagara Falls, New York*, 45–46, box 3, Conference Papers, YMCA Professional Secretaries Records.

41. Ibid., 32, 33.

42. Warburton, "A Study of the Success of the Railroad Work of the Young Men's Christian Association from the Standpoint of the Men," *Railroad Men* 18 (March 1904): 226; David G. Latshaw, "What Makes a Man," *Railroad Association Magazine* 3 (November 1913): 17. On domestic sentiment, see Halttunen, *Confidence Men and Painted Women*, 57–59.

43. For the complaints about "unwise wives," see Moore, "Study of His Failures and Successes," in *Increase of Efficiency*, 12, 13, box 2, Conference Papers, YMCA Professional Secretaries Records. For the statement by a secretarial spouse, agreeing with this, see Mrs. I. E. Brown, "The Traveling Secretary's Wife: Her Relation to His Work," *Proceedings of the First Conference of Wives of Secretaries of the Young Men's Christian Associations of North America, Thousand Island Park, New York, June 7–9, 1900* (n.p.: n.p., 1900), 9, box 1, Conference Papers, YMCA Professional Secretaries Records.

44. "Statement Regarding the Railroad Situation at Decatur, Ill.," *Railroad Men* 15 (November 1901): 62; "The Decatur Situation," *Railroad Men* 14 (July 1901): 477.

45. See Cecil L. Gates, "Woman's Work for Y.M.C.A.," *Helps for Christian Workers: A Quarterly Magazine* (April 1889): 10, box 1, Early Pamphlets, 1887–1892, YMCA Work with Women and Girls, YMCA Archives. On the activities of the Collinwood YMCA Women's Auxiliary, see *Proceedings of the Twenty-second Annual Convention of the Young Men's Christian Associations of the United States and British Provinces, Held at Louisville, Ky., June 6–10, 1877* (New York: Executive Committee, 1877), 22. On the role of the Women's Auxiliaries, see Hopkins, *History of the Y.M.C.A. in North America*, 39, 234, 241–42. Generally, for the role of women in the YMCA during the Gilded Age and the Progressive Era, see Mary Ross Hall and Helen Firman Sweet, *Women in the Y.M.C.A. Record* (New York: Association Press, 1947), 23–66; Jodi Vandenberg-Daves, "The Manly Pursuit of a Partnership between the Sexes: The Debate over YMCA Programs for Women and Girls, 1914–1933," *Journal of American History* 78 (March 1992): 1324–46.

46. Gates, "Woman's Work for Y.M.C.A.," in *Helps for Christian Workers: A Quarterly Magazine* (April 1889): 5, box 1, Early Pamphlets, 1887–1892, YMCA Work with Women and Girls.

47. Mrs. H. D. Dickson, "The Sacrifices and Joys of a Secretary's Wife," *Proceedings of the First Conference of Wives of Secretaries of the Young Men's Christian Associations of North America, Thousand Island Park, New York, June 7–9, 1900* (n.p.: n.p., 1900), 8, box 1, Conference Papers, YMCA Professional Secretaries Records.

48. Mrs. J. P. Garbrance, "Our Auxiliaries—Their Strength," *Report of the Proceedings of the Second Annual Conference of Women's Auxiliaries of the Railroad Young Men's Chris-*

tian Associations of New York State, October 4–6, 1892 (n.p.: n.d.), 19, box 1, YMCA Work with Women and Girls.

49. For this prevailing theme in U.S. women's history in the nineteenth century, see, for example, Cott, *Bonds of Womanhood;* Keith Melder, *Beginnings of Sisterhood: The American Women's Rights Movement, 1800–1850* (New York: Schocken Books, 1977); Barbara J. Berg, *The Remembered Gate: Origins of American Feminism: The Woman and the City, 1800–1860* (New York: Oxford University Press, 1978); Hewitt, *Women's Activism and Social Change;* Ginzberg, *Women and the Work of Benevolence.*

50. Mrs. J. P. Garbrance, "Our Auxiliaries—Their Strength," in *Report of the Proceedings of the Second Annual Conference of Women's Auxiliaries of the Railroad Young Men's Christian Associations of New York State, October 4–6, 1892* (n.p.: n.d.), 19–20, box 1, YMCA Work with Women and Girls. For the perception of the role of YMCA Women's Auxiliaries by a leading male YMCA secretary, see Gates, "Woman's Work for Y.M.C.A.," *Helps for Christian Workers: A Quarterly Magazine* (April 1889), 10, box 1, Early Pamphlets, 1887–1892, YMCA Work with Women and Girls.

51. Mrs. N. Waterman, "Our Auxiliaries—Their Object," in *Report of the Proceedings of the Second Annual Conference of Women's Auxiliaries of the Railroad Young Men's Christian Associations of New York State, October 4–6, 1892* (n.p.: n.d.), 17, box 1, YMCA Work with Women and Girls.

52. Ibid., 18; Mrs. F. H. Chapman, "Influence and Opportunities of Woman," *Report of the Proceedings of the Second Annual Conference of Women's Auxiliaries of the Railroad Young Men's Christian Associations of New York State, October 4–6, 1892* (n.p.: n.d.), 20, YMCA Work with Women and Girls.

53. *Proceedings of the First Conference of Wives of Secretaries of the Young Men's Christian Associations of North America, Thousand Island Park, New York, June 7–9, 1900* (n.p.: n.p., 1900), 19, box 1, Conference Papers, YMCA Professional Secretaries Records. For the notion of "maternal union," see Blake, *Beloved Community,* 32.

54. Quoted in Ward W. Adair, *Memories of George Warburton* (New York, J. J. Little & Ives, n.d.), 27–28.

55. Halttunen, *Confidence Men and Painted Women,* 204, 205.

56. See *Roster of Paid Secretaries.* Determining an exact date for this change is difficult. The second volume of the *Roster* traces the employment of YMCA secretaries only until 1905, but the remark on reasons for dismissal may have been entered later. For developments after 1900, see Charles K. Ober, "Men Who Will Make Secretaries," *Association Men* 37 (October 1911): 23.

57. "Pets and Patronage," *Association Men* 29 (May 1904): 362.

58. On YMCA secretaries as "man-culturists," see "From the Editor's Viewpoint," *Association Men* 26 (January 1901): 135. On "manhood engineering," see Charles K. Ober, "Manhood Engineering," *Association Men* 36 (March 1911): 256.

59. See Warburton, "Secretary's Self Culture," in *Second Conference of Metropolitan General Secretaries, December 6–9, 1912, Niagara Falls, New York,* 32, 33, box 3, Conference Papers, YMCA Professional Secretaries Records; Warburton, "Railroad Secretaryship," 12; L. L. Pierce, "How Best to Unify the Metropolitan Work," in *Second Conference of Metropolitan General Secretaries, December 6–9, 1912, Niagara Falls, New York* (December 1912), 17, box 3, Conference Papers, YMCA Professional Secretaries Records.

60. The relative cultural convergence of notions of manhood and of womanhood in corporate workplaces with the ascent of corporate capitalism also has been noted by Kwolek-Folland, *Engendering Business*, 43, 53–54.

Chapter 7

1. For a summary of these currents of thought, see Glenn C. Altschuler, *Race, Ethnicity, and Class in American Social Thought, 1865–1919* (Arlington Heights, Ill.: Harlan Davidson, 1982).

2. Halttunen, *Confidence Men and Painted Women*, 195.

3. Report of C. C. Michener, Secretary, Industrial Department, September 1905, box 11, Monthly Reports, 1903–1911, Departmental Reports, 1903–1911, YMCA Industrial Records.

4. Report of C. C. Michener, September 1906.

5. Ibid.

6. Report of C. C. Michener, September 1903.

7. Report of C. C. Michener, September 1905.

8. Report of C. C. Michener, September 1906.

9. Ibid.

10. On the "confidence man" of Victorian advice literature, see Halttunen, *Confidence Men and Painted Women*, 1–32.

11. Report of C. C. Michener, September 1903.

12. Report of C. C. Michener, September 1906.

13. *Principles and Methods of Religious Work for Men and Boys*, Atlantic City Edition (New York: Association Press, 1912), 10–11, 118, 119.

14. "Shop Bible Classes," *Association Men* 27 (October 1901): 17. On the date for the first Cleveland Shop Bible Class, see "Shop Bible Classes," 37, YMCA of Cleveland II. On the role of shop Bible classes in YMCA industrial work, see Hopkins, *History of the Y.M.C.A. in North America*, 504, 507.

15. Michener is quoted in Report of C. C. Michener, September 1906. For attendance figures, see *Yearbook 1903–1904*, 134–76; *Yearbook 1906–1907*, 98–142. On the function of shop Bible classes as an entrance point at a company, see Extracts from International Committee Minutes, 8 October 1903, box 11, Monthly Reports, 1903–1911, Departmental Reports, 1903–1911, YMCA Industrial Records. See also Report of the Industrial Committee, [January 1904], YMCA Industrial Records.

16. "An Adequate Attempt to Evangelize the Men of the City: A Study of Cleveland's Undertaking," *Association Men* 30 (April 1905): 302. On the nonpolitical content of such meetings, see also *Yearbook: State Young Men's Christian Association of Wisconsin, 1909*, 31, box 54, Annual Reports, 1903–1909, YMCA State and Regional Records.

17. "Shop Bible Classes," 8–9, YMCA of Cleveland II; "An Adequate Attempt to Evangelize the Men of a City," 302, 304.

18. "An Adequate Attempt to Evangelize the Men of a City," 304; "Shop Bible Classes," 16, YMCA of Cleveland II.

19. Quoted in Charles G. Reade, "Shop Meetings and Bible Classes," *Association Men* 25 (June 1900): 294.

20. "Shop Bible Classes," 6, 15, YMCA of Cleveland II.

21. Soares, *Vocation with a Future*, 7–8, 10, box 2, Conference Papers, YMCA Professional Secretaries Records.

22. "Shop Bible Classes," 8, 11, 13, 16, YMCA of Cleveland II.

23. My argument about the meaning of personality owes much to Rockefeller, *John Dewey*, 97; see also 49, 74, 99, 121, 142, 213, 353–56, 578–79 n. 67.

24. Soares, *Vocation with a Future*, 33, box 2, Conference Papers, YMCA Professional Secretaries Records.

25. Doggett et al., *Life Problems*, 3, YMCA International Committee Pamphlet Collection.

26. On the idea of a heightened sense of self and a notion of self-expression, see Rotundo, *American Manhood*, 279–81. The shift described here was also reflected in changing perceptions about the character of emotions, such as anger. See Peter N. Stearns, *American Cool: Constructing a Twentieth-Century Emotional Style* (New York: New York University Press, 1994), 95–138.

27. Wiebe, *Search for Order*, 113, 4; emphasis added. On character, personality, and self-expression, see Lystra, *Searching the Heart*, 37–42.

28. See Hopkins, *History of the Y.M.C.A. in North America*, 479; Morse, *History of the North American Young Men's Christian Associations*, 216.

29. For the following episode, see Charles R. Towson, "With the Men of the Open: The Joy of Working with Rugged, Responsive Men," *Association Men* 39 (May 1914): 402–3.

30. This concern with workers' bodies, I suggest, was related to a changing emphasis in middle-class manhood, demanding physical fitness from men. While the work environment of middle-class men no longer provided a source for a man's self-identification, workingmen retained the close cultural association between work and manhood. In a time when middle-class ideals of manhood began to emphasize toughness and physical strength, workers, whose manhood was manifest physically and retained the relation to work, became objects of both admiration and envy to middle-class men. See Stearns, *Be A Man!* 109.

31. Towson, "With the Men of the Open," *Association Men* 39 (May 1914): 402–3.

32. Towson, "The Good Work of Good Will," *Association Men* 39 (February 1914): 236–37.

33. Towson, "Jim, There's Money in It!" *Association Men* 39 (November 1913): 71.

34. Towson, "Good Work of Good Will," 237.

35. I reconstructed this account from Adair, *Lure of the Iron Trail*, 193–94; and "How He Won the Bull-Cook: A Letter from Sellwood," *Association Men* 37 (May 1912): 385–86.

36. My argument about the meaning of these narratives builds on Moon, "Gentle Boy from the Dangerous Classes," 88–89, 90, 107.

37. On the YMCA's efforts at Pontis, see "The Expanding Industrial Department," *Association Men* 33 (March 1908): 266–67. For the following accounts of the activities of one William H. Morrison, YMCA secretary at Pontis, South Dakota, and Taft, Montana, see William H. Day, "Reconstruction in a Construction Camp," *Association Men* 33

(May 1908): 372–74; Day, "The Story of the Taft Tunnel Gang," *Association Men* 34 (April 1909): 301–2.

38. My interpretation of this scenario and the shift in the gendering of sentiment is informed by my reading of Sedgwick, *Epistemology of the Closet*, 142, 146; and, more generally, Carole Pateman, *The Sexual Contract* (Stanford, Calif.: Stanford University Press, 1988); and Kann, *On the Man Question*. On the importance of the home as expression and transmitter of cultural values in Victorian American culture, see Kathryn Kish Sklar, *Catherine Beecher: A Study in American Domesticity* (New Haven, Conn.: Yale University Press, 1973).

39. Day, "Story of the Taft Tunnel Gang," *Association Men* 34 (April 1909): 301–2.

40. *Among Industrial Workers*, 23.

41. Frederick Harris, ed., *Service With Fighting Men: An Account of the American Young Men's Christian Associations in the World War* (New York: Association Press, 1929), 215. On the labor relations during World War I, see Neill A. Wynn, *From Progressivism to Prosperity: World War I and American Society* (New York: Holmes and Meier, 1986), 86–132; Jacoby, *Employing Bureaucracy*, 133–66; Montgomery, *Fall of the House of Labor*, 370–410; Frank L. Grubbs, Jr., *The Struggle for Labor Loyalty: Gompers, the A.F. of L., and the Pacifists, 1917–1920* (Durham: Duke University Press, 1968).

42. "A Time for Leadership," *Service* 1 (November 1918): 1.

43. John W. Prins, "The Singing Shipbuilders," undated brochure, 6, box 1, Departmental Materials, 1899–1932, YMCA Industrial Records.

44. "What Can the Association Substitute for the Saloon?" *Service* 2 (June 1919): 2. See also "Musical Shop Meetings at Chester, Pa.," *Service* 2 (May 1919): 3. The volume numbers of *Service* are irregular, and sometimes no volume number is given. Therefore, I have cited this publication always as given.

45. Towson, "A Needed Supplement to Industrial Housing—Part I," *American Architect* (May 1918): 621; Towson, "A Summary of Industrial Progress," *Service* 2 (July 1919): 1.

46. "A Time for Leadership," *Service* 1 (November 1918): 1. On the widespread fear of radicals in American society and government actions against it, see William J. Preston, Jr., *Aliens and Dissenters: Federal Suppression of Radicals, 1903–1933* (New York: Harper Torchbooks, 1966); Robert K. Murray, *Red Scare: A Study in National Hysteria, 1919–1920* (Minneapolis: University of Minnesota Press, 1955); John Higham, *Strangers in the Land: Patterns of American Nativism, 1860–1925* (New Brunswick, N.J.: Rutgers University Press, 1955), 222–33.

47. "The Opportunity of the Hour," *Service* 2 (January 1919): 1.

48. "Satisfying the Industrial Worker," *Service* (September 1918): 6. On recapitulation theory, see Cynthia Eagle Russett, *Sexual Science: The Victorian Construction of Womanhood* (Cambridge, Mass.: Harvard University Press, 1989), 50–63. See also Laura Otis, *Organic Memory: History and the Body in Late Nineteenth and Early Twentieth Centuries* (Lincoln, Neb.: University of Nebraska Press, 1994).

49. For discussions of recapitulation theory and organized play, see Dominick Cavallo, *Muscles and Morals: Organized Playgrounds and Urban Reform, 1880–1920* (Philadelphia: University of Pennsylvania Press, 1981), 76–84; David I. McLeod, *Building Character in the American Boy* (Madison: University of Wisconsin Press, 1983), 99–101, 104–14,

116, 143; Benjamin G. Rader, "The Recapitulation Theory of Play: Motor Behaviour, Moral Reflexes and Manly Attitudes in Urban America, 1880–1920," in *Manliness and Morality: Middle-Class Masculinity in Britain and America, 1880–1940*, ed. J. A. Mangan and James Walvin (New York: St. Martin's Press, 1987), 123–34.

50. "Industrial Men," *Association Men* 44 (January 1919): 389. For emphasis on self-expression as a main goal of YMCA wartime programs, see also "Organizing an Industry for Americanization," *Service* 2 (May 1919): 5; "The Association in New Haven Industries," *Service* 2 (May 1919): 1.

51. "Music in Industry," *Service* 2 (May 1919): 1–2. On the significance of emotional bonds between individuals and in groups to overcome social differences in liberal protestant thought, see Richard Wightman Fox, "The Culture of Liberal Protestant Progressivism," *Journal of Interdisciplinary History* 23 (Winter 1993): 649.

52. *Among Industrial Workers*, 80.

53. "Music in Industry," *Service* 2 (May 1919), 1–2.

54. Towson, "Industrial Work in War Time," *Association Men* 44 (November 1918): 228, 230.

55. "Harmony," *Service* 1 (July 1918): 1. On the music director's success, see *Among Industrial Workers (Ways and Means): A Handbook for Associations in Industrial Fields*, rev. ed. (New York: International Committee of YMCAs, 1920), 83.

56. On the image of the crowd as a fantasy for middle-class professionals, promising understanding of their social roles and fulfillment, see Gregory W. Bush, *Lord of Attention: Gerald Stanley Lee and the Crowd Metaphor in Industrializing America* (Amherst: University of Massachusetts Press, 1991), 8–30.

57. "Music in Industry," *Service* (May 1919): 1–2.

58. J. W. Prins, "The Singing Shipbuilders," 18, undated brochure, box 1, Departmental Materials, 1899–1932, YMCA Industrial Records. My interpretation of the group experience described and its relation to gender follows Blake, *Beloved Community*, 10–48; and Lears, *No Place of Grace*, 248–50.

59. W. H. Warren, "From Now On, I'm Your Friend," *Association Men* 44 (January 1919): 389.

60. For the concept of the "pious consumer," see Lori Merish, "'The Hand of Refined Taste' in the Frontier Landscape: Caroline Kirkland's *A New Home, Who'll Follow?* and the Feminization of American Consumerism," *American Quarterly* 45 (December 1993): 487. I am relying here on the broad definition of "consumption," used by Richard Wightman Fox and Jackson Lears, which, as I would argue, calls for an equally broad definition of production at a time when traditional boundaries between these realms became increasingly porous: "Consumers are not only buyers of goods but recipients of professional advice, marketing strategies, government programs, electoral choices, and advertisers' images of happiness" (introduction to *Culture of Consumption*, ed. Fox and Lears, xii).

61. For the following episode, see Edward A. Steiner, *The Immigrant Tide: Its Ebb and Flow* (New York: Fleming H. Revell, 1909), 253–58.

62. The Bureau of Motion Pictures and Exhibits, Industrial Department. *Use of Industrial and Educational Motion Pictures in the Y.M.C.A. Practical Program* (New York: International Committee Y.M.C.A., Industrial Department Bureau of Motion Pictures,

1920), 7, box 2, Motion Picture Pamphlets, YMCA Industrial Records. On the use of group singings in prisons, see Richard Polenberg, *Fighting Faiths: The Abrams Case, the Supreme Court, and Free Speech* (New York: Penguin, 1987), 288.

Conclusion

1. Theweleit, *Male Fantasies*, 270.

2. Lears, *No Place of Grace*, 35.

3. Wiebe, *Search for Order*, 113. On gender and Wiebe's *Search for Order*, see also Robyn Muncy, *"The Search for Order* Reconsidered," paper delivered at the Annual Meeting of the American Historical Association, 1997, panel: "Robert Wiebe's *Search for Order*: A Thirty-Year Retrospective."

4. See, for example, Robyn Muncy, *Creating a Female Dominion in American Reform, 1890–1935* (New York: Oxford University Press, 1991); Molly Ladd-Taylor, *Mother-Work: Women, Child Welfare, and the State, 1890–1930* (Urbana: University of Illinois Press, 1994); Mary Odem, *Delinquent Daughters: Protecting and Policing Adolescent Female Sexuality in the United States, 1885–1920* (Chapel Hill: University of North Carolina Press, 1995); Kriste Lindenmeyer, *A Right to Childhood: The U.S. Children's Bureau and Child Welfare, 1912–1946* (Urbana: University of Illinois Press, 1997). See also Muncy, *"Search for Order* Reconsidered."

5. For elaborations on an emerging focus on entrepreneurship in middle-class ideals of manhood, eclipsing notions of the independent producer as hallmark of manhood in that time period, see Kwolek-Folland, *Engendering Business*, 47–51; for "corporate man" and "team player," see p. 47. See also Hilkey, *Character Is Capital*, 143.

6. See R. L. Dickinson, "Foreword," *Service* (January 1925): 1; Fred H. Rindge, Jr., "What Is Our Field and Our Force?" *Service* (June 1928): 15; *Report on a Survey of the International Committee of Young Men's Christian Associations of North America* (New York: n.p., 1923), 1, 175–76, box 27, Record Group II, Welfare-Youth, Rockefeller Family Archives; Hopkins, *History of the Y.M.C.A. in North America*, 477, 570–71.

PRIMARY SOURCES

Archival Materials

Kautz Family YMCA Archives, University Libraries, University of Minnesota, Twin Cities
     Roster of Paid Secretaries, 2 vols., 1880–1905.
     YMCA Biographical Files.
     YMCA Professional Secretaries' Records.
     YMCA Industrial Department Records, 1889–1980.
     YMCA International Committee Pamphlet Collection.
     YMCA State and Regional Records.
     YMCA Railroad/Transportation Department Records, 1877–1987.
     YMCA Work with Women and Girls.
Chicago Historical Society, Chicago, Illinois
     YMCA of Metropolitan Chicago Papers.
Western Reserve Historical Society, Cleveland, Ohio
     YMCA of Cleveland Records.
     YMCA of Cleveland Records, series II.
Newberry Library, Chicago, Illinois
     Chicago, Burlington & Quincy Railroad Company Archives.
     Illinois Central Railroad Company Archives.
Rockefeller Archive Center, North Tarrytown, New York.
     Colorado, Fuel & Iron, Business Interests, Record Group III 2c, Rockefeller Family Papers, Office of the Messrs. Rockefeller.
     Welfare Interests/Youth, Record Group II, Rockefeller Family Papers, Office of the Messrs. Rockefeller.

Census Material and Government Documents

Olmsted, Victor H. "The Betterment of Industrial Conditions." *Bulletin of the Department of Labor* 5 (November 1900): 1156.

U.S. Census Office. Eighth Census, 1860. Reel 460, Maryland, Baltimore.

———. Eighth Census, 1860. Reel 727, New York, Cayuga County, City of Auburn.

———. Eighth Census, 1860. Reel 762, New York, Jefferson County (part).

———. Eighth Census, 1860. Reel 1437, Wisconsin, Winnebago and Woud Counties.

———. Ninth Census, 1870. Reel 460, Maryland, Baltimore.

———. Tenth Census, 1880, Population. Reel 835, New York, Fulton (part) and Genesee Counties.

U.S. Department of Commerce. *Statistical Abstract of the United States, 1920.* Washington, D.C.: GPO, 1921, 279.

U.S. Department of Commerce and Labor. *Statistical Abstract of the United States, 1910.* Washington, D.C.: GPO, 1911, 226

U.S. Department of Labor, Bureau of Labor Statistics. *Welfare Work for Employees in Industrial Establishments in the United States. Bulletin of the United States Bureau of Labor Statistics,* misc. series, no. 250. Washington, D.C.: Government Printing Office, February 1919.

Periodicals

Association Forum, 1921.

Association Men, 1898–1921.

Cleveland Plain Dealer, 1877.

Coal Age, 1913.

Eastern Laborer, 1907.

Iron Moulders Journal, 1876.

Men, 1898–1899.

New York, New Haven, & Hartford Railroad News, 1905.

New York Railroad Men, 1891–1896.

New York Times, 1932.

Pennsylvania Railroad Men's News, 1898.

Railroad Association Magazine, 1911–1919.

Railroad Men, 1896–1921.

Service, 1918–1921.

Survey, 1912.

Trades Union News, 1905.

Union Pacific Employee Magazine, 1890.

United Mine Workers Journal, 1912.

Watchman, 1881.

Published Materials, Books, and Theses

Adair, Ward W. *Memories of George Warburton.* New York: J. J. Little & Ives, n.d.

———. *The Lure of the Iron Trail.* New York: Association Press, 1912.

———. *The Road to New York.* New York: Association Press, 1936.

Among Industrial Workers (Ways and Means): A Handbook for Associations in Industrial Fields. New York: International Committee of Young Men's Christian Associations, 1916.

Among Industrial Workers (Ways and Means): A Handbook for Associations in Industrial Fields. Rev. ed. New York: International Committee of Young Men's Christian Associations, 1920.

Brown, Herbert E. "The History of the Railroad Young Men's Christian Association." Graduation thesis, Institute and Training School of Young Men's Christian Associations, Chicago, Illinois, 25 May 1905.

Conference on Welfare Work, Held at the Waldorf-Astoria, New York City, March 16, 1904, under the Auspices of the Welfare Department of the National Civic Federation. New York: Andrew H. Kellogg, 1904.

Dacus, J. A. *Annals of the Great Strikes of the United States: A Reliable History and Graphic Description of the Causes and Thrilling Events of Labor Strikes and Riots of 1877.* New York: Burt Franklin, 1877.

Daniels, John. *America via the Neighborhood.* 1920; reprint Montclair, N.J.: Patterson Smith, 1971.

Finney, Charles Grandison. *Memoirs of Rev. Charles G. Finney, Written by Himself.* New York: Fleming H. Revell, 1876.

Fisher, Galen M. *Public Affairs and the YMCA: 1844–1944.* New York: Association Press, 1948.

Foster, William Z. *The Great Steel Strike and Its Lessons.* New York: B. W. Huebsch, 1920.

Hall, Mary Ross, and Helen Firman Sweet. *Women in the Y.M.C.A. Record.* New York: Association Press, 1947.

Harris, Frederick, ed. *Service with Fighting Men: An Account of the American Young Men's Christian Associations in the World War.* New York: Association Press, 1929.

Hicks, Clarence J. *My Life in Industrial Relations: Fifty Years in the Growth of a Profession.* New York: Harper & Brothers, 1941.

Hine, Charles DeLano. *Letters from an Old Railway Official to His Son, a Division Superintendent.* Chicago: Railway Age, 1904.

Knebel, Aaron G. *Four Decades with Men and Boys.* New York: Association Press, 1936.

Latta, Samuel. *Rest Houses for Railroad Men: The Pennsylvania's Provision for the Welfare of Its Conductors, Engineers, Firemen, and Trainmen—How the Railroad Men Regard Such Convenience—A Model Hospital Car.* New York: National Civic Federation Welfare Department, 1906.

Lewis, W. Everett. "A History of the Industrial Work of the Young Men's Christian Association." Thesis, International Young Men's Christian Association Training School, Springfield, Mass., 1904.

Moore, John F. *The Story of the Railroad "Y."* New York: Association Press, 1930.

Morse, Richard C. *History of the North American Young Men's Christian Associations.* New York: Association Press, 1919.

———. *My Life with Young Men: Fifty Years in the Young Men's Christian Association.* New York: Association Press, 1918.

Ninde, H. S., J. T. Bowne, and Erskine Uhl, eds. *A Handbook of the History, Organization, and Methods of Work of the Young Men's Christian Association.* New York: International Committee of Young Men's Christian Associations, 1892.

Pence, Owen. *The Y.M.C.A. and Social Need: A Study of Institutional Adaptation.* New York: Association Press, 1939.

Principles and Methods of Religious Work for Men and Boys, Atlantic City Edition. New York: Association Press, 1912.

Proceedings of the Twenty-second Annual Convention of the Young Men's Christian Associations of the United States and British Provinces, Held at Louisville, Ky., June 6–10, 1877. New York: Executive Committee, 1877.

Proceedings of the Twenty-fourth International Convention of Young Men's Christian Associations, Held at Cleveland, O., May 28–29, 1881. New York: International Committee of Young Men's Christian Associations, 1881.

Proceedings of the Twenty-fifth International Convention of Young Men's Christian Associations, Held at Milwaukee, Wis., May 16–20, 1883. New York: International Committee of Young Men's Christian Associations, 1883.

Proceedings of the Twenty-sixth International Convention of Young Men's Christian Associations of the United States and British Provinces, Held in Atlanta, Ga., May 13–17, 1885. New York: International Committee of Young Men's Christian Associations, 1885.

Proceedings of the Thirty-first International Convention of the Young Men's Christian Associations of North America, Held in Springfield, Mass., May 8–12, 1895. New York: International Committee of Young Men's Christian Associations, 1895.

Proceedings of the Thirty-fifth International Convention of the Young Men's Christian Association of North America, Held at Buffalo, New York, 11–15 May 1904. New York: International Committee of Young Men's Christian Associations, 1904.

Proceedings of the Fortieth International Convention of Young Men's Christian Associations of North America, Held at Detroit, Michigan, November 19–23, 1919. New York: Association Press, 1920.

Rea, Charles T. "The History of the Railroad Young Men's Christian Association." Thesis, International Young Men's Christian Association Training School, Springfield, Mass., 1904.

Report of the International Committee of the Young Men's Christian Associations to the Thirty-ninth International Convention at Cleveland, Ohio, May 12–16, 1916. New York: Association Press, 1917.

Rindge, Fred Hamilton, Jr. "The Young Men's Christian Association and Industrial Betterment." Master's thesis, Columbia University, 1909.

Schwenning, Gustav Theodor. "A History of the Industrial Work of the Young Men's Christian Association." Ph.D. dissertation, Clark University, 1925.

Shedd, Clarence P. *Two Centuries of Student Christian Movements: Their Origin and Intercollegiate Life.* New York: Association Press, 1934.

Steiner, Edward A. *The Immigrant Tide: Its Ebb and Flow.* New York: Fleming H. Revell, 1909.

Super, Paul. *Formative Ideas in the YMCA.* New York: Association Press, 1929.

Wallace, W. Stewart, ed. *A Dictionary of North American Authors Deceased Before 1950.* Toronto: Ryerson Press, 1968.

Warburton, George A. "James Stokes and the Association Work among Railroad Men." In *James Stokes: Pioneer of Young Men's Christian Associations,* edited by Frank W. Ober. New York: Association Press, 1921.

Who Was Who among North American Authors, 1921–1939, vol. 2. Detroit: Gale Research, 1976.

Who Was Who in America, vol. 1, 1897–1942. Chicago: Marquis Who's Who, 1943.

Wilson, William B. *History of the Pennsylvania Railroad Department of the Young Men's Christian Association.* Philadelphia: Stephen Greene, 1911.

Woods Baltimore City Directory. N.p.: John H. Woods, 1860.

Yearbook of Young Men's Christian Associations of North America, 1882–1921.

SECONDARY SOURCES

Aaron, Cindy Sondik. *Ladies and Gentlemen of the Civil Service: Middle-Class Workers in Victorian America.* New York: Oxford University Press, 1987.

Adams, Graham, Jr. *Age of Industrial Violence, 1910–15: The Activities and Findings of the United States Commission on Industrial Relations.* New York: Columbia University Press, 1966.

Altschuler, Glenn C. *Race, Ethnicity, and Class in American Social Thought, 1865–1919.* Arlington Heights, Ill.: Harlan Davidson, 1982.

Andrews, F. Emerson. *Corporation Giving.* New York: Russell Sage Foundation, 1952.

Barker-Benfield, Graham J. *The Horrors of the Half-Known Life: Male Attitudes toward Women and Sexuality in Nineteenth-Century America.* New York: Harper & Row, 1976.

Barney, William L. *The Passage of the Republic: An Interdisciplinary History of Nineteenth-Century America.* Lexington, Mass.: D. C. Heath, 1987.

Baron, Ava. "An 'Other' Side of Gender Antagonism at Work: Men, Boys, and the Re-masculinization of Printers' Work, 1830–1920." In *Work Engendered,* edited by Ava Baron, 47–69. Ithaca, N.Y.: Cornell University Press, 1991.

———. "Questions of Gender: Deskilling and Demasculinization in the U.S. Printing Industry, 1830–1915." *Gender and History* 1 (Summer 1989): 178–99.

———, ed. *Work Engendered: Toward a New History of American Labor.* Ithaca, N.Y.: Cornell University Press, 1991.

Bederman, Gail. *Manliness and Civilization: A Cultural History of Gender and Race in the United States, 1880–1917.* Chicago: University of Chicago Press, 1995.

———. "'The Women Have Had Charge of the Church Work Long Enough': The Men and Religion Forward Movement of 1911–1912 and the Masculinization of Middle-Class Protestantism." *American Quarterly* 41 (September 1989): 432–65.

Bensman, David. *The Practice of Solidarity: American Hat Finishers in the Nineteenth Century*. Urbana: University of Illinois Press, 1985.

Berg, Barbara J. *The Remembered Gate: Origins of American Feminism: The Woman and the City, 1800–1860*. New York: Oxford University Press, 1978.

Bilhartz, Terry D. *Urban Religion and the Second Great Awakening: Church and Society in Early National Baltimore*. Rutherford, N.J.: Farleigh Dickinson University Press, 1986.

Black, Vincent. "The Development of Management Personnel Policies on the Burlington Railroad, 1860–1900." Ph.D. dissertation, University of Wisconsin–Madison, 1982.

Blake, Casey Nelson. *Beloved Community: The Cultural Criticism of Randolph Bourne, Van Wyck Brooks, Waldo Frank, and Lewis Mumford*. Chapel Hill: University of North Carolina Press, 1990.

Bledstein, Burton J. *The Culture of Professionalism: The Middle Class and the Development of Higher Education in America*. New York: Norton, 1976.

Blumin, Stuart M. *The Emergence of the Middle Class: Social Experience in the American City, 1760–1900*. Cambridge: Cambridge University Press, 1989.

Bourdieu, Pierre. *Language and Symbolic Power*. Edited by John B. Thompson. Cambridge, Mass.: Harvard University Press, 1991.

———. *The Logic of Practice*. Translated by Richard Nice. Stanford, Calif.: Stanford University Press, 1990.

Boyer, Paul. *Urban Masses and Moral Order, 1820–1920*. Cambridge, Mass.: Harvard University Press, 1978.

Brandes, Stuart D. *American Welfare Capitalism, 1880–1940*. Chicago: University of Chicago Press, 1976.

Bristow, Nancy K. *Making Men Moral: Social Engineering during the Great War*. New York: New York University Press, 1996.

Brod, Harry, ed. *The Making of Masculinities: The New Men's Studies*. Boston: Allen & Unwin, 1987.

Brody, David. "The Rise and Decline of American Welfare Capitalism." In *Change and Continuity in Twentieth-Century America: The 1920s*, edited by John Braeman, Robert H. Bremner, and David Brody, 147–78. Columbus: Ohio State University Press, 1968.

———. *Steelworkers in America: The Non-Union Era*. Cambridge, Mass.: Harvard University Press, 1960.

Brown, Gillian. *Domestic Individualism: Imagining Self in Nineteenth-Century America*. Berkeley: University of California Press, 1990.

Bruce, Robert V. *1877: Year of Violence*. Indianapolis, Ind.: Bobbs-Merrill, 1959.

Budd, Michael Anton. *The Sculpture Machine: Physical Culture and Body Politics in the Age of Empire*. New York: New York University Press, 1997.

Burke, Martin J. *The Conundrum of Class: Public Discourse on the Social Order in America*. Chicago: University of Chicago Press, 1995.

Burns, Rex. *Success in America: The Yeoman Dream and the Industrial Revolution*. Amherst: University of Massachusetts Press, 1976.

Bush, Gregory W. *Lord of Attention: Gerald Stanley Lee and the Crowd Metaphor in Industrializing America*. Amherst: University of Massachusetts Press, 1991.

Butler, Judith. *Gender Trouble: Feminism and the Subversion of Identity*. New York: Routledge, 1990.

Carnes, Mark C. *Secret Ritual and Manhood in Victorian America*. New Haven, Conn.: Yale University Press, 1989.

Carnes, Mark C., and Clyde Griffen, eds. *Meanings for Manhood: Constructions of Masculinity in Victorian America*. Chicago: University of Chicago Press, 1990.

Carter, Paul A. *The Spiritual Crisis of the Gilded Age*. DeKalb: Northern Illinois University Press, 1971.

Cashman, Sean Dennis. *America in the Age of the Titans: The Progressive Era and World War I*. New York: New York University Press, 1988.

————. *America in the Gilded Age: From the Death of Lincoln to the Rise of Theodore Roosevelt*. 3d ed. New York: New York University Press, 1993.

Cavallo, Dominick. *Muscles and Morals: Organized Playgrounds and Urban Reform, 1880–1920*. Philadelphia: University of Pennsylvania Press, 1981.

Cawelti, John G. *Apostles of the Self-Made Man*. Chicago: University of Chicago Press, 1965.

Chandler, Alfred DuPont. *The Visible Hand*. Cambridge, Mass.: Belknap Press, Harvard University Press, 1977.

————, ed. *The Railroads: The Nation's First Big Business*. New York: Harcourt, Brace & World, 1965.

Chateauvert, Melinda. *Marching Together: Women of the Brotherhood of Sleeping Car Porters*. Urbana: University of Illinois Press, 1998.

Chauncey, George. *Gay New York: Gender, Urban Culture, and the Making of the Gay Male World, 1890–1940*. New York: Basic Books, 1994.

Clawson, Mary Ann. *Constructing Brotherhood: Class, Gender, and Fraternalism*. Princeton, N.J.: Princeton University Press, 1989.

Coontz, Stephanie. *The Social Origins of Private Life: American Families, 1600–1900*. New York: Verso, 1988.

Cooper, Patricia A. *Once a Cigar Maker: Men, Women, and Work Culture in American Cigar Factories, 1900–1919*. Urbana: University of Illinois Press, 1987.

Cott, Nancy. *The Bonds of Womanhood: "Woman's Sphere" in New England, 1778–1835*. New Haven, Conn.: Yale University Press, 1977.

Cross, Whitney R. *The Burned-Over District: The Social and Intellectual History of Enthusiastic Religion in Western New York, 1800–1850*. Ithaca, N.Y.: Cornell University Press, 1950.

Crunden, Robert M. *Ministers of Reform: The Progressives' Achievement in American Civilization, 1889–1920*. New York: Basic Books, 1982.

Curtis, Susan. *A Consuming Faith: The Social Gospel and Modern American Culture*. Baltimore: Johns Hopkins University Press, 1991.

Cutlip, Scott M. *Fund Raising in the United States: Its Role in American Philanthropy*. New Brunswick, N.J.: Rutgers University Press, 1965.

Davidoff, Leonore, and Catherine Hall. *Family Fortunes: Men and Women of the Middle Class, 1760–1850.* Chicago: University of Chicago Press, 1987.

Drury, Clifford M. *San Francisco Y.M.C.A.: 100 Years by the Golden Gate, 1853–1953.* Glendale, Calif.: Arthur H. Clark, 1963.

DeVault, Ileen A. *Sons and Daughters of Labor: Class and Clerical Work in Turn-of-the-Century Pittsburgh.* Ithaca, N.Y.: Cornell University Press, 1990.

Dimock, Wai Chee. "Class, Gender, and a History of Metonymy." In *Rethinking Class: Literary Studies and Social Formations,* edited by Wai Chee Dimock and Michael T. Gilmore, 57–104. New York: Columbia University Press, 1994.

Diner, Steven J. *A Very Different Age: Americans of the Progressive Era.* New York: Hill & Wang, 1998.

Donaghue, Terry. *An Event on Mercer Street: A Brief History of the YMCA of the City of New York.* New York: n.p., 1952.

Douglas, Ann. *The Feminization of American Culture.* New York: Alfred A. Knopf, 1979.

Drury, Clifford M. *100 Years at the Golden Gate: The San Francisco YMCA.* (Glendale, Calif.: Arthur H. Clark, 1963).

Dubbert, Joe. *Men's Places: Masculinity in Transition.* Englewood Cliffs, N.J.: Prentice Hall, 1979.

———. "Progressivism and the Masculinity Crisis." In *The American Man,* edited by Elizabeth H. Pleck and Joseph H. Pleck, 303–20. Englewood Cliffs, N.J.: Prentice Hall, 1980.

Dulles, Foster Rhea, and Melvyn Dubofsky. *Labor in America: A History.* 1949; Wheeling, Ill.: Harlan Davidson, 1993.

Edwards, Paul K. *Strikes in the United States, 1881–1974.* New York: St. Martin's Press, 1981.

Eley, Geoff. "Nations, Publics, and Political Cultures: Placing Habermas in the Nineteenth Century." In *Culture/Power/History: A Reader in Contemporary Social Theory,* edited by Nicholas B. Dirks, Geoff Eley, and Sherry B. Ortner, 297–335. Princeton, N.J.: Princeton University Press, 1993.

Elias, Norbert. *The Civilizing Process.* 1939; Oxford: Blackwell, 1994.

Epstein, Barbara. *The Politics of Domesticity: Women, Evangelism, and Temperance in Nineteenth-Century America.* Middletown, Conn.: Wesleyan University Press, 1981.

Fabian, Ann. *Card Sharps, Dream Books, and Bucket Shops: Gambling in Nineteenth-Century America.* Ithaca, N.Y.: Cornell University Press, 1990.

Filene, Peter Gabriel. *Him/Her/Self: Sex Roles in Modern America.* Baltimore: Johns Hopkins University Press, 1986.

Fine, Lisa M. "'Our Big Factory Family': Masculinity and Paternalism at the REO Car Company of Lansing, Michigan." *Labor History* 34 (Spring-Summer 1993): 274–91.

Fones-Wolf, Kenneth. *Trade-Union Gospel: Christianity and Labor in Industrial Philadelphia, 1865–1915.* Philadelphia: Temple University Press, 1989.

Foucault, Michel. *History of Sexuality.* Vol. 1, *An Introduction.* New York: Vintage, 1980.

Fox, Richard Wightman. "The Culture of Liberal Protestant Progressivism." *Journal of Interdisciplinary History* 23 (Winter 1993): 639–60.

Fox, Richard Wightman, and T. J. Jackson Lears. Introduction to *The Culture of Consumption: Critical Essays in American History, 1880–1980*. Edited by Richard W. Fox and T. J. Jackson Lears. New York: Pantheon, 1983.

Fredrickson, George M. *The Inner Civil War: Northern Intellectuals and the Crisis of the Union*. New York: Harper & Row, 1965.

Gay, Peter. *The Bourgeois Experience: Victoria to Freud: The Cultivation of Hatred*. New York: Norton, 1990.

Giddens, Anthony. *The Class Structure of the Advanced Societies*. New York: Harper & Row, 1975.

Ginger, Ray. *The Age of Excess: The United States from 1877–1914*. 2d ed. New York: Macmillan, 1975.

Ginzberg, Lori. *Women and the Work of Benevolence: Morality, Politics, and Class in the Nineteenth-Century United States*. New Haven, Conn.: Yale University Press, 1990.

Gitelman, Howard M. *Legacy of the Ludlow Massacre: A Chapter in American Industrial Relations*. Philadelphia: University of Pennsylvania Press, 1988.

———. "Welfare Capitalism Reconsidered." *Labor History* 33 (Winter 1992): 5–31.

Gorn, Elliot J. *The Manly Art: Bare-Knuckle Prize Fighting in America*. Ithaca, N.Y.: Cornell University Press, 1986.

Gorrell, Donald K. *The Age of Responsibility: The Social Gospel in the Progressive Era, 1900–1920*. Macon, Ga.: Mercer University Press, 1988.

Green, James R. *The World of the Worker: Labor in Twentieth-Century America*. New York: Hill & Wang, 1980.

Green, Marguerite. *The National Civic Federation and the American Labor Movement, 1900–1925*. Westport, Conn.: Greenwood Press, 1973.

Griffen, Clyde. "Reconstructing Masculinity from the Evangelical Revival to the Waning of Progressivism: A Speculative Synthesis." In *Meanings for Manhood: Constructions of Masculinity in Victorian America*, edited by Mark Carnes and Clyde Griffen, 183–204. Chicago: University of Chicago Press, 1990.

Griswold, Robert. *Fatherhood in America: A History*. New York: Basic Books, 1993.

Grubbs, Frank L., Jr. *The Struggle for Labor Loyalty: Gompers, the A.F. of L., and the Pacifists, 1917–1920*. Durham, N.C.: Duke University Press, 1968.

Gustav-Wrathall, John Donald. *Take the Young Stranger by the Hand: Same-Sex Relations and the YMCA*. Chicago: University of Chicago Press, 1998.

Gutman, Herbert George. "Protestantism and the American Labor Movement: The Christian Spirit in the Gilded Age." *American Historical Review* 72 (October 1966): 74–101.

Haber, Samuel. *The Quest for Authority and Honor in the American Professions, 1750–1900*. Chicago: University of Chicago Press, 1991.

Habermas, Jürgen. *The Structural Transformation of the Public Sphere: An Inquiry into a Category of Bourgeois Society*. Cambridge, Mass.: MIT Press, 1989.

Hall, Jacquelyn Dowd, et al. *Like a Family: The Making of a Southern Cotton Mill World*. Chapel Hill: University of North Carolina Press, 1987.

Haller, John S., Jr., and Robin M. Haller. *The Physician and Sexuality in Victorian America*. Urbana: University of Illinois Press, 1974.

Halttunen, Karen. *Confidence Men and Painted Women: A Study of Middle-Class Culture in America, 1830–1870.* New Haven, Conn.: Yale University Press, 1982.

Hays, Samuel P. *The Response to Industrialism, 1885–1914.* Chicago: University of Chicago Press, 1957.

Heald, Morrell. *The Social Responsibilities of Business: Company and Community, 1900–1960.* 2d ed. New Brunswick, N.J.: Transaction Books, 1987.

Herring, Harriet L. *Welfare Work in Mill Villages: The Story of Extra-Mill Activities in North Carolina.* Montclair, N.J.: Patterson Smith, 1968.

Hewitt, Nancy A. *Women's Activism and Social Change: Rochester, New York, 1822–1872.* Ithaca, N.Y.: Cornell University Press, 1984.

Higham, John. *Writing American History: Essays on Modern Scholarship.* Bloomington: Indiana University Press, 1970.

———. *Strangers in the Land: Patterns of American Nativism, 1860–1925.* New Brunswick, N.J.: Rutgers University Press, 1955.

Hilkey, Judy. *Character Is Capital: Success Manuals and Manhood in Gilded Age America.* Chapel Hill: University of North Carolina Press, 1997.

Hill, Christopher. *A Century of Revolution, 1603–1714.* Rev. ed. New York: Norton, 1980.

Hobsbawm, Eric J. *The Age of Revolution, 1789–1848.* London: Weidenfeld & Nicholson, 1962.

Hofstadter, Richard. *Social Darwinism in American Thought.* Rev. ed. Boston: Beacon Press, 1955.

Hoganson, Kristin L. *Fighting for American Manhood: How Gender Politics Provoked the Spanish-American and Philippine-American Wars.* New Haven, Conn.: Yale University Press, 1998.

Hopkins, C. Howard. *History of the Y.M.C.A. in North America.* New York: Association Press, 1951.

Horlick, Allan Stanley. *Country Boys and Merchant Princes: The Social Control of Young Men in New York.* Lewisburg, Pa.: Bucknell University Press, 1975.

Howe, Daniel Walker. *Making the American Self: Jonathan Edwards to Abraham Lincoln.* Cambridge, Mass.: Harvard University Press, 1997.

Huber, Richard M. *The American Myth of Success.* New York: McGraw-Hill, 1971.

Irigaray, Luce. *This Sex Which Is Not One.* Ithaca, N.Y.: Cornell University Press, 1985.

Jacoby, Sanford. *Employing Bureaucracy: Managers, Unions, and the Transformation of Work in American Industry, 1900–1945.* New York: Columbia University Press, 1985.

Jaher, Frederic Cople. *Doubters and Dissenters: Cataclysmic Thought in America, 1885–1918.* London: Free Press of Glencoe, 1964.

Johnson, Paul E. *A Shopkeeper's Millennium: Society and Revivals in Rochester, New York, 1815–1837.* New York: Hill & Wang, 1978.

Kann, Mark E. *On the Man Question: Gender and Civic Virtue in America.* Philadelphia: Temple University Press, 1991.

———. *A Republic of Men: The American Founders, Gendered Language, and Patriarchal Politics.* New York: New York University Press, 1998.

Kimmel, Michael S. *Manhood in America: A Cultural History.* New York: Free Press, 1996.

————. "The Feminization of American Culture and the Recreation of the Male Body, 1832–1920." *Michigan Quarterly Review* 33 (Winter 1994): 7–35.

Klein, H. M. J. *The Pennsylvania Young Men's Christian Association: A History, 1854–1950.* Kennett Square, Pa.: Kennett News and Advertiser Press, 1950.

Kocka, Jürgen. *White Collar Workers in America, 1890–1940: A Social-Political History in International Perspective.* London: Sage, 1980.

Kwolek-Folland, Angel. *Engendering Business: Men and Women in the Corporate Office, 1870–1930.* Baltimore: Johns Hopkins University Press, 1994.

Laclau, Ernesto. *Political Ideology in Marxist Theory.* London: Verso, 1979.

Ladd-Taylor, Molly. *Mother-Work: Women, Child Welfare, and the State, 1890–1930.* Urbana: University of Illinois Press, 1994.

Laurie, Bruce. *Artisans into Workers: Labor in Nineteenth-Century America.* New York: Noonday Press, 1989.

Lears, T. J. Jackson. "The Concept of Cultural Hegemony: Problems and Possibilities." *American Historical Review* 90 (June 1985): 567–93.

————. "From Salvation to Self-Realization: Advertising and the Roots of the Consumer Culture, 1880–1930." In *The Culture of Consumption: Critical Essays in American History, 1880–1980*, edited by Richard Wightman Fox and T. J. Jackson Lears, 1–38. New York: Pantheon Books, 1983.

————. *No Place of Grace: Antimodernism and the Transformation of American Culture, 1880–1920.* New York: Pantheon Books, 1982.

Lerner, Gerda. *The Creation of Patriarchy.* New York: Oxford University Press, 1986.

Leverenz, David. *Manhood and the American Renaissance.* Ithaca, N.Y.: Cornell University Press, 1989.

Licht, Walter. *Industrializing America: The Nineteenth Century.* Baltimore: Johns Hopkins University Press, 1995.

————. *Working for the Railroad: The Organization of Work in the Nineteenth Century.* Princeton, N.J.: Princeton University Press, 1983.

Lightner, David L. *Labor on the Illinois Central Railroad, 1852–1900: The Evolution of an Industrial Environment.* New York: Arno Press, 1977.

Lindenmeyer, Kriste. *A Right to Childhood: The U.S. Children's Bureau and Child Welfare, 1912–1946.* Urbana: University of Illinois Press, 1997.

Lupkin, Paula. "Manhood Factories: Architecture, Business, and the Evolving Urban Role of the YMCA, 1865–1925." In *Men and Women Adrift: The YMCA and the YWCA in the City*, edited by Nina Mjagkij and Margaret Spratt, 40–64. New York: New York University Press, 1997.

Lystra, Karen. *Searching the Heart: Women, Men, and Romantic Love in Nineteenth-Century America.* New York: Oxford University Press, 1989.

Matthews, Jean V. *Toward a New Society: American Thought and Culture, 1800–1830.* Boston: Twayne Publishers, 1991.

May, Henry F. *Protestant Churches and Industrial America.* New York: Harper & Row, 1949.

McBride, Paul. *Culture Clash: Immigrants and Reformers, 1880–1920.* San Francisco: R & E Research Associates, 1975.

————. "Peter Roberts and the YMCA Americanization Program, 1907–World War I." *Pennsylvania History* 44 (1977): 145–62.

McCall, Laura, and Donald Yacovone, eds. *A Shared Experience: Men, Women, and the History of Gender*. New York: New York University Press, 1998.

McCarthy, Kathleen D. *Noblesse Oblige*. Chicago: University of Chicago Press, 1982.

McClay, Wilfred M. *The Masterless: Self and Society in Modern America*. Chapel Hill: University of North Carolina Press, 1994.

McGaw, Judith A. *Most Wonderful Machine: Mechanization and Social Change in Berkshire Paper Making, 1801–1885*. Princeton, N.J.: Princeton University Press, 1987.

McLaren, Angus. *The Trials of Masculinity: Policing Sexual Boundaries, 1870–1930*. Chicago: University of Chicago Press, 1997.

McLeod, David I. *Building Character in the American Boy: The Boy Scouts, YMCA, and Their Forerunners*. Madison: University of Wisconsin Press, 1983.

Melder, Keith. *Beginnings of Sisterhood: The American Women's Rights Movement, 1800–1850*. New York: Schocken Books, 1977.

Melosh, Barbara, ed. *Gender and American History since 1890*. London: Routledge, 1993.

Merish, Lori. "'The Hand of Refined Taste' in the Frontier Landscape: Caroline Kirkland's *A New Home, Who'll Follow?* and the Feminization of American Consumerism." *American Quarterly* 45 (December 1993): 485–523.

Meyer, Stephen, III, *The Five Dollar Day: Labor Management and Social Control in the Ford Motor Company, 1908–1921*. Albany: State University of New York Press, 1981.

Mjagkij, Nina. *Light in the Darkness: African Americans and the YMCA, 1852–1946*. Lexington: University of Kentucky Press, 1994.

Mohl, Raymond A. *The New City: Urban America in the Industrial Age, 1860–1920*. Arlington Heights, Ill.: Harlan Davidson, 1985.

Montgomery, David. *Citizen Worker: The Experience of Workers in the United States with Democracy and the Free Market during the Nineteenth Century*. Cambridge: Cambridge University Press, 1993.

————. *The Fall of the House of Labor: The Workplace, the State, and American Labor Activism, 1860–1925*. Cambridge: Cambridge University Press, 1987.

————. *Workers' Control in America: Studies in the History of Work, Technology, and Labor Struggles*. New York: Cambridge University Press, 1979.

————. "Workers' Control of Machine Production in the Nineteenth Century." *Labor History* 17 (Fall 1976): 485–509.

Moon, Michael. "'The Gentle Boy from the Dangerous Classes': Pederasty, Domesticity, and Capitalism in Horatio Alger." *Representations* 19 (1987): 87–110.

Muncy, Robyn. *Creating a Female Dominion in American Reform, 1890–1935*. New York: Oxford University Press, 1991.

————. "*The Search for Order* Reconsidered." Paper delivered at the Annual Meeting of the American Historical Association, 1997. Panel: "Robert Wiebe's *Search for Order*: A Thirty-Year Retrospective."

Murphy, Kevin P. "Socrates in the Slums: Homoerotics, Gender, and Settlement House Reform." In *A Shared Experience: Men, Women, and the History of Gender*, edited by

Laura McCall and Donald Yacovone, 273–96. New York: New York University Press, 1998.

Murray, Robert K. *Red Scare: A Study in National Hysteria, 1919–1920.* Minneapolis: University of Minnesota Press, 1955.

Nelson, Daniel. *Managers and Workers: Origins of the New Factory System in the United States, 1880–1920.* Madison: University of Wisconsin Press, 1975.

Nestor, Oscar. *A History of Personnel Administration, 1890–1910.* New York: Garland Publishing, 1986.

Nye, David E. *Image Worlds: Corporate Identities at General Electric, 1890–1930.* Cambridge, Mass.: MIT Press, 1985.

Oberdeck, Kathryn J. "Religion, Culture, and the Politics of Class: Alexander Irvine's Mission to Turn-of-the-Century New Haven." *American Quarterly* 47 (June 1995): 236–79.

Odem, Mary. *Delinquent Daughters: Protecting and Policing Adolescent Female Sexuality in the United States, 1885–1920.* Chapel Hill: University of North Carolina Press, 1995.

Otis, Laura. *Organic Memory: History and the Body in Late Nineteenth and Early Twentieth Centuries.* Lincoln: University of Nebraska Press, 1994.

Ozanne, Robert. *A Century of Labor-Management Relations at McCormick and International Harvester.* Madison: University of Wisconsin Press, 1967.

Painter, Nell Irvin. *Standing at Armageddon: The United States, 1877–1919.* New York: Norton, 1987.

Palmer, Bryan D. *Descent into Discourse: The Reification of Language and the Writing of Social History.* Philadelphia: Temple University Press, 1990.

Palmer, Robert Roswell. *The Age of Democratic Revolutions: A Political History of Europe and America, 1760–1800.* 2 vols. Princeton, N.J.: Princeton University Press, 1959–1964.

Pateman, Carole. *The Sexual Contract.* Stanford, Calif.: Stanford University Press, 1988.

Peck, Gunther. "Manly Gambles: The Politics of Risk on the Comstock Lode, 1860–1880." *Journal of Social History* 26 (Summer 1993): 701–23.

Pleck, Elizabeth H., and Joseph H. Pleck, eds. *The American Man.* Englewood Cliffs, N.J.: Prentice Hall, 1980.

Polanyi, Karl. *The Great Transformation: The Political and Economic Origins of Our Time.* Boston: Beacon Press, 1957.

Polenberg, Richard. *Fighting Faiths: The Abrams Case, the Supreme Court, and Free Speech.* New York: Penguin, 1987.

Preston, William J., Jr. *Aliens and Dissenters: Federal Suppression of Radicals, 1903–1933.* New York: Harper Torchbooks, 1966.

Przeworski, Adam. *Capitalism and Social Democracy.* Cambridge: Cambridge University Press, 1985.

Putney, Clifford Wallace. "Character Building in the YMCA, 1880–1930." *Mid-America: An Historical Review* 73 (January 1991): 49–70.

———. *Muscular Christianity: Manhood and Sports in Protestant America, 1880–1920.* Cambridge, Mass.: Harvard University Press, 2001.

Quandt, Jean. *From the Small Town to the Great Community: The Social Thought of Progressive Individuals.* New Brunswick, N.J.: Rutgers University Press, 1970.

Rader, Benjamin G. "The Recapitulation Theory of Play: Motor Behaviour, Moral Reflexes, and Manly Attitudes in Urban America, 1880–1920." In *Manliness and Morality: Middle-Class Masculinity in Britain and America, 1880–1940,* edited by J. A. Mangan and James Walvin, 123–34. New York: St. Martin's Press, 1987.

Ramirez, Bruno. *When Workers Fight: The Politics of Industrial Relations in the Progressive Era, 1898–1916.* Westport, Conn.: Greenwood Press, 1978.

Roberts, Gerald Franklin. "The Strenuous Life: The Cult of Masculinity in the Era of Theodore Roosevelt." Ph.D. dissertation, Michigan State University, 1970.

Rockefeller, Steven C. *John Dewey: Religious Faith and Democratic Humanism.* New York: Columbia University Press, 1991.

Rodgers, Daniel T. *The Work Ethic in Industrial America, 1850–1920.* Chicago: University of Chicago Press, 1978.

Rose, Anne C. *Victorian America and the Civil War.* Cambridge: Cambridge University Press, 1992.

———. *Voices of the Marketplace: American Thought and Culture, 1830–1860.* New York: Twayne, 1995.

Rosenberg, Charles E. "Sexuality, Class, and Role in Nineteenth-Century America." *American Quarterly* 25 (May 1973): 131–53.

Rosenzweig, Roy. *Eight Hours for What We Will: Workers and Leisure in an Industrial City, 1870–1920.* (Cambridge: Cambridge University Press, 1983.

Rotundo, E. Anthony. *American Manhood: Transformations in Masculinity from the Revolution to the Modern Era.* New York: Basic Books, 1993.

———. "Body and Soul: Changing Ideals of American Middle-Class Manhood, 1770–1920." *Journal of Social History* 16 (Summer 1983): 23–38.

Rubin, Joan Shelley. *The Making of Middle-Brow Culture.* Chapel Hill: University of North Carolina Press, 1992.

Russett, Cynthia Eagle. *Darwin in America: The Intellectual Response, 1865–1912.* San Francisco: W. H. Freeman, 1976.

———. *Sexual Science: The Victorian Construction of Womanhood.* Cambridge, Mass.: Harvard University Press, 1989.

Ryan, Mary P. *Cradle of the Middle Class: The Family in Oneida County, New York, 1790–1865.* Cambridge: Cambridge University Press, 1981.

Said, Edward. *Orientalism.* New York: Pantheon, 1978.

Salvatore, Nick. *Eugene V. Debs: Citizen and Socialist.* Urbana: University of Illinois Press, 1982.

Schaeffer, Ronald. *America in the Great War: The Rise of the War Welfare State.* New York: Oxford University Press, 1991.

Scheinberg, Stephen J. *Employees and Reformers: The Development of Corporation Labor Policy, 1900–1940.* New York: Garland Publishing, 1986.

Schudson, Michael. "Was There Ever a Public Sphere? If So, When? Reflections on the American Case." In *Habermas and the Public Sphere,* edited by Craig Calhoun. Cambridge, Mass.: MIT Press, 1992.

Scobey, David. "Anatomy of the Promenade: The Politics of Bourgeois Sociability in Nineteenth-Century New York." *Journal of Social History* 17 (May 1992): 203–27.

Scott, James C. *Domination and the Arts of Resistance: Hidden Transcripts.* New Haven, Conn.: Yale University Press, 1991.

Scott, Joan Wallach. "Deconstructing Equality-Versus-Difference: or, The Uses of Post-structuralist Theory for Feminism." *Feminist Studies* 14 (Spring 1988): 33–50.

———. "Gender: A Useful Category of Historical Analysis." *American Historical Review* 91 (December 1986): 1053–75.

———. "On Language, Gender, and Working Class History." With responses by Bryan D. Palmer, Christine Stansell, and Anson Rabinbach. *International Labor and Working Class History* 31 (Spring 1987): 1–36.

———. "A Reply to Criticism." *International Labor and Working Class History* 32 (Fall 1987): 39–45.

Scranton, Philip. *Proprietary Capitalism: The Textile Manufacturer at Philadelphia, 1800–1885.* Philadelphia: Temple University Press, 1983.

Sedgwick, Eve Kosofsky. *Between Men: English Literature and Male Homosocial Desire.* New York: Columbia University Press, 1985.

———. *Epistemology of the Closet.* New York: Columbia University Press, 1990.

Sellers, Charles. *The Market Revolution: Jacksonian America, 1815–1846.* New York: Oxford University Press, 1991.

Shi, David. *The Simple Life: Plain Living and High Thinking in American Culture.* New York: Oxford University Press, 1985.

Singleton, Gregory H. "Protestant Voluntary Organizations and the Shaping of Victorian America." *American Quarterly* 27 (Winter 1975): 549–60.

Sklar, Kathryn Kish. *Catherine Beecher: A Study in American Domesticity.* New Haven, Conn.: Yale University Press, 1973.

Sklar, Martin J. *The Corporate Reconstruction of American Capitalism, 1890–1916: The Market, the Law, and Politics.* Cambridge: Cambridge University Press, 1988.

Slotkin, Richard. *The Fatal Environment: The Myth of the Frontier in the Age of Industrialization, 1800–1890.* New York: Atheneum, 1985.

Stearns, Peter N. *Be a Man! Males in Modern Society.* 2d rev. ed. London: Holmes & Meier, 1990.

———. *American Cool: Constructing a Twentieth-Century Emotional Style.* New York: New York University Press, 1994.

Steinberg, Marc W. "The Dialogue of Struggle: The Contest over Ideological Boundaries in the Case of the London Silk Weavers in the Early Nineteenth Century." *Social Science History* 18 (Winter 1994): 505–42.

Stromquist, Shelton. *A Generation of Boomers: The Pattern of Railroad Labor Conflict in Nineteenth-Century America.* Urbana: University of Illinois Press, 1987.

Summers, Mark Whalgren. *The Gilded Age, or the Hazard of New Functions.* Upper Saddle River, N.J.: Prentice Hall, 1997.

Susman, Warren I. *Culture as History: The Transformation of American Society in the Twentieth Century.* New York: Pantheon Books, 1984.

Taylor, Charles. *Sources of the Self: The Making of the Modern Identity.* Cambridge, Mass.: Harvard University Press, 1989.

Theweleit, Klaus. *Male Fantasies.* Vol. 1, *Women, Floods, Bodies, History.* Translated by Stephen Conway. Minneapolis: University of Minnesota Press, 1987.

Thompson, E. P. *The Making of the English Working Class.* Reprint with a new preface. London: Penguin, 1980.

Tone, Andrea. *The Business of Benevolence: Industrial Paternalism in Progressive America.* Ithaca, N.Y.: Cornell University Press, 1997.

Townsend, Kim. *Manhood at Harvard: William James and Others.* New York: Norton, 1996.

Trachtenberg, Alan. *The Incorporation of America: Culture and Society in the Gilded Age.* New York: Hill & Wang, 1982.

Traister, Bryce. "Academic Viagra: The Rise of American Masculinity Studies." *American Quarterly* 52 (June 2000): 274–304.

Vandenberg-Daves, Jodi. "The Manly Pursuit of a Partnership between the Sexes: The Debate over YMCA Programs for Women and Girls, 1914–1933." *Journal of American History* 78 (March 1992): 1324–46.

Wade, Louise C. *Graham Taylor: Pioneer for Social Justice, 1851–1938.* Chicago: University of Chicago Press, 1964.

Wallace, Anthony F. C. *Rockdale: The Growth of an American Village in the Early Industrial Revolution.* New York: Alfred A. Knopf, 1980.

Watts, Sarah Lyons. *Order against Chaos: Business Culture and Labor Ideology in America, 1880–1915.* Westport, Conn.: Greenwood Press, 1991.

Weinstein, James. *The Corporate Ideal in the Liberal State, 1900–1918.* Boston: Beacon Press, 1968.

Weir, Robert M. *Beyond Labor's Veil: The Culture of the Knights of Labor.* University Park: Pennsylvania State University Press, 1996.

Weiss, Richard. *The American Myth of Success: From Horatio Alger to Norman Vincent Peale.* New York: Basic Books, 1969.

White, Kevin. *The First Sexual Revolution: The Emergence of Male Heterosexuality in Modern America.* New York: New York University Press, 1993.

White, W. Thomas. "Race, Ethnicity, and Gender in the Railroad Work Force: The Case of the Far Northwest, 1883–1918." *Western Historical Quarterly* 16 (July 1985): 265–83.

Wiebe, Robert. *The Search for Order, 1877–1920.* New York: Hill & Wang, 1967.

Williams, Pierce, and Frederick E. Croxton. *Corporation Contributions to Organized Community Welfare Service.* New York: National Bureau of Economic Research, 1930.

Williams, Raymond. "Personality." In *Keywords: A Vocabulary of Culture and Society,* rev. ed., 232–35. New York: Oxford University Press, 1983.

Wilson, Raymond Jackson. *In Quest of Community: Social Philosophy in the United States, 1860–1920.* New York: Oxford University Press, 1968.

Worman, E. Clark. *History of the Brooklyn and Queens Young Men's Christian Association, 1853–1949.* New York: Association Press, 1952.

Wyllie, Irvin G. *The Self-Made Man in America: The Myth of Rags to Riches*. New York: Free Press, 1966.

Wynn, Neill A. *From Progressivism to Prosperity: World War I and American Society*. New York: Holmes & Meier, 1986.

Yacovone, Donald. "Abolitionists and the 'Language of Fraternal Love.'" In *Meanings for Manhood: Constructions of Masculinity in Victorian America*, edited by Mark C. Carnes and Clyde Griffen, 85–95. Chicago: University of Chicago Press, 1990.

———. "'Surpassing the Love of Women': Victorian Manhood and the Language of Fraternal Love." In *A Shared Experience: Men, Women, and the History of Gender*, edited by Laura McCall and Donald Yacovone, 195–221. New York: New York University Press, 1998.

Zahavi, Gerald. *Workers, Managers, and Welfare Capitalism: The Shoeworkers and Tanners of Endicott Johnson, 1890–1950*. Urbana: University of Illinois Press, 1987.

Zunz, Olivier. *Making America Corporate, 1870–1920*. Chicago: University of Chicago Press, 1990.